The Limits of Victory

WRITTEN UNDER THE AUSPICES OF THE
CENTER FOR INTERNATIONAL AFFAIRS,
HARVARD UNIVERSITY

The Limits of Victory

THE RATIFICATION OF THE PANAMA CANAL TREATIES

George D. Moffett III

CORNELL UNIVERSITY PRESS

Ithaca and London

First published 1985 by Cornell University Press.
Published in the United Kingdom by
Cornell University Press Ltd., London.

International Standard Book Number 0-8014-1737-6
Library of Congress Catalog Card Number 84-14920
Printed in the United States of America
Librarians: Library of Congress cataloging information
appears on the last page of the book.

The paper in this book is acid-free and meets the guidelines
for permanence and durability of the Committee on Production
Guidelines for Book Longevity of the Council on Library Resources.

To my mother and father,
with a grateful heart

Contents

Preface

This book addresses three questions regarding the ratification of the Panama Canal treaties of 1977–78. The first is why the exhaustive efforts of the administration of Jimmy Carter, despite nearly every apparent advantage, almost failed to secure Senate ratification of the Canal treaties. The second is how, having almost failed, the administration ultimately succeeded in gaining the necessary two-thirds support. The third is why success on the treaties came to the Carter administration at such a formidably high price. The book purports to be neither a history of the thirteen-year-long negotiations that led up to the ratification debate nor a study in executive-congressional relations per se. Rather, it describes the political environment within which the ratification contest occurred and shows how that environment influenced the nature and eventual outcome of the debate. It considers the Canal debate as a case study of the difficulties involved in trying to force a major policy initiative on an unwilling public and a reluctant Congress.[1]

Beginning in August 1977, the Carter administration devoted nearly seven months to an intensive campaign to win public and congressional approval for the Panama treaties. What stands out in reevaluating the politically charged events of the period is the striking contrast between the administration's advantageous political position at the start of the ratification debate and the enormous effort and cost that finally proved necessary to pull together a fragile two-thirds majority for approval in the Senate.

Taken at face value, at least, the available evidence suggests that the president managed the ratification campaign from a position of unusual strength. The treaties, the product of negotiations conducted by four successive Republican and Democratic administrations, had

9

built-in bipartisan backing. In response to concessions made to the Pentagon during the negotiations, they had gained the full and active support of the Defense Department and the Joint Chiefs of Staff. In Congress the president had the benefit of a Senate controlled by his own party and from January 1978 on profited from the active support and parliamentary skill of both the majority and the minority leadership in the Senate. Within the ranks of the nation's Establishment foreign-policy elite, the treaties were the object of the first broad-based consensus since the Vietnam War. By the time of the two votes[2] editorial endorsements in the nation's press were running by margins of two-to-one in favor of ratification; supportive opinion was all but unanimous among such influential newspapers as the *New York Times*, among leading columnists on both the Right and the Left, and among leading newspaper chains, including the traditionally conservative Hearst and Scripps-Howard syndicates. There was almost universal support for the treaties among the nation's leading corporate, banking, and religious institutions and labor, minority, civic, and public-interest organizations. By the end of the ratification debate there were even indications that a massive public relations campaign mounted by the administration to win popular backing for the treaties was beginning to pay dividends.

Moreover, the only organized activity directed against the treaties issued largely from outside the political mainstream. It was led by mostly new, relatively untested umbrella organizations of the so-called New Right, abetted only by a few scattered veterans' organizations and patriotic societies, supported by a comparatively small minority of the nation's media, and forced to operate without any strong base in the opposition Republican party.

The administration skillfully capitalized on all these advantages. It orchestrated the ratification campaign with a high degree of energy and political dexterity, in the process ensuring that political alliances potentially strong enough to defeat the treaties were never allowed to coalesce. Yet, and the point is central to the chapters that follow, the treaties were nearly defeated. They received the barest margin of Senate approval in spite of the general competence of the president's political management, in spite of the unusually high degree of bureaucratic unanimity that prevailed within the administration on behalf of ratification, and in spite of the broad support of public, press, elite, and institutional opinion. After thirteen years of negotiations, over forty days of congressional hearings in six committees, and the longest floor debate in the Senate in over half a century, the two-thirds coalition for ratification was patched together by hard-pressed administration lobbyists with literally only minutes to spare.

When victory did come, moreover, it came at a debilitatingly high political price. The treaties, by the president's own estimate, may have done more than any other issue to compromise his chances for reelection in 1980.[3] He later wrote in his memoirs that the treaty fight was "the most difficult political battle I had ever faced, including my long campaign as President."[4] In the opinion of one White House lobbyist, the treaty debate effectively catalyzed the political energies of the New Right and "without any question cost the Democrats the Senate in 1980."[5] Whether or not these assessments are accurate, it is clear that the price of success was unexpectedly high. My purpose, then, is to describe the causes and consequences of this fundamental paradox of the ratification debate. I hope to explain how, in the end, the fight waged to gain approval for the 1977 Panama Canal treaties resulted in one of the most significant Pyrrhic victories in recent American politics.

Not least of many remarkable aspects of the debate over the Canal treaties is that the fate of a 75-year-old, largely outmoded canal in Central America could become an issue at all, much less the object of some of the most heated passions in modern diplomatic history. Part of the explanation is to be found in the deep, visceral attachment Americans have historically felt toward the Canal, once described by Franklin D. Roosevelt as "this wonder of the world, greater than the Tower of Babel or the Pyramids."[6] Reflecting pride in the great technical and humanitarian achievement associated with construction and with the eradication of disease, the Canal has remained "despite time and circumstance," in historian David McCullough's words, "a huge American Success."[7] Reflecting the license taken to create the political arrangements necessary to begin the work of construction, it has also remained, as Senator Frank Church put it, the unrivaled symbol "of a time when we [Americans] did pretty much as we pleased."[8]

But if traditional attachments contributed to the ratification troubles faced by the Carter administration, the problem was clearly exacerbated by the *timing* of the ratification debate. It came just as Americans were learning, for the first time, that the United States could *not* do pretty much as it pleased, and just as all around, there were clear indications that America's postwar dominance was coming to an end. The central problem for the Carter administration lay in the fact that just as the contest for public opinion was about to begin, major events—

defeat in Vietnam, the attainment of strategic parity by the Soviet Union, the changing complexion of the United Nations, the new challenge to American energy security posed by the Arab oil cartel, the advent of a confusing new international environment in which, in Harlan Cleveland's words, "no one was in general charge"[9]—were producing one of the rare crises of confidence in American history.

The new mood produced by these changes was not exactly bellicose. As recorded in major studies of public attitudes conducted in the mid-1970s,[10] it did, however, express a kind of insecurity that found outlet in demands for a stronger national defense, in a preoccupation with the position of the United States as "the preeminent global power,"[11] in a "quickening nationalist spirit at home,"[12] and in a heightened sensitivity to the imperatives of national honor. Thus the peculiar passions aroused by efforts to "give away" the prized possession of the Canal may be properly understood as the product of a kind of "frustrated nationalism," a part of what journalist Kevin Phillips describes as the "pathology of the national response" to the "forced retreat of U.S. global power over the last two decades."[13]

As chapter 1 illustrates, there was growing evidence dating from the Eisenhower administration that with respect to Panama policy the views of policy makers and public were evolving in opposite directions. By 1976 it was clear that whoever was destined to occupy the White House in 1977 would face an enormously difficult task of reconciliation. For Jimmy Carter, to whom that task fell, the problem was made exponentially more difficult by the determination of millions of Americans to rally doggedly behind the symbol of the Canal— even as the reality behind the symbol was slipping irretrievably away. As a result, there was no raw material with which to fashion a consensus, either for the Panama policy specifically or for the larger conception of foreign policy that the new treaties expressed. The core of the administration's ratification problems, therefore, was that at the very time international pressures were making the conclusion of new treaties almost inevitable, domestic pressures were making ratification of new treaties almost impossible.

As a closer look at public opinion suggests, only a relatively small percentage of Americans may ever have been deeply concerned about the Canal issue itself. Only among elements on the far Right was the issue ever regarded as a matter of "national survival,"[14] "America's second Pearl Harbor,"[15] or "the most disastrous decision. . .of our entire diplomatic history."[16] Still, if such apocalyptic views were not widely representative of the national response to the treaties, the restrictive new climate of opinion—like the isolationism of the 1930s that constrained the "all-aid-short-of-war" policies of the Roosevelt administration—may have given concerns voiced on the Right a synergistic effect.

In the end the administration was able to salvage a victory in the Senate, in part because of a skillful effort to sustain bipartisanship and in part because the president was willing to adopt a flexible policy on treaty amendments. Nevertheless, the issue became something the administration never intended. Instead of producing a quick legislative victory, it became the object of the longest foreign-policy debate since the Versailles Treaty of 1919–20. Instead of christening the Carter foreign-policy agenda, it largely compromised it. Instead of providing the opportunity for a knock-out blow against the Right, the treaty debate regenerated the political Right as a major force in American politics. Instead of contributing to the creation of a new foreign-policy consensus, the debate exacerbated the old divisions left over from the Vietnam War.

In a less wrenching way, perhaps, the debate over the Canal treaties may be understood as a counterpart to the painful domestic transitions that occurred during the 1950s in France after Vietnam and Algeria and in Britain after Suez. For the United States, a comparable reconciliation of new realities and old myths occurred within the crucible of ratification politics. For the administration of Jimmy Carter, the task of managing this reconciliation was to become a demanding and costly ordeal. It is to this subject that the following chapters are devoted.

The caveats with which an author attempts to anticipate and deflect the reproaches of critics are more necessary than usual in the present work, and for four specific reasons.

The first is that this book is not the product of an entirely neutral party. I was for a time research director of a small citizens' committee that organized to abet the ratification effort. (It is described briefly in chapter 3.) I later served on the White House staff of President Jimmy Carter between 1978 and 1981. That said, interpretations advanced in this book do purport to be, as much as possible, the work of a scholar, not of a partisan. If at occasional points my personal preference for ratification may still be apparent, I hope that they will not be so frequent as to compromise the integrity of the research.

Second, there are obvious limitations associated with treating a topic so recently a part of the public agenda. Foremost among them is the scarcity of primary source material and the commensurate necessity of relying to an ususually large extent on published secondary sources. As the reader will quickly discover, this book draws heavily on contemporary newspaper and journal accounts and on the few books so far published which treat the ratification debate. To compensate for these methodological limitations, I have broadened the research base with personal interviews with over fifty participants in the debate. Their observations and the lively interest they have shown in the research have been invaluable. To the extent that this retelling of the Panama story proves useful, it owes much to the insights they have so generously provided. I have also relied on my extensive notes on documents from the Carter White House. Interviews are detailed in Appendix C, "Primary Sources," which also lists the archives in which materials of especial use to future researchers are now deposited.

Third, though a historian, I have ventured into the realm of the public opinion analyst, the interest-group theorist, the political economist, and the scholar of the American Right. Practitioners in these fields may find imperfections in the parts of the present work with which they are most familiar. I hope, however, that the gist of the arguments herein, if not my mastery of specific theory or lexicon, will be sufficient to justify the time invested in these pages.

Finally, any such contemporary account will eventually be fair game for revision, in part because additional documentation will become available and in part because later historians will be able to define the Canal debate in a fuller historical context.

Still, I find myself confident about the individual threads of which this story is woven. I shall be surprised if new evidence substantially disproves that the failure of five administrations beginning in the late 1950s to make an effective public defense of incremental changes in Panama policy contributed substantially to the difficulties encountered by Jimmy Carter in winning popular and congressional support for the final 1977 draft treaties (chapter 1); that part of the reason support for ratification proved so hard to come by was that the Carter administration's foreign policy was itself so widely misunderstood (chapter 2); that the general skill with which the administration managed the ratification effort was substantially offset by a climate of opinion that was largely nonpermissive (chapter 3); that notwithstanding extensive public relations efforts, the administration was never successful in winning public acceptance of the case for ratification (chapter 4); that no *supportive* interest group had a sufficiently direct stake in the outcome of the treaty debate to engage in the kind of high-priority lobbying that might have eased the administration's task in the Senate, while, on the Right, forces in *opposition* worked effectively to retard the ratification effort (chapter 5); or, finally, that the case for the treaties was needlessly jeopardized by the inability of the administration to respond to concerns voiced by various maritime interests regarding the possible economic consequences of ratification (chapter 6).

In the course of writing this book, I quickly discovered that, as with any major enterprise, the work could not have been completed without the invaluable help of numerous supportive friends. In particular I extend thanks to the following for their special contributions: Professors Leo P. Ribuffo, Anna K. Nelson, and William H. Becker of George Washington University for their constructive comments and criticism and for the interest they have shown at every stage of the writing; Samuel P. Huntington, who graciously provided the opportunity to pursue the research and writing in the hospitable environment of Harvard's Center for International Affairs; Governor W. Averell Harriman and Pamela Harriman for expressions of great personal kindness in the course of the research; Phillip Chamberlain, who typed, Sara Goodgame, who proofread, and Roger Haydon, who edited, and who each contributed so much; and participants in the Panama debate who gave so willingly of their time and insights.

Finally, special thanks go to three people who played major supporting roles. First, to Barbara McAdoo, whose abiding interest has been an unfailing support from the beginning. Second, to Elizabeth Beck, who ever so patiently instructed me in the fine points of writing and to whom full credit goes for whatever stylistic quality these pages may display. Finally, to Diane Powell. Of Diane it may truly be said that without her unflagging confidence, gentle strength, and devoted interest this book would never have been written. For them, and for family and friends who never allowed me to doubt that the work was a step of progress, no words of gratitude are sufficient.

GEORGE D. MOFFETT III

Washington, D.C.

Acronyms

AFL-CIO	American Federation of Labor/Congress of Industrial Organizations
AIMS	American Institute of Merchant Shipping
API	American Petroleum Institute
CBS	Columbia Broadcasting System
CEO	chief executive officer
CFR	Council on Foreign Relations
COACT	Committee of Americans for the Canal Treaties, Inc.
ILA	International Longshoremen's Association
IMF	International Monetary Fund
JCS	Joint Chiefs of Staff
NAM	National Association of Manufacturers
NATO	North Atlantic Treaty Organization
NBC	National Broadcasting Company
NIEO	New International Economic Order
NSC	National Security Council
OAS	Organization of American States
OPEC	Organization of Petroleum Exporting Countries
ORC	Opinion Research Corporation
PRC	Policy Review Committee
PRM	Presidential Review Memorandum
SALT	Strategic Arms Limitation Treaty
SEATO	Southeast Asia Treaty Organization
UAW	United Auto Workers
UN	United Nations

The Limits of Victory

CHAPTER 1

Historical Background: The
Divergence of Policy and Opinion

The dream of bridging the Central American isthmus—"this peremptory non-intercourse act of nature," as one nineteenth-century visitor to Panama called it—has ancient origins.[1] At least since the advent of Spanish rule in the isthmus in 1501, and probably for centuries earlier among the local inhabitants of the region, the prospect of finishing the task that nature itself came so close to completing has fired the imaginations of innumerable statesmen, explorers, and engineers.

In spite of persistent interest in such a project, for four hundred years after the arrival of the Spanish the division of the isthmus remained a dream. Its fulfillment was delayed not only by the absence of a practicable technology but also by the prudent judgment of a succession of Spanish monarchs that to open the isthmus would increase the vulnerability of Spain's rich dominions in Peru and Mexico. Through much of the nineteenth century, following the end of Spanish colonial rule in 1821, the dream was a casualty of a different kind of politics, as the question of who should construct a canal was subordinated by the new contending powers in the region, Great Britain and the United States, to the question of how such a canal should be controlled.[2]

In the United States active interest in a canal also had remote origins. But it was the acquisition of California from Mexico in 1848, and the discovery of gold in California a year later that first made an isthmian passage the object of serious political interest by placing a premium on a faster route to the Pacific. As historian Dwight Miner writes, after mid-century the matter was taken up with unprecedented urgency and thereafter was never allowed to rest.[3] By the 1890s it had become a virtual strategic imperative, as the United States embarked on a course of overseas expansion. Motivated by the dictates of trade and missionary diplomacy and by a desire to emulate British greatness through the acquisition of seapower and colonies, the United States assembled a far-flung empire by 1900 that, adorned with the spoils of the Spanish-American War, stretched from the Philippines to Puerto Rico.

The key to the maintenance of such an empire according to the logic formulated by naval theorist Alfred Thayer Mahan and embraced by President Theodore Roosevelt, was strategic control of the Caribbean plus a navy capable of securing American interests in both the Caribbean and the Pacific. The prerequisite to both objectives was a waterway through the isthmus. Private French interests had tried and failed to construct a sea-level canal through Panama in the 1880s, at a staggering loss in lives and capital. Now the opportunity lay with the United States, and for the first time in four centuries of imperial interest in the isthmus all of the necessary factors converged to make the great work a practical possibility. With the diplomatic acquiescence of the British, the technical expertise, the medical knowledge to protect the labor force from the ravages of malaria and yellow fever, and most of all the political commitment of the U.S. government, the dream of building the canal could now be realized.

Theodore Roosevelt, reflecting his sense of urgency about the project and his impatience with the ways of politics and diplomacy, boasted in later years that "I took the Canal and let Congress debate."[4] In one of the remarkable ironies of the history of U.S. relations with Panama, the manner of that taking almost immediately produced the germ of the very political counterforce in Panama that, in time, would prove strong enough to compel the United States to relinquish its position in the Canal Zone. Within Theodore Roosevelt's own lifetime the first practical expressions of Woodrow Wilson's principle of "self-determination" were signaling the beginning of the end of the great age of imperialism. One of the final casualties of the anticolonial movement that followed and that reached its zenith after World War II was the very treaty, signed in 1903, by which the United States acquired the rights to build and operate the Panama Canal.

This chapter will examine the dissatisfactions produced by the treaty of 1903 and evaluate their implications for the ratification debate of 1977–78. Specifically, the chapter will explore four issues: first, how from the beginning the terms by which the United States secured rights to construct and administer the Canal became the source of deep resentment in Panama; second, how circumstances in the years following World War II made it possible for the Panamanians to translate their dissatisfaction into politically effective demands for an end to the 1903 treaty; third, how American policy grew by stages more responsive to these escalating pressures; and fourth, how changes in official U.S. policy toward the Canal, and the failure of five successive presidential administrations to justify these changes, led to the deep political divisions that characterized the 1977–78 ratification debate in the United States.

[1]

As to the roots of Panamanian discontent, it seems clear in retrospect that the complications which grew out of the 1903 Hay–Bunau-Varilla Treaty—for seventy-five years the centerpiece of U.S. relations with Panama—could have been avoided. Had the agreement been the product of normal bilateral negotiations, many of the offending provisions, which in time generated irresistible pressures for reform, might have been omitted. As it was, the treaty was written under extraordinary circumstances by an interested third party, a Frenchman named Philippe Bunau-Varilla. His personal financial stake in the outcome of the negotiations effectively precluded the possibility of equitable terms for Panama.[5]

For a brief period Bunau-Varilla had been chief engineer of the private French company that made the first serious effort, beginning in 1880, to construct an isthmian canal through Panama. Under the constraints of topography and climate the company had fallen into bankruptcy and receivership. In 1894 it was re-formed by a group of the original stockholders, including Bunau-Varilla, who entertained hopes of recouping their losses by persuading the United States to purchase the company's remaining assets and construction rights. To advance this objective, Bunau-Varilla put his personal stamp on all the events leading to the ratification of the 1903 treaty. When Congress voted a preference for a canal through Nicaragua, it was Bunau-Varilla, with the strong support of the Roosevelt administration, who successfully led the lobby in Congress for the alternative route through Panama.[6] When Colombia, of which Panama was province, rebuffed a U.S. treaty offer for rights to build through Panama, it was Bunau-Varilla who helped plan the revolution that in November 1903 made Panama an independent nation. And when the revolution was over, it was Bunau-Varilla who drafted the canal treaty between the United

States and Panama, and on terms that, in effect, pegged the survival of Panamanian independence to the satisfaction of French claims.

There is little evidence to suggest that the final terms of the Hay-Bunau-Varilla Treaty bore any resemblance to what the Panamanians themselves had in mind. Immediately after the revolution the provisional government sent a delegation headed by President Manuel Amador to Washington, with explicit instructions not to enter into any agreement that would impair the new nation's sovereignty or territorial integrity. The enterprising Bunau-Varilla, however, had other ideas. Reckoning that the only sure protection for French interests was a treaty the U.S. Senate could not refuse, and anticipating that the key to such a treaty was a grant, *in perpetuity*, of the very sovereignty the Panamanian delegation was steaming north to protect, the Frenchman seized the initiative[7] and contrary to the expressed wishes of the provisional government entered into hasty and unilateral negotiations with Secretary of State John Hay. When the Panamanian delegation finally arrived in Washington, it was presented with a fait accompli in the form of the signed Hay–Bunau-Varilla Treaty. By Bunau-Varilla's own recounting, Amador, on reading the terms of the treaty, "nearly swooned on the platform of the station."[8] Later, when the Panamanians threatened not to ratify, Bunau-Varilla warned of dire consequences. "If the government does not think [it] possible to take this minimum but sufficient step," he wired the government in Panama, "I do not wish to appear responsible for calamities which certainly will result from this situation, the most probable being the immediate suspension of [American] protection."[9] David McCullough's prize-winning history of the constitution of the Canal states that this threat was "the ultimate knife at the throat and wholly spurious.... Nothing of the kind was even remotely contemplated at the White House or the State Department."[10] Nevertheless, no such confidence prevailed in Panama. Fearful of calling Bunau-Varilla's bluff, the government, under duress, gave its approval to the new pact.

Bunau-Varilla harbored no false modesty about his work. "I not only signed the treaty," he claimed, "but I wrote it from the first line to the last."[11] He later summarized the import of his accomplishment: "I had safeguarded the work of French genius.... I had served France."[12] In serving France, however, he had severely compromised the interests of the Panamanians. By the terms of the Hay–Bunau-Varilla Treaty, signed on 19 November 1903, the United States was given exclusive jurisdictional rights in perpetuity within a ten-mile-wide strip of territory where the Canal was to be dug. In return,

Panama was granted a flat sum of $10 million plus an annuity of $250,000. For Bunau-Varilla's efforts the French company received $40 million for its rights and assets sold to the United States.

Bunau-Varilla described the treaty "from a practical point of view [as] identical for Panama with the Hay-Herran Treaty," by which the United States had sought to secure construction rights from Colombia in 1903, before the Panamanian revolution.[13] In fact, the treaty that the Colombian Congress rejected had exacted neither sovereignty nor the hated perpetuity clause, and the inequity of the arrangement ruffled Panamanian sensibilities from the very beginning. The 1903 treaty, by Bunau-Varilla's own admission, "met with a cold reception in Panama."[14] Hay himself understood that it was "vastly advantageous to the U.S. and we must confess with what face we can muster . . . not so advantageous to Panama. . . . You and I know too well," he wrote to President Roosevelt, "how many points there are in this treaty to which a Panamanian patriot could object."[15]

Vocal objections to the 1903 treaty began almost at once, as Panamanians realized that, in the words of historian William D. McCain, "they were victims of a pact negotiated and signed . . . by an American who knew little of their interests and needs, and by a Frenchman who probably cared less."[16] The practical import of the Hay–Bunau-Varilla Treaty for the Panamanians was the necessity of tolerating foreign control over 550 square miles of Panama's best real estate, including the nation's prime deep-water port locations and potentially profitable commercial opportunities in the Zone, from which Panamanian citizens were excluded. The symbolic import ran deeper still, as Panamanians chafed at the indignity posed by the existence of what amounted to an American colony within Panama's national borders. Although the Panamanian government would be controlled by politicians and elites loyal to the United States for the next forty years, the inequity of the 1903 treaty spawned popular dissatisfactions that, as early as 1924 spilled over into periodic episodes of anti-American violence.

Through years of political dependence on the United States, Panama was unable to obtain more than minor adjustments in the terms of the 1903 treaty.[17] Nevertheless, dissatisfaction with the high price exacted for the benefits of having the Canal in Panama generated growing pressures for change. Although few Americans understood the point, the annuities granted under the treaty were never for most Panamanians to be an adequate substitute for the loss of sovereignty, nor for the chance to have substantive, eventually exclusive, control over the operation of the Canal. "We value our dignity and national pride as much as you do," one Panamanian wrote years later to an American friend, "and we simply cannot allow a foreign country to exercise independent authority inside our country."[18] For seventy-five years American officials were forced to cope with the growing pressures that such opposition produced. After World War II it would become apparent—to policy makers if not to the American public—that however well the 1903 agreement suited American interests, it engendered resentments in Panama that were not to be contained indefinitely.

[2]

Although the fact did not become apparent until later, the policy of the United States toward Panama was destined to be radically influenced by the powerful forces of change unleashed by World War II. The weakening of the European colonial powers during the war, the growth of nationalism in the subject regions of Asia and Africa, new demands for racial and economic equality, all gave rise to a new "international egalitarianism" that after 1945 completely transformed colonial relations around the globe.[19]

In Latin America the contagious nature of postwar nationalism was abetted by a variety of entrenched economic and social discontents. These discontents were first thrust on the attention of most Americans by events in Cuba after 1959. The Castro revolution triggered a long-overdue reevaluation of American policy in the hemisphere, which began in the last year of the second Eisenhower administration.

In Panama the harbinger of such pressures, and of more militant opposition to U.S. treaty rights in the Canal Zone, was the gradual ascendency of middle-class politics in the years after the war. As Walter LaFeber writes, the middle class was the engine of postwar Panamanian nationalism, and it was fueled by opposition both to the nation's traditional ruling oligarchy and to the special political and economic privileges that the United States enjoyed in the Canal Zone. Arnolfo Arias, "El Hombre" to his followers and three-time president of Panama, was the first to shake the foundations of the old politics. Beginning in the 1930s he mobilized Panama's small but growing middle class behind a reformist platform of "government by Panamanians for the happiness of the Panamanian people."[20] Before Arias, the oligarchy had survived by skillfully diverting pressures for domestic reform into opposition to the American presence in the Zone; because of the oligarchy's own close ties to the United States, however, such opposition was largely perfunctory and without political significance.[21] After Arias, and especially after the mid-1950s, pressures for changes in the 1903 treaty were no longer the sport of the oligarchs and hence no longer harmless diversions. In the hands of middle-class politicians nationalism and domestic reform were coupled in a political program that had an "explosive" effect, producing pressures for treaty reform that could no longer be ignored.[22]

These pressures were reinforced by the sudden deterioration of economic conditions in Panama after 1945. Wartime demand for the primary products of Latin America had brought unprecedented prosperity to the region and high hopes that the preferential treatment extended by the United States during the wartime emergency would become a permanent fixture of hemispheric relations. But no sooner did the war end than American interest and American aid shifted to Europe and eventually to the Far East; Latin America was set adrift to cope with economic problems that almost overnight assumed prewar severity. "When the dreams were shattered," writes historian Donald Dozer, "Latin Americans not only blamed the United States for having permitted the dreams to be dreamed at all but also tended to blame it for all their economic and social ills."[23] Faced with this relapse into dependency, politically active middle-class Panamanians responded by constructing an equation that linked the need for independence to the need for modernization, the need for modernization to the need for capital, and the need for capital to the need for greater access to the revenues of the Canal. Economic hardship thus worked to sharpen the traditional antagonism to American sovereignty in the Zone, and by the 1950s the political changes reflected in the rise of middle-class nationalism were creating the wherewithal, for the first time in half a century, to make effective demands on the United States for the termination of the 1903 treaty.

The implications of such changes were indicated by the Panamanian reaction to the terms of a treaty negotiated and ratified in 1955, which made revisions (technical adjustments, for the most part) in the Hay-Bunau-Varilla Treaty.[24] In the United States it was presumed that the agreement of 1955 would dissipate pressures for treaty reform and keep Panamanian relations on the back burner for the indefinite future. Instead, within just four years frustration in Panama over U.S. privileges in the Zone boiled over into violent anti-American demonstrations and into the new demands, this time not for further cosmetic changes but for the end of the 1903 treaty altogether. After the 1950s no Panamanian government would ever bargain for less than some tangible recognition of sovereignty over the Zone.

Ironically, these new pressures were the local expression of a global impulse that the United States itself had done much to encourage. During World War II the United States had been openly critical of the overseas empires of its European allies, and afterward had acted as midwife to the United Nations, one of the most important forums for the expression of the anticolonialist persuasion. As the Panamanians caught the mood, John Major suggests, Americans were thus "hoist with their own petard," especially as Panama began to use the United Nations to build international support for its negotiating position against the United States.[25]

America's willingness to countenance the dismemberment of European empires, however, was no guarantee of support at home for a policy of retreat from the Canal. Indeed, the imposition of new international realities on cherished old positions was no more welcome in America than in Europe. After six decades the Canal remained an indispensable symbol of American power. By the time of the ratification debate in 1977–78 it was perhaps the only place where, as columnist Stephen Rosenfeld suggested, Americans could find "respite from cares that plague all our other international dealings. There alone we can play out the fantasies of our national adolescence. By our technology, our money, our power, we spread progress and enlightenment and receive gratitude and praise." There alone, said Rosenfeld, could we "still indulge a dream of benevolent imperialism."[26]

Thus the necessity of accommodating Panamanian nationalism, of adjusting to new limits, was met with the same resistance and produced the same kind of political and psychological strains that attended the loss of empire in Europe. Under the circumstances it was not surprising that the controversy over ratification would become a gaudy rhetorical spectacle and that on the Right, opposition to the new treaties would take the form of a protracted requiem for America's lost greatness as a world power. Nor was it surprising that, before it was over, the contest over the Canal treaties would become a full-dress debate over America's role in the post-Vietnam era.

[3]

Perhaps no single factor weighed so heavily in the balance against ratification of the 1977 treaties as the near-total absence of public understanding of the circumstances that made these changes in U.S. Canal policy necessary. As we have seen, one such circumstance was the depth of popular dissatisfaction in Panama with the arrangements of the 1903 treaty. A second was the economic and political forces that, especially in the postwar years, gave new strength to Panamanian demands for treaty reform. We now turn to the third and fourth considerations raised in this chapter, examining the process by which, from the late 1950s onward, the United States was forced to abandon old positions in Panama, and the reaction to this process that developed in Congress and in public opinion.

The character of the period after the mid-1950s can be summarized by noting three trends. The first, described above, was the growth of internal pressure within Panama for the end of American control over the Canal Zone. This pressure was accompanied by successful Panamanian efforts (especially under General Omar Torrijos during the mid-1970s) to build broad international diplomatic support for revision of the 1903 Hay–Bunau-Varilla Treaty.

The second trend was growing sentiment within the policy–making echelons of six successive American presidential administrations in favor of revisions in the 1903 treaty with Panama. Initially the proposed changes were largely cosmetic and symbolic. By the time of the Kennedy administration a consensus had formed to find a substitute for the 1903 agreement. The Johnson administration adjusted the policy effort toward the actual restoration of Panamanian sovereignty over the Canal Zone. By the second Nixon administration, in 1974, the outlines of the final 1977 settlement had been pieced together in an agreement negotiated by Secretary of State Henry Kissinger and Panamanian foreign minister Juan Tack. In all, there were five attempts to alter the old treaty before the 1977 draft was completed. Each attempt progressively compromised positions defined in 1903.[27]

The third trend was the growth of domestic opposition to treaty reform within Congress and the public (and for a time within the executive branch itself). Successive attempts to alter the treaty met volatile reactions, harbingers of the organized opposition that would pour forth in response to President Jimmy Carter's efforts to secure Senate ratification of the 1977 draft treaty.

Policy makers who had to deal with the issue were thus caught between two fixed forces—the growing international pressure to end the last vestige of outright American imperialism in the Western hemisphere and the opposition of conservative groups at home for whom the perpetuation of treaty rights in Panama was the sine qua non, politically and symbolically, of sustaining American predominance in world affairs. Trapped between the proverbial rock and a hard place, America officials were forced to work out the most tenable compromise possible, one that would bring an end to seventy-five years of

American jurisdiction over the Zone while preserving some measure of practical control over the short-term operation and long-term defense of the Canal itself. Predictably, no one would be entirely happy with the results when the process was all over. For conservatives the 1977 treaty represented a tragic strategic concession; for many liberals it was little more than a tactical alteration that perpetuated the purpose, if not the form, of American imperial control in the isthmus.

The cost and divisiveness of the final struggle over Panama policy in 1977–78 were partly the result of the failure of five successive administrations to explain to Congress and to the American people the reasons why the treaty in 1903 had so rapidly become an anachronism. To that failure may be attributed both the intensity of the opposition that greeted successive changes in Canal policy and what Stephen Rosenfeld calls the "ambivalence of purpose" that became the inescapable attribute of more than twelve years of negotiations on a new regime for the Canal.[28] It is to the history of these negotiations that we now turn.

[4]

The rioting that occurred in May 1958 was significant as a testament to the growing political pressures that were stiffening the determination of successive governments in Panama to press for sweeping revisions of the 1903 treaty. As late as 1955 the American government was able to contain the Panama problem by making the kind of technical adjustments prescribed in the treaty of that year, but after 1958 the issue was never to be less than sovereignty itself. Beginning with the Eisenhower administration no American president could escape the escalating pressures for treaty reform. As Margaret Scranton writes, "Whether one views the erosion of United States control over the Canal and the Canal Zone as the beginning of the end of its world power status or as the beginning of a new era in hemispheric relations, the second Eisenhower Administration is the place to begin searching for an explanation of the changes in canal policy which culminated in ratification of the 1978 canal treaties."[29]

The riots of 1958 retrieved U.S. policy in Panama from neglect just as the hostile reception given Vice President Nixon's state visit to Latin America in 1958 and the Cuban revolution of 1959 were forcing a reevaluation of policy for the entire hemisphere. American policy toward Panama would come to be characterized by a certain built-in, perhaps inescapable, contradiction as successive administrations searched for ways to bow to the inevitable without completely relinquishing effective prerogatives over the operation and defense of the Canal.

For the Eisenhower administration the principal effect of the Cuban revolution and the outbreaks of civil unrest in Panama was to reinforce its disposition not to make basic concessions to Panamanian nationalists regarding sovereignty and defense rights. But on one issue the administration did make a key concession to the Panamanians. This concession, doubtless influenced by the president's brother, Dr. Milton Eisenhower, may in retrospect be identified as the first clear step on the road to the treaties initialed by President Carter and General Torrijos in Washington in 1977.

In July 1958 the younger Eisenhower visited Panama as part of a Latin American fact-finding tour. In Panama he reportedly confided to one senior government official that the United States would recognize titular Panamanian sovereignty over the Canal Zone on Panamanian Independence Day, 3 November 1959. Whether true or apocryphal, the news spread widely enough to generate expectations that, when dashed, were the cause of new rioting in 1959. The rioting culminated in a pitched battle between students and contingents of U.S. Army Troops and Canal Zone police at Ancon Hill, inside the Zone.[30]

It seems clear that the president himself was favorably disposed toward making some conciliatory gesture on the matter of titular sovereignty. "We should be generous in all small administrative details," he told Dulles. "Our firmness should be in holding fast to basic principles and purposes of [the] treaty."[31] He told a press conference in December 1959 that "in some form or other we should have visual evidence that Panama does have titular sovereignty over the region." Secretary of State Christian Herter accordingly announced that "sympathetic consideration" was being given to the possibility of allowing one Panamanian flag to fly within the Zone.[32] The new flag policy was announced in a statement that emphasized its "voluntary and unilateral" nature, on 17 September 1960. Four days later a single Panamanian flag was hoisted at a location called Shaler Triangle, just inside the Zone and within sight of downtown Panama City. In the words of one writer the policy was "the most momentous of any since 1903."[33]

The response to the flag concession revealed the breadth and strength of domestic opposition to changes in the status of American power in the isthmus, opposition that was to retard the evolution of Panama policy for the next two decades. Milton Eisenhower wrote that "When

29

Congress got word of [the flag concession] there were violent protests.... They saw flying the flags as the first step; next Panama would want police power in the Zone; soon we would be without complete jurisdiction and the efficiency of the canal operations and its readiness for security actions might be jeopardized."[34] Even before the formal announcement, the House of Representatives voted by a lopsided margin of 390 to 12—in February 1961—to condemn Eisenhower's intentions on the matter.[35] Representative Daniel Flood of Pennsylvania, the leading congressional spokesman for the American community in the Zone and a man described by the *Chicago Tribune* as "one of the best informed in Congress on the issue," depicted the rioting that prompted the concession as "probes of our government's will power to stand up for the just and indispensable rights of the United States at Panama."[36] He pronounced Herter's assessment that recognition of titular sovereignty represented no surrender of actual sovereignty "a naivety that is incomprehensible."[37] The concessions, he said, "did not beguile Panamanian radicals but simply whetted their appetites for more concessions."[38] As he summed up the implications of the policy, "The day [the Panamanian flag] is formally hoisted marks the beginning of the end of exclusive control over the Panama Canal."[39] Arch-conservative New Hampshire publisher William Loeb was thrown—in the words of former senator Thomas McIntyre—into "high dudgeon" over the matter. "Believe it or not," complained Loeb, "the Panamanian flag is to fly above the Stars and Stripes in the Panama Canal Zone on certain occasions. The trick was sneaked over the American public so quietly that most Americans are probably not aware of this shocking and fantastic order by the State Department. Can you imagine putting the American flag below any other flag on American territory? This gives you some idea of how nearly insane are the people who run our foreign policy."[40] Echoed Flood: "In the years of American history, impeachment of Presidents has been urged for less than this. This action ... is a further appalling example of American diplomatic appeasement, loss of leadership and weakened integrity in the eyes of the world."[41]

More serious was opposition to the policy expressed within the executive branch itself. "It is very simple," testified the vice chief of naval operations on the proposed change in flag policy. "We don't think it should be done...It symbolizes the resumption of sovereignty which is not in accord with the terms of the treaty we have with the Panamanians."[42] The governor of the Canal Zone, Major General William E. Potter, concurred in assessing the risks: "I am sure that the flying of the flag is not an ultimate step; it is merely the next step."[43]

Voices in opposition to the Eisenhower policy were heard even from the academy. Writing in *U.S. News and World Report,* Yale diplomatic historian Samuel Flagg Bemis described the stakes in a larger context: "Scarcely anything, short of withdrawal of American forces from Europe and the Asiatic littoral, or the dissolution of NATO ... or SEATO ... would please the Red imperialists more than neutralization of the Panama Canal or the transfer of its control and defense to the Republic of Panama, like the Suez Canal to Egypt.... The Communist conspiracy is on its toes today in Panama trying to dislodge the United States from control of this still-vital American lifeline."[44]

On at least one point there was agreement between Panamanian nationalists and American conservatives. As one Panamanian newspaper put it, "Sovereignty, like virginity, is or is not—there is no halfway measure."[45] For critics of the Eisenhower policy the decision to fly the flag called forth immediate fears of the beginning of the end, even as events in Cuba were raising the specter of the first serious challenge to the integrity of the Monroe Doctrine in one hundred fifty years. "I'm not the sort of fellow who looks for Bolsheviki with whiskers under my bed with bombs every night," disclaimed Flood. "But the fact remains that whenever you have a situation like this, the Reds move in."[46] Even President Eisenhower confessed that it was "a little perplexing" that the Panamanians were so hostile so soon after the concessions made in the 1955 agreement. The riots, he concluded, were instigated by "an excitable group; people that are extremists."[47]

Nevertheless, with the announcement of the new flag policy the Eisenhower administration had made a major tactical adjustment against the backdrop of a fixed strategy designed to preserve the rights granted in the 1903 treaty; by 1960 the first cycle of pressure, response, and opposition was complete. American policy had inched in a symbolic but significant way toward concessions written into the 1977 treaties. As a result of the flag decision, concludes Laurence Ealy, "there could no longer be doubt that the North American authority in the Canal Zone was simply that of a lessee-custodian of a part of the Republic of Panama's national territory."[48]

[5]

The dilemmas inherent in the Eisenhower policies appeared again during the Kennedy administration. In hemispheric affairs Kennedy adopted a two-pronged strategy for dealing with the dread contagion

tóbal on the Atlantic. When the riots ended three days later, the casualty figures showed twenty-five dead and damage of over $2 million, much of it to American property in the Zone.

The episode offers an instructive example in the political uses of violence. Despite repeated requests for the government to call out the National Guard, including one request directly from Johnson himself, the violence was allowed to go unchecked, consistent with Milton Eisenhower's understanding that "the way to get action out of the United States is to stir up trouble or threaten to turn to Moscow for help."[53] With an eye to the latter, Chiari did nothing to discourage rumors of Communist participation in the riots, though he steadfastly maintained his own opposition to communism. The strategy clearly heightened Washington's assessment of the stakes.[54] Moreover, Chiari seized the occasion to draw world attention to the deepening crisis: he dramatically broke diplomatic relations with the United States on 8 January and charged the United States with a violation of the Rio Pact for an "unprovoked armed attack" on Panamanian territory.[55] Thereafter he appealed to the UN Security Council and to the Council of Ministers of the Organization of American States. A five-nation investigating team sent by the OAS predictably found blame on both sides and refused to cite the United States for an act of aggression. Nevertheless, Panama had made its point in two international forums, thereby increasing the pressures for change and decreasing the operating leverage (in the manner of the Eisenhower and Kennedy flag concessions) of Johnson and his successors.

Johnson's reaction to his first major foreign-policy crisis was largely defined by the countervailing domestic and international pressures at work; in the end he drew American policy closer to the final compromise defined in the 1977 draft treaty. First he renewed the call, this time in earnest, for an inquiry into the possibility of a new sea-level canal, speaking freely, and with an obvious diplomatic purpose, of building it in Nicaragua or Colombia. In April 1964 he appointed an Atlantic-Pacific Interoceanic Canal Study Commission to make a comprehensive site and feasibility study for an alternative, sea-level route.

With the commission's work in progress, Johnson moved to revise the arrangements governing the existing Canal. Citing the endorsement of former presidents Eisenhower and Truman, he announced plans on 18 December 1964 to begin negotiations on a new treaty to replace the 1903 agreement with its controversial grant of perpetual American sovereignty. Robert B. Anderson, a Republican and former secretary of the treasury under Eisenhower, was appointed chief U.S. negotiator.

Within a year, in September 1965, the two parties announced an agreement in principle. The agreement called for the abrogation of the 1903 treaty; the recognition by the United States of Panamanian sovereignty over the Canal Zone; and a new treaty with a fixed termination date to coincide with the opening of the hoped-for sea-level canal. In addition U.S. troops were for the first time put under a Status of Forces Agreement that, as Margaret Scranton notes, "elevated Panama's status from occupied status to defense partner."[56] In return the United States was to retain primary defense rights and a predominant role in a new administrative agency to oversee the day-to-day operations of the Canal. Speaking for critics of the administration's plans, columnist James J. Kilpatrick complained that the new policy was "simply surrender, abject surrender, to a gang of blackmailers whose bluff came down to this: Throw in your hand or we'll riot again."[57]

The negotiators worked for two years defining the terms of transition to eventual Panamanian control of the waterway, and on 29 June 1967 Johnson and Chiari's successor, Winston Robles, announced the conclusion of three draft treaties and plans for a Rose Garden signing ceremony on 23 July. But before the signing could be held, the contents of the draft treaties were leaked to the *Chicago Tribune*, on 7 July. The agreements were swept away in the flood tide of angry criticism that followed.

The House of Representatives immediately issued a condemnatory resolution signed by one hundred fifty members. Opposition was led by Lenore Sullivan (D.-Mo.), who predicted that if the Canal were given to Panama, it would "rot and decay" like "everything else turned over to them."[58] Another House member invoked the threat of Soviet intervention: "We are throwing wide the doors for the Soviet Union to come in and take over...and they will."[59] Responding to the announced treaty package, House minority leader Gerald R. Ford cautioned that "with Cuba under control of the Soviet Union via Castro and increased Communist subversion in Latin America, a Communist threat to the Canal is a real danger."[60] The peripatetic Congressman Flood, "who has thoroly [sic] studied the issue,"[61] called the new policy "appeasement" and "absolutely suicidal,"[62] a "direct outgrowth of the Bolshevik Revolution of 1917 and the international Communist conspiracy."[63]

For our officials to proclaim that Panama, which since 1955 has not been able to collect its own garbage from the streets of Panama City and Colón, is a partner of this great interoceanic public utility is, to say the least, unrealistic and really astounding....

The President's announcement, indeed, marks a sad day for the United States, although it may bring rejoicing at Peiping and Moscow. He has completely yielded to the council of his advisers, sappers and appeasers, who must be made to bear basic responsibility for what has occurred. Moreover, I predict that the expressed willingness to surrender control over the Panama Canal will be taken as a signal for accelerated activity among communistic revolutionary elements all over Latin America and the Caribbean.[64]

Outside Congress the response to the treaties was no warmer. Veterans' groups, patriotic societies such as the Daughters of the American Revolution, traditional right-wing groups like the Liberty Lobby and the American Security Council, all warned that the only way to safeguard vital U.S. interests in the Canal was to retain control of it. Opponents universally echoed Flood's concern that to abandon the waterway was to invite a Communist takeover. These sentiments were duplicated in resolutions passed by several state legislatures. This time, moreover, the powerful maritime lobby weighed in with a warning against changes that would impair the efficiency of the Canal. Representing the maritime industry, the American Institute of Merchant Shipping reported that it would "strongly oppose" the 1967 draft treaty: "AIMS takes the position that the United States must retain exclusive control and sovereignty over the Panama Canal and Canal Zone, including determination of toll rates and should oppose any proposals for the establishment of a joint Administration which would replace the Panama Canal Company in the operation, maintenance and improvement of the Canal."[65] Noting that tolls were "far from a light burden" and fearing the eventual transfer of toll-setting authority to Panama, AIMS spokesmen declared that "we would find no alternative" to the present treaty and that it was necessary to "maintain sovereignty as a precondition to operation."[66]

In the face of this outpouring of public opposition, complicated by growing pressures in Vietnam and the onset of election season in both Panama and the United States, Johnson was forced to cancel the signing ceremony, and efforts to secure Senate ratification were postponed until after the 1968 election. As it happened, neither Johnson nor Robles survived the year's elections, and in September 1970 a new government in Panama notified the United States that the draft treaties of 1967 were no longer acceptable as a basis for resuming negotiations.

The Johnson years offered dramatic evidence of the extent to which policy makers and public were drafting apart in their perceptions of an appropriate solution to the Canal crisis. Diverging responses to the flag riots within the administration and among vocal congressional opponents and interest-group spokesmen were of central significance in the Johnson years and an omen of the enormously difficult public relations task that would face Jimmy Carter. For Johnson the riots were a signal to compromise while compromise was still attainable. For critics the riots were a clarion call to stand firm in the face of adversity.

By the end of the Johnson administration another salient fact was becoming apparent. Trapped between conflicting sets of domestic and international pressures, policy makers from the Eisenhower administration onward were consistently more responsive to international concerns. To be sure, negotiations on the 1967 treaties make it clear that U.S. concessions on sovereignty in the Zone were hedged about with preconditions designed to keep operational and defense rights alive for a far longer time than the Panamanians were willing to accept. Nevertheless, by 1967 a trend was unmistakable. Where Eisenhower sought to retain unilateral power according to the terms of the 1903 treaty, and where Kennedy sought to retain control through a multilateralized, inter-American scheme, Johnson devised a bilateral arrangement that, despite its provision for the short-term retention of defense and administration rights, did make the concession on sovereignty which was the heart of the Canal issue. The concession once made, no government in Panama could settle for less as the basis for future negotiations. After 1967 the question was no longer if, but only when and in what specific manner, the old principle of American control would be relinquished forever.

Finally, by 1967 it was clear that domestic politics was lagging far behind America's bilateral diplomacy with Panama. Each new retreat from positions enshrined in the 1903 treaty, like lightning on a summer's night, illuminated the landscape of public and congressional opposition, revealing widening and deepening resistance to positions held within the executive branch. Even so, efforts to build a base of domestic political support for new approaches to the Panama problem still lay a decade ahead. When the task was finally undertaken during the Carter administration, to win support for ratification of the 1977 treaties, negotiator Sol Linowitz would conclude that marshaling public approval was "a very consuming job, in many ways more arduous than the negotiations themselves and in many ways more painful."[67]

[7]

Preoccupied with the Vietnam War the first Nixon administration consigned relations with Latin America to a period of benign neglect, and progress on the treaties languished. Negotiations were begun again in June 1971 and continued off and on for two years, but the effort was largely inconclusive. Retreating from the more generous bargaining positions of 1965–67, U.S. negotiators adhered to the "irreducible minimums" of retaining "sufficient rights to continue to operate, maintain, and defend this canal and expand it when we need it."[68] As the State Department announced at the resumption of the talks, there was a "willingness to make adjustments" but "no intention of yielding control and defense of the Canal to the threat of violence."[69] Under the circumstances there was little likelihood of substantial progress.

Panama's first military coup, in 1968, brought to power the head of the influential National Guard, Brigadier General Omar Torrijos Herrara. Torrijos was typical of a new generation of left-leaning, reform-minded Latin American "caudillos," whose political base was anchored in lower- and middle-class support. His nationalism found expression in heightened opposition to the continuing American presence in the Zone. It was to Torrijos that the task would now fall of breaking the stalemate at the bargaining table.

Though the possibility of renewed violence was always an implicit bargaining chip for the Panamanians, Torrijos adopted a *diplomatic* offensive to force the United States back into productive negotiations.[70] One Panamanian explained the rationale behind the strategy in these terms: "General Torrijos understood that a struggle for national liberation carried out only at the bilateral level was a struggle without a future for the very simple reason that it was the struggle of a very small country against the major power in the world. Thus he decided . . . that the problem of Panama, the Canal problem, would not be a real problem until it became a problem of the American continents and of the world."[71]

To make it a problem of the world, Torrijos invited the UN Security Council to meet in special session in Panama, in March 1972. For six days representatives of the fifteen member-nations were subjected to a carefully orchestrated round of speeches and site visits that dramatized Panamanian dissatisfaction with U.S. treaty rights in the Zone. By the time the session was over, the American delegation was isolated even from old allies and was forced to veto a UN resolution calling for a treaty that would "guarantee full respect for Panama's effective sovereignty over all of its territory."[72] Over the next four years similar expressions of support were culled from the ranks of the OAS, the conference of nonaligned nations, and individual world leaders. Warned one, Venezuelan president Carlos Andres Pérez, it is "the unanimous opinion of all Latin America that the United States should return sovereignty over the Canal to Panama." Otherwise, "Panama can become a keg of dynamite."[73]

The Panamanian strategy was a striking success. Suddenly, reported Steven Rosenfeld in 1975, "the issue has become an international fixture.... The propaganda and political beating administered in the United Nations [has] helped transform the issue within the U.S. government from a modest regional matter, which could safely be left in a state of stagnation, into a major priority."[74]

As quickly as the issue had subsided after 1968, it now came to life again, this time reflecting the convergence of all the circumstances necessary to make a final agreement possible: the diplomatic support systematically garnered by Torrijos; the end of the Vietnam War; the growing U.S. interest in upgrading relations with Latin America (and in the economic benefits that would stem from such a policy); and a bottom-line assessment that, increasingly, there was everything to gain and little to lose by making the long-postponed concessions on sovereignty and control.[75] Moreover, there was renewed personal interest in the issue on the part of Secretary of State Kissinger. Rosenfeld indicates that Kissinger "had been tentatively searching since Vietnam for a way for the United States to deal effectively with the insistent nationalism of smaller and weaker states."[76] With Panama he had an issue made to order.

Inspired to new action, the Nixon administration set about the task of solving the Panama problem with renewed determination. It scrapped the draft treaty under negotiation since 1971, appointed a new negotiator, former business executive and international troubleshooter Ellsworth Bunker, and, significantly, agreed to produce a joint statement with Panama on the principles to guide a new (and presumably final) round of negotiations. This task was completed in February 1974, when Secretary Kissinger flew to Panama to initial formally eight guidelines that represented the last major milestone on the road to the 1977 treaties. In Panama Kissinger explained the motives behind the new, conciliatory position of the United States: "a stable world cannot be imposed by force; it must derive from consensus. Mankind can only achieve community on the basis of shared objectives.... In the past our negotiation would have been determined by relative strength. Today we have come together in an act of conciliation. We recognize that no agreement can endure unless the parties want to maintain it. Participation in partnership is far preferable to reluctant acquiescence."[77]

The principles agreed to in Panama represented the final break in

39

U.S. policy toward Panama, first, by formally renouncing sovereignty and second, by making explicit the assumption implicit in the 1967 draft treaties that security for American interests in the Canal was increasingly a function of consent and not coercion. As Bunker explained, "In our negotiations we are attempting to lay the foundations for a new, more modern relationship which will enlist Panamanian cooperation and better protect our interests. Unless we succeed, I believe that Panama's consent to our presence will continue to decline, and at an even more rapid rate. Some form of conflict in Panama would seem virtually certain."[78] Moreover, the Kissinger-Tack principles effectively abandoned plans for the construction of a sea-level canal, at least for the time being; the United States thereby jettisoned the fallback position that had made earlier concessions on the administration and control of the existing Canal and the Zone an acceptable political risk. By 1974 there was no mistaking the serious intention of the United States to relinquish, without qualification, positions held since 1903.

The so-called Kissinger-Tack Agreement[79] prefigured the final outlines of the treaty that Jimmy Carter would submit to the U.S. Senate in 1977. It called for the abrogation of the 1903 treaty and its replacement by a new treaty with a fixed termination date; for the end of U.S. jurisdiction over Panamanian territory; for the return of the Canal Zone to Panama, with certain specified rights to be extended to the United States during the yet-to-be determined life of the new treaty; for full Panamanian participation in the administration of the Canal during the transition period; and for some "just and equitable" share of the benefits of the Canal's operation to go to Panama.[80]

Denison Kitchel writes of the Kissinger-Tack principles that it was "unusual for one of the two nations in bilateral treaty negotiations to throw away its major trading positions before negotiations commence."[81] Indeed, it seems clear that the bargaining room that once existed had been forfeited by 1964, when Lyndon Johnson agreed to abandon the perpetuity clause of the 1903 treaty as the basis for future talks. Notwithstanding some latitude for give and take in the resolution of countless matters of detail, it was evident by 1974 that there could be but one quid and one quo in any serious future negotiations: the eventual, final relinquishment of American rights in the Zone and the international goodwill and cooperation from Panama, which, at least by the reckoning of the State Department, the sacrifice of old rights would guarantee. Thus for whatever future administration would finally bring the matter to a conclusion, there lay ahead the most difficult of all public relations tasks—winning support for a treaty that would exchange tangible rights for abstract gains. But by 1974, perhaps by 1964, there was no turning back. The diplomats inexorably pressed on with the job of negotiating a new treaty. Justifying their work would be a problem for the future.

[8]

With agreement on the Kissinger-Tack principles in hand, the evolution of Canal policy was all but complete, and the stage was set for one of the major ratification contests in American history. On one side was an undetermined but apparently growing number of Americans inside and outside Congress who were opposed to any concessions to Panama on the status of the waterway.[82] On the other side were policy makers and a small, largely liberal community of supporters inside and outside Congress who were responsive to the demands of a new international environment and to the ceaseless efforts of the Panamanians to be done with the offending American presence in the Canal Zone.

As long as Canal policy was the sole prerogative of the executive branch, concessions could be made in an environment relatively free from domestic political pressures. Throughout the negotiation period, however, evidence was mounting of the strength and breadth of countervailing opinion, opinion that was certain to be mobilized once a final draft treaty was submitted to the Senate for ratification.

Significantly, the outbreaks of public and congressional opposition that occurred in response to changes in the flags policy in 1960 and 1962, to the negotiating principles announced in 1964, to the draft treaties of 1967, and now to the Kissinger-Tack Agreement, revealed widespread dissatisfaction not only with the concessions themselves but with the rationale that made such concessions a matter of logic— indeed, a matter of some urgency—to U.S. policy makers. After the ratification debate was finally won, Robert Pastor, President Jimmy Carter's National Security Council specialist on Latin America, would observe that the heart of the administration's problem was the difficulty of selling the counterintuitive premise that the way to protect American interests in the Zone was to relinquish American jurisdiction over the Zone.[83] *Newsday* described it as the paradox of "giving up the Canal to save it."[84] It was this very position that Kissinger and Bunker began to articulate in 1974 and that the Carter administration would have to defend to an uncomprehending public through the eight months of the Senate debate in 1977–78. Nearer to the public's understanding was the more intuitive premise, urged by such critics as Flood and eventually Ronald Reagan, that ownership was a virtual precondition to the long-term security of American interests in the Canal.

On Capitol Hill the concessions made by Secretary Kissinger amounted, in Stephen Rosenfeld's words, to a "call to the barricades."[85] This time the opposition was broader and better organized than ever before. In March 1974, in direct response to the Kissinger-Tack Agreement, Senator Strom Thurmond of South Carolina rounded up thirty-four cosponsors for a Senate resolution urging that "the government of the United States should maintain and protect its sovereign rights and jurisdiction over the Canal and Zone and should in no way cede, dilute, forfeit, negotiate or transfer any of these sovereign rights."[86] Thurmond wrote in defense of the resolution that "In in my judgment the secretary [Kissinger] committed an egregious blunder in committing the United States to a course of action on a new Panama treaty without a reasonable assurance that the requisite two-thirds majority of the Senate supported the abrogation of sovereignty."[87] A year later two-thirds support looked less likely than ever. In May 1975 the Thurmond Resolution was reintroduced, this time attracting thirty-seven sponsors, three more than necessary to defeat any treaty submitted to the Senate. In June 1975 the House of Representatives weighed in on its own with an amendment to the State Department appropriations bill to prohibit funding for negotiations that would lead to the relinquishment of U.S. rights in the Zone. The amendment, sponsored by Kentucky congressman Gene Synder, passed by a comfortable 246 to 164 margin. When a conference report later reduced the language to a simple disclaimer that such negotiations should protect the "vital interests" of the United States in the Canal, it was passed in the House by a 212 to 201 majority.[88]

In a letter to Foreign Minister Juan Tack, Kissinger described the opposition in Congress as a "tribute to the success of what you and I have been trying to achieve. . . . In view of the fact that we have had success and significant progress up to the present time, this has inspired those who do not want progress to do all in their power to impede or discourage new advances."[89] In fact, by 1975 the congressional power to impede progress on the negotiations was showing signs of running out of steam, at least for the short term. As LaFeber suggests, the passage of the Snyder Amendment probably represented the "high-water mark" of congressional opposition to the negotiating positions staked out by Kissinger and Tack in 1974.[90] In July

Senator Harry Byrd of Virginia was forced to abandon efforts to round up support in the Senate for his own version of the Snyder Amendment, and in 1976 Snyder himself was heavily outvoted in a second attempt to secure modifying language that would mandate the retention of U.S. sovereignty in the Canal Zone. One final attempt by Snyder in 1977 was disposed of by voice vote.

In the longer term, however, there were no grounds for complacency, in part because Kissinger-Tack was only a dress rehearsal but also because no evidence suggested any growing appreciation in Congress of the logic of the protreaty argument. As Robert Pastor writes, treaty supporters in the Senate expected that the Ford administration would mount an offensive of some kind in 1975 to counteract the threat posed by the Thurmond Resolution.[91] But while an information campaign was mapped out at the State Department, it was never implemented, and on 4 March 1975 the second Thurmond Resolution passed without effective opposition from the administration.[92] Congressional briefings were eventually scheduled in an effort to fend off the Snyder Amendment, but even then the effort was too little and too late—and, for that matter, largely off the point. When administration lobbyists finally did take up the fight, they argued not on the merits of the Kissinger-Tack principles but on the grounds that the president's treaty power should not be circumscribed by the legislative branch. The final draft of the conference report on the State Department appropriations bill for 1976 therefore duly explained that qualifying language was "not intended to derogate in any way the President's constitutionally mandated power to negotiate treaties."[93] Thus although congressional opposition to the Kissinger-Tack Agreement finally did subside, the episode bequeathed no promising legacy to the Carter administration. As Pastor concluded in 1975,

> the [State] Department fails to see . . . that the time has long passed when the domestic and international negotiating tracks can be pursued separately, the first after the second. The two tracks are inextricably intertwined and concentrating on one to the exclusion of the other will doom the entire effort. . . . State's obsolete attitudes and institutional lethargy have contributed to what may become one of the most significant foreign policy failures of the decade.[94]

As if to underscore the point, one congressman prophetically warned the present and future administrations, "Whatever you do, you are going to have to come back to Congress . . . and unless you look behind you and look ahead of you, you are going to make a real

43

mistake. . . . I think the State Department must understand necessarily
that they have equally as large problems with the United States Senate
and with this House as they do with . . . the Panamanian people and
the Zonians."[95]

If congressional opinion was not exactly primed for the treaty fight
that lay ahead, public opinion was even more impervious to the rationale adopted by the architects of U.S. policy on the Canal. The
only sounding of public opinion prior to 1975 was taken by the Gallup
Organization in the aftermath of the 1964 rioting in Panama, and it
offers striking evidence on the point. Gallup found that among the
64 percent of the population aware of the issue, opposition to relinquishing control over the Canal was running at a margin of six to
one.[96] Thirteen years later, on the eve of the ratification debate, public
support had slipped even further. Polling results published by Opinion Research Corporation of Princeton, New Jersey, in May 1977
showed opposition to relinquishing "ownership and control" of the
Canal up to 78 percent.[97] In spite of these warning signals, however,
there was no more concerted effort at the State Department to build
a public case for the Kissinger-Tack principles than there had been
to stem opposition in Congress. In 1975 Kissinger, Bunker, and other
administration officials belatedly addressed a variety of university and
foreign-policy forums, but the effort was a mere hint of the kind of
serious public relations offensive that would be required to support
the work of the diplomats who were now on the verge of final success.
As Paul B. Ryan writes of the implications:

> The failure of Lyndon Johnson and succeeding Presidents as well to
> heed this signal is puzzling. Perhaps over the years the Panama problem
> paled into insignificance when compared to the Vietnam War, the Mid-
> dle-East flare-ups, the SALT talks, China, or inflation. Whatever the
> reason, the Johnson, Nixon, and Ford Administrations successively ne-
> glected to obtain strong support from the Congress and the public for
> what many interpreted as the ultimate surrender of complete control of
> the Canal. This oversight, with its intimations of secret diplomacy, vir-
> tually preordained the public uproar that erupted during the 1976 Pres-
> idential campaign.[98]

That uproar was occasioned by Ronald Reagan's almost accidental
discovery of the electric response evoked by the Panama Canal issue.
As the Snyder and Thurmond resolutions defined the breadth of
congressional opposition, the Reagan campaign shed light as nothing

had before on the strength of latent public antagonism to the course of the negotiations.

Columnist Mary McGrory reports that the issue first surfaced in New Hampshire. "I saw it born in New Hampshire in the Presidential primary of 1976. I watched Ronald Reagan say 'We built it, we paid for it, it's ours'. . . and I saw the response. He looked stunned. . . . He stepped back from the microphone, blinked. . .and then he smiled. He knew he had an issue."[99] Other accounts place the genesis of the issue in North Carolina, Texas, and Florida. Wherever it started, Reagan's evocative hints of State Department perfidy were precursors of the full-blown conspiracy theories that would characterize much of the public opposition to ratification during the Carter administration. As Reagan said before a Sun City retirement community near Tampa, Florida:

> State Department actions for several years now have suggested that they are intimidated by the propaganda of Panama's military dictator, Fidel Castro's good friend, Omar Torrijos. Our State Department apparently believes the hints regularly dispensed by the leftist Torrijos regime that the Canal will be sabotaged if we don't hand it over. Our government has maintained a mouselike silence as criticisms of the giveaway have increased. I don't understand how the State Department can suggest we pay blackmail to this dictator, for blackmail is what it is. When it comes to the Canal, we built it, we paid for it, it's ours, and we should tell Torrijos and company that we're going to keep it.

The response, according to one observer, was "bedlam." One campaign aide reported that "Reagan, who knows his audience very well, was so taken aback that he lost his place."[100]

Wherever the issue first began to draw such lively responses, the salient point is that it was Reagan, and not the government, who made the treaty negotiations a major national issue for the first time; and it was Reagan who effectively defined the terms on which the debate over the Canal would be waged down to the last day of the Senate ratification drive. Into the vacuum of public understanding of the motives of five presidential administrations, Reagan skillfully planted doubts about the wisdom and, always by indirection, about the loyalty of public officials whose management of the issue for close to two decades had become a repetitious pattern of concessions and backsliding. The earnest, self-evident logic of the Reagan critique, more genial than Representative Flood's blunt verbal assaults, crystalized the half-formed doubts of millions of Americans and gave expression to a growing disposition to hold on in Panama to what events in Vietnam and elsewhere had so forcefully called into question, namely, the symbol and substance of America's preeminent place in world affairs.

Thus by the eve of the Carter administration we may define Panama policy in precisely the same terms as those that obtained during the second Eisenhower administration, when the first symbolic gesture to Panamanian nationalism was made in the form of a seemingly inconsequential revision of flags policy. After twenty years the framers of U.S. policy toward Panama were still caught in the trap produced by conflicting domestic and international pressures. Warning of new threats of violence, the Panamanian government now urgently pressed for translation of the Kissinger-Tack principles into a draft treaty. At home, opposition to further concessions was strong enough to keep the negotiations on hold through the long election season of 1976.

As long as diplomacy and domestic politics were on separate tracks, there was always a means of escape, if only by the course of deferral that the Ford administration chose in 1976. But once diplomacy and politics converged, as they were destined to do during the Carter administration, some fundamental adjustment would have to be made. By 1976 it was possible to predict with some certainty that the burden of adjustment would have to fall to domestic opinion. By 1976 it was equally clear that the failure of five administrations properly to condition public attitudes would all but guarantee a costly and divisive ratification debate when new treaties were finally completed. Indeed, so far had policy evolved in one direction and so far had opinion evolved in the other, so contrary were the lessons drawn from postwar history, that one writer summarized the situation on the eve of the Carter presidency by describing the evolution of two worlds. "On one hand ... a majority of the American people is instinctively opposed to giving up our rights and position in Panama—call it the world of public opinion—and on the other, in the official world [there is] an even clearer indication that those rights and that position are going to be given up.... Both worlds are real. They are on a collision course."[101] With 1976 elections behind and a new president in the White House, that collision was now at hand. For Jimmy Carter the job of building a bridge between policy and opinion would require all the political dexterity his young administration could muster. The difficulty of the task was underscored by the growing evidence of public and congressional opposition to the goal of reforming the 1903 treaty to which Carter, in the tradition of his three immediate predecessors, would soon be committed. The urgency of the task was demonstrated by the proliferating international pressures for change. As for events in Panama itself, concluded the *New Republic*'s TRB, "the tinder only awaits a spark."[102]

CHAPTER 2

The End of Containment: The Foreign Policy of Jimmy Carter

Dissatisfaction in Panama with the treaty arrangements of 1903 produced a series of escalating pressures that, by the postwar period, could no longer be denied. Beginning with sporadic outbursts of rioting in the late 1950s and culminating at the time of the 1976 elections, these pressures became the focus of international diplomatic attention. During the same period U.S. policy evolved with extraordinary speed from steadfast reaffirmations of the principle of continued American sovereignty in the Zone in the 1950s to the renunciation of that principle embodied in the Kissinger-Tack Agreement of 1974. By the latter year the days of American jurisdiction in the Zone appeared to be numbered.

Still, the matter was not completely settled. Concessions at the policy-making level were met with spirited reactions from apparent majorities in the American public and on Capitol Hill, and by 1976 the positions staked out by Kissinger and Tack were drawing sizable election-year fire. Under the pressure of events the Ford administration was forced to consign the movement for treaty reform, so strong only two years earlier, to a kind of diplomatic limbo.

Nor was reluctance to face the issue confined to the Ford administration. Through the months of the longest presidential campaign in American history, pronouncements on the issue from Democratic front-runner Jimmy Carter were models of studied ambivalence, raising questions as to whether, if elected, he would be the president to make good on the promise of the Kissinger-Tack Agreement. As Carter explains in his memoirs, his stated position on the issue was that "we could share responsibilities more equitably without giving up practical control of the Canal."[1] The point was first elaborated before a Democratic party conference in November 1975:

> I would try to work out some arrangement within these two limitations: First of all, I would not be in favor of relinquishing actual control of the Panama Canal or its use to any other nation, including Panama. I think we've got to retain that actual practical control. On the other hand, I think there are several things that can be done to assuage the feelings among the Panamanians that they've been excluded or perhaps even outtraded back in the 1903 period. So I would be glad to yield part of the sovereignty over the Panama Canal Zone to Panama. I would certainly be willing to renegotiate the payment terms to Panama and I would also be willing to remove the word "perpetuity" from the present agreement.[2]

A year later, in New York, Carter expressed the same sentiments. "I believe the Panamanians will respond to open and continued negotiations and the sharing of sovereignty and control, recognizing their rights in that respect. I would certainly look with favor on the possible reduction of the number of bases ... possibly a reduction in the number of military forces we have there.... [However] I would never give up full control of the Panama Canal as long as it had any contribution to make to our national security."[3]

Carter's position, apart from his stated willingness to relinquish the "in perpetuity" clause of the 1903 treaty, was a sizable step back from that staked out by President Ford, who stated during the campaign that he wished only to retain *access* to the Canal and not control of it.[4] To continue the negotiations without giving up control of the Canal, as Carter was suggesting, was a "contradiction in terms," complained columnist Marquis Childs, "since the negotiations are about giving up sovereignty."[5] Carter's intentions are "worse than President Ford's, " echoed the *Washington Post*; Carter would "renege on the Ford Administration's promise to give Panama full control when a new treaty's fixed term expires some decades hence. Instead, Mr. Carter proposed a 'sharing of sovereignty'—a phrase that, if it is not simply mumbo jumbo, amounts to a step backward, since the U.S. does not contend now that it exercises 'sovereignty' in the Canal Zone, only rights."[6]

There was little more clarity in Carter's position by the time of the long-awaited television debates between Carter and Ford. In the second debate, on 7 October Carter reiterated that he would never give up complete control or practical control of the Panama Canal Zone, but I would continue to negotiate with the Panamanians.... I would be willing to go ahead with negotiations. I believe that we could share more fully responsibilities for the Panama Canal Zone with Panama. I would be willing to continue to raise the payment for shipment of goods through the Panama Canal Zone. I might even be willing to reduce to some degree our military emplacements in the Panama Canal Zone, but *I would not relinquish practical control of the Panama Canal Zone any time in the foreseeable future.*[7]

However, within two months of his election Carter, in a remarkable about-face, suddenly embraced the very positions he had so recently foresworn as candidate. Carter writes in his memoirs that, "as I conferred with my foreign-policy advisors after the election, it seemed clear that...[an] eventual agreement would have to include a phasing out of our absolute control of the Canal, as well as the acknowledgement of Panamanian sovereignty."[8] With a speed and sense of urgency that were hardly predictable, he thus began to set in motion events that would within eight months produce the very treaty envisioned by Kissinger and Tack and that finally and definitively swept away positions enshrined in the 1903 agreement and defended during the 1976 presidential campaign.

On 12 January he announced to a gathering of House members at the Smithsonian Institution in Washington that he would resume negotiations on a new treaty immediately upon taking office. The negotiations, he said, were to proceed from the Kissinger-Tack Agreement and were to have a target completion date of June 1977. On 21 January, Carter's first full day in office, he ordered the first Presidential Review Memorandum (PRM 1) to "undertake a review of our interests and objectives with regard to concluding new Canal treaties in Panama."[9] On 27 January an interagency Policy Review Committee (PRC) recommended that negotiations be brought to the earliest possible conclusion and made the first tentative recommendations regarding the organization of a congressional and public relations campaign to generate support for the new treaties. The PRC's recommendations included the establishment of a blue-ribbon citizens' committee to spearhead the drive for public support and the scheduling of a presidential address to the nation to explain the purposes and goals of the negotiations.

Meanwhile, on 15–16 January, Carter had announced the appointment of Washington attorney Sol M. Linowitz—a former ambassador to the OAS and former chairman of the Xerox Corporation—to act as conegotiator with Ambassador Ellsworth Bunker in the new round of negotiations. Secretary of State Cyrus Vance and Panamanian foreign minister Aquilino Boyd held a preliminary review of the status of the negotiations on 31 January and announced plans for a "sustained and continuous effort" to conclude a new treaty at an early date based on the Kissinger-Tack principles.[10] The talks were formally resumed on 14 February. In April Carter explained in his first major foreign-policy address on Latin America, to the Organization of American States, that the Canal issue was one of the problems "that plague us from the past" and pronounced the 1903 treaty "no longer appropriate or effective. . . . I am firmly committed," he said, "to negotiating in as timely a fashion as possible a new treaty which will take into account Panama's legitimate needs as a sovereign nation. . . ."[11]

That this striking reversal may actually have been more apparent than real is suggested by several facts. For one thing, it seems obvious that no candidate would have lightly risked a public endorsement of the Kissinger-Tack principles given the strength of public opposition to treaty reform that the Reagan campaign had revealed. We must therefore discount some of Carter's ambivalence as the predictable casualty of a close election.

For another, there is suggestive evidence that positions Carter took publicly during the campaign were not a wholly reliable index of his ultimate intentions.[12] Sol Linowitz recounts that the day after the second candidates' debate he was approached at a luncheon in New York by Panamanian foreign minister Aquilino Boyd. Boyd described the concern aroused in Panama by Carter's statement that he would not relinquish effective control of the Canal and asked Linowitz to make an effort to secure clarifying language. As Linowitz describes it, he raised the issue with Cyrus Vance, then a foreign policy advisor to candidate Carter, and was given reassurances that Carter was fully aware of the implications of the Panamanian situation. "Campaign talk is sometimes imprecise," Vance explained, adding that if Carter were elected he would "certainly want to do the right thing in connection with the Panama Canal situation." A day later Linowitz received similar assurances from Carter's principal domestic advisor, Stuart Eizenstat, which were passed back through private channels to Torrijos. "Frankly," Linowitz concludes, discounting any change of heart on Carter's part, "I don't think he had studied [the issue] in depth at the time he made his statement. By effective control he probably meant nothing more than defense rights."[13]

Perhaps the most convincing evidence that there was no significant reversal is the fact that Jimmy Carter brought to the presidency a world view which reflected all the assumptions built into the Kissinger-Tack Agreement. The process of formulating that world view effectively began for Carter in 1973, when he was appointed the first governor and one of only six Southerners to the Trilateral Commission.

The commission was a private-sector study group founded by David Rockefeller in response to actions of the Nixon administration that ended free trade and fixed exchange rates (the so-called Nixon shocks) in 1973, the advent of OPEC, and to growing demands from the developing world for a "new international economic order." As Richard Ullman suggests, the last prompted a perceived need for "closing ranks against the oncoming hordes of the poor," the former two for "a hunkering down within the Western camp."[14] Doing the principal hunkering were some one hundred eighty bankers, businessmen, scholars, and government officials from the three sectors of the industrialized world, the United States, Western Europe, and Japan, and they were bound together by a shared objective: defining new strategies to preserve unrestricted trade and investment opportunities in the new international environment of the post-Vietnam era. Their deliberations were, as John Oakes says, a consummate expression of the "transnational outlook of the multinational corporations."[15]

If "liberal internationalism" was the "creed" of the Trilateralists, as C. Fred Bergsten notes, then Jimmy Carter was undoubtedly its "prophet."[16] As a Trilateral member Carter was an earnest student, "silent but assiduous ... a careful notetaker and offstage brainpicker," who absorbed his education in international relations—much of it at the hands of the commission's executive director, Zbigniew Brzezinski—with quickness and alacrity.[17] Numerous Trilateralists were eventually to become Carter intimates, and twenty of them would come to occupy virtually all the senior-level foreign-policy posts in the Carter administration, including Vice-President Walter Mondale; Secretry of State Cyrus Vance; National Security Advisor Brzezinski; Defense Secretary Harold Brown; UN Ambassador Andrew Young; Treasury Secretary Michael Blumenthal; Deputy Secretary of State Warren Christopher; Treaty Negotiator Sol Linowitz; and Treasury Under-Secretary Richard Cooper. Together they indelibly colored the new administration's emerging outlook.

In their tolerance of political diversity and in their respect for the forces of global change, they challenged many of the fundamental assumptions of the postwar doctrine of containment. Under the circumstances it was all but inevitable that a new Panama treaty, fashioned along the lines of the Kissinger-Tack Agreement, would be a high priority on the new administration's foreign-policy agenda. What was not so predictable was that the accommodationist policies of the Trilateralists would themselves become the object of growing opposition and that the treaty debate would become the means by which the "transnational" outlook of the new administration would be largely discredited, at least in the public mind. It is to this subject that we now turn.

[1]

The liberal internationalists[18] who shaped the Carter administration's world view bridged the generational gap between those veterans of the Wall Street–Ivy League establishment whose foreign-policy beliefs were in transition for the first time since World War II and a group of younger scholars who were weaned in the 1960s on outspoken opposition to the Vietnam policies of the Johnson and Nixon administrations.[19] For both groups the Vietnam War was a watershed, a fault line that separated two worlds, one, the fixed international system defined by the architects of the postwar international system, the other, an ever-shifting amalgam of political patterns that they were groping to understand and elucidate even as Jimmy Carter took office. Together these liberal internationalists defined a new, more diverse, less internally coherent body of assumptions and policy prescriptions to guide America through the post-Vietnam era. Collectively they spearheaded the first successful rebellion in twenty-five years against the old and tried first principle of containment.

Since the onset of the Cold War the policy of containment was the "strategic core" of the world view of the American foreign-policy establishment, the "basic organizing principle," in Zbigniew Brzezinski's words, which provided the rationale for America's debut as a world power.[20] First publicly articulated by George Kennan in the pages of *Foreign Affairs*,[21] provided its operational accoutrements in National Security Council Memorandum no. 68 (NSC-68) and the Korean War, and universalized in the policies of the Truman and later administrations, containment became the adjunct of the tense postwar world of two superpowers, fixed alliances, quiescent hinterlands, and a trade and monetary system fashioned at Bretton Woods to preserve and perpetuate, within the "free" world at least, the unchallenged economic and political supremacy of the United States.

For containment threorists the starting point of American policy was Soviet aggression and Munich its central diplomatic reference point. The effort to keep the Soviets from filling strategically important "power vacuums" in Europe, Asia, and the Middle East was its inescapable end.

The governing assumption was that all change within the international system was of the zero-sum variety, that "every gain for the Soviet Union, or for 'world communism,' was a loss for us."[22] Primacy over the forces of change was therefore not a luxury but a virtual precondition to survival, since every tip of the scales threatened to produce the very chain reaction described in the theory of dominoes. Consequently, whether in a primary theater such as Western Europe or in a secondary theater such as Southeast Asia, threats posed by forces of change not directly accountable to the United States called forth identical levels of response. The practitioners of containment, unable to differentiate between central and peripheral interests, were thus led eventually to put American power on the line in the jungles of Vietnam. In the process they produced a crisis of faith and authority within their own ranks.

The light at the end of the tunnel of Vietnam, wrote Warren Manshel in 1975, was the funeral pyre of a policy widely discredited by its failure to calculate local circumstances.[23] From its ashes came a major effort to fashion a new "organizing principle," a revisionist view of the world that found its most influential expression in the perceptions and policies of the administration of Jimmy Carter.

The intellectual foundations of this view, as Carl Gershman writes in the pages of *Commentary*,[24] were largely hammered out by a group of writers associated with *Foreign Policy*, a journal founded in 1970 to "stimulate rational discussion of the new directions required in American foreign policy after Vietnam."[25] Many of these theorists would come to occupy positions of influence in the Carter administration— Zbigniew Brzezinski at the National Security Council, C. Fred Bergsten at Treasury, Paul Warnke, Richard Holbrooke, Richard Cooper, Leslie Gelb, and Anthony Lake at the State Department. As Stanley Hoffmann of Harvard described them, they were "a kind of expectant establishment in exile."[26] While their writings reflected a wide range of opinions, the common denominator was a repudiation of containment, of policies based on ideology and traditional spheres of influence as an acceptable basis for the reconstruction of American foreign policy in the post-Vietnam world.[27]

Their basic criticism of containment was that it had lapsed into irrelevance as a result of extraordinary changes in the balance, distribution, and diversification of world power. Over one hundred new developing nations, old nations with new economic clout such as Japan and the countries of Western Europe, and strong new "transnational" actors, principally corporate and banking entities, were together demonstrating a growing capacity to make vigorous demands on the international system. In the process they created within that system powerful centrifugal forces, which completely reconfigured the orderly world of the containment theorists.

For the architects of the revisionist view of world politics the implications of these changes were obvious. "The age of grandiose blueprints is dead," wrote Hoffmann. "What is needed today is a new international system that goes beyond past forms of ... balance of power eras."[28] Just what the new agenda of international politics would be, or at least what its guiding principles would be, the critique of containment itself suggested. At its core was the central argument that in a new world where power was calculated more in economic than strategic terms, the primary threat to American security was no longer defined simply, or even primarily, by military imbalances and Soviet expansion, indeed, was no longer the exclusive function of East-West relations. "How to deal with the Communist world remains a key problem for the U.S.," wrote Brzezinski, "but it may no longer be the *central* threat."[29] The central problem was change itself, the constant flux in a world made unpredictable and dangerous by resource scarcities, by the diffusion of nuclear capabilities, by strident demands for political and economic justice in the Third World, by traditional regional disputes made exponentially more threatening by the spread of sophisticated weapons. And if the problem was change, then the fundamental policy prescription was a call to pay closer, more patient attention to the dynamics of change, to deal with change on its own terms, and to foreswear the temptation to impose simplistic views on a world that was now, in Hoffmann's words, "reduced to a complex set of processes with no inherent essence."[30]

For the writers who described these changes, and whose views were so deeply imprinted on the Carter administration, the emerging outlines of a new foreign policy represented a revision of old premises.

Where the containment theorists thought primarily in strategic terms and focused on competing ideologies, alliance systems, and power balances, these newer writers were particularists who viewed the world from the bottom up, focusing on individual nations or clusters of nations made influential by technology or resources. They abandoned the Cold War fixation with Soviet aggression and warned instead of the proliferation of new factors that now had bearing on American security interests. They largely ignored communism and looked to nationalism as the primary motive force in world affairs. They abjured the "misguided universalism"[31] that had led American policy to Vietnam and urged, with Richard J. Barnet, that policy makers reflect a "greater willingness to accept the existence of local politics and local issues and less readiness to see the Kremlin's hand in every revolutionary movement."[32]

Likewise, where containment theorists often feared global change, the revisionists argued that the processes of change needed to be viewed with greater tolerance or actually channeled in constructive directions when they served the end of the old principle of "legitimacy" so cherished by liberal internationalists since the days of Woodrow Wilson. The revisionists argued that security for American interests lay in a world order that was no longer a function of the static process of maintaining arms and power balances but the function of the more dynamic process of helping satisfy legitimate demands for political and economic justice around the globe. Thus they maintained that American policy was to be put to the service of democracy and human rights, of greater equity in international economic arrangements, and of fair, negotiated resolutions to disruptive local conflicts.

Moreover, where containment theorists defined power in military terms, the revisionists took political and especially economic power as the coin of the new realm. They defined security as a function no longer of hegemony but of accommodation to the broad range of "multiple and cross-cutting coalitions"[33] that were forming around commodity interests and regional economic and security concerns. Instead of what Arnold Wolfers calls the traditional "possession" goals of foreign policy (i.e., bases, territory), they spoke of new "milieu" goals (a favorable environment for trade and investment and continued safe access to raw materials) and of the diminished utility of military power to achieve them.[34] They concurred with Joseph Nye that to understand what is changing, it is necessary to "distinguish between power over *others* from power over *outcomes*,"[35] and with Hoffmann that in the postcontainment era *"influence* rather than *control* is at the heart of the process."[36]

A presidential commission summarized the revisionist outlook in a report issued in 1980:

> It will no longer be possible for this country to conduct its foreign policies on the assumption that its unilateral objectives can be realized without also accommodating the legitimate needs and aspirations of other nations.... Significant competing forces have now arisen throughout the modern world. Our reaction to international events must be guided by

a sensitive understanding of the changes that have taken place, an intelligent awareness of the uses and limitations of American power and a renewed determination to pursue American foreign policy objectives in the context of an increasingly complex and interdependent environment.[37]

[2]

At least for the first two years of the Carter administration, and arguably beyond, American foreign policy was indelibly influenced by this revisionist reaction to containment and by the transnational outlook of the Trilateral Commission where Carter's own foreign-policy education was acquired. In May 1977, in a widely noted address delivered at the University of Notre Dame, the president elucidated the administration's new approach to dealing with international affairs. Gershman describes the speech as "the perfect synthesis" of the views of the "new foreign policy establishment."[38] It was a testament as well to the extent to which Carter would try to associate U.S. policy with the forces of global change.

As Carter defined it, the new policy had its roots in the "strands which connect our actions overseas with our essential character as a nation."[39] He said that Vietnam had been a "profound moral crisis," demonstrating the "intellectual and moral poverty" of old policies. From that failure came the promise of a new beginning: "We have now found our way back to our own principles and values, and we have regained lost confidence." What was needed, he said, was a new policy tailored to the realities of a new world. The world has changed "dramatically"; the "lives and aspirations of most human beings have been transformed," producing "a worldwide determination to achieve social justice." It followed that "we can no longer separate the traditional issues of war and peace from the new global questions of justice, equity, and human rights." We need fresh policies, said the president, in which "dignity and freedom are fundamental spiritual requirements" and where "the power of words and of the ideas that words embody" are not to be undervalued. Such policies would involve elements of cooperation and competition with the Soviet Union, efforts to settle regional disputes, collaboration with old allies on the global issues of energy, hunger, nuclear proliferation, and the international environment—in short, policies "derived from the larger view of global change" and "rooted in our moral values which never change."

"Not for thirty years has there been so much new music in a Presidential pronouncement on foreign policy," wrote Richard J. Barnet of Carter's Notre Dame speech.[40] By the president's new conception, "the sin of Vietnam would be expunged by working for redemption in the rest of the world."[41] The policy was a "bold new departure," according to Stanley Hoffmann:

> While the United States would of course remain strong, it would shed its obsession with communism and turn from the politics of competition to the politics of building a moderate world order. The Soviet-American relationship would no longer be treated as the dominant issue of world politics, either for confrontation or detente. Attention would be focused on the new global agenda filled with issues that have little to do with East-West relations, involving primarily the capitalist industrialist powers and the countries of the Third World—or else, as in the case of human rights, transcending ordinary distinctions between friends and foes, rich and poor.[42]

Undoubtedly there was little in the past to provide direction for this, the first post-Vietnam presidency. The old diplomatic certainties and ground rules, and even many of the old practitioners themselves, were discredited by the extension of containment into Southeast Asia. Thus as the very time a new foreign policy was needed to take the place of the old, the prospects for finding just the right formula seemed more remote than ever. In place of the fixed diplomatic landscape of the high years of the Cold War, Jimmy Carter faced an international environment characterized by an extraordinary paradox of fragmentation and interdependence, of proliferating power centers and emerging new global issues.

In response to these new circumstances Carter fashioned policies that had two distinguishing characteristics. The first was a new accent on morality, a determination that American policy should have a "higher cause than mere equilibrium,"[43] in Peter Jay's words, or "simple survival," in the president's own.[44] The second was respect for legitimacy, or what the president described as "justice" and "equity."[45]

As the administration set its sights on majority rule in southern Africa, or human rights in Latin America, or relinquishing the Canal in Panama (the last in response to a violation of *territorial* legitimacy), therefore, it was not the logic of containment but the logic of accommodation of the forces of history that gave such policies meaning. There was, to be sure, by the administration's reasoning a clear link between legitimacy and security, for tensions generated by political, economic, and racial inequality constantly threatened to draw the great powers into their vortex. As the president warned at Notre Dame, "the world is threatened by the danger that we will not resolve the differences of race and wealth without violence or without drawing into combat the major military powers."[46] Therefore the fruit of accommodation, of what Thomas L. Hughes describes as a kind of "anticipatory, precrisis diplomacy," would be the attenuation of such threats, as well as the resulting political support, which would be fungible in international forums such as the United Nations and which would help keep open critically important lines of trade and access to raw materials.[47] Nevertheless, the real heart of the policy was the conviction the president voiced at Notre Dame, that "dignity and freedom are fundamental spiritual requirements."[48] It was a policy in which, in Hughes's words, the "equity issues" were to claim precedence over the "security issues."[49]

In its accent on morality and legitimacy the policy had a pronounced Wilsonian aspect, and with respect to the principle of legitimacy there was in Peter Jay's words an instructive "undeclared intellectual consensus" between Carter and Henry Kissinger.[50] As Hedley Bull writes, "For Kissinger, as for his heroes, Metternich and Bismarck, foreign policy is the pursuit of national interest, but the national interest points toward the development of a legitimate order acceptable to others."[51] Kissinger himself writes that "The problem of political legitimacy is the key to political stability in regions containing two-thirds of the world's population.... Nor should we define the problem as how to prevent the spread of Communism. Our goal should be to build a moral consensus which can make a pluralistic world creative rather than destructive."[52]

But it is significant that, while Kissinger and Carter both understood the contribution legitimacy could make to political stability, Kissinger's definition of legitimacy had been largely anchored to a foreign policy based on the security themes of containment. That Carter's definition was not—or at least seemed not to be—suggests a crucial part of the reason why the struggle for public acceptance of the Panama treaties was so arduous. Where Kissinger had adopted a "geopolitical" approach to the Third World of which regionalism was a part, Carter all but erased the distinction. He fashioned a foreign policy tailored almost completely to the exigencies of a pluralistic world and to the moral themes that administration officials hoped would give credence to such a policy. Where Kissinger had continued to see the Soviet Union as the central reference point in foreign policy ("The problem of our age," he wrote, "is how to manage the emergence of the Soviet Union as a superpower") and evaluated Third

59

World policy in terms of East-West relations, Carter effectively abandoned detente and containment. He dealt with the Soviets on a largely ad hoc basis and kept attention fixed on policy along the North-South axis, that is, on relations between the developed and underdeveloped worlds.[53] Where Kissinger abandoned bipolarity for "strategic triangles" and "pentagonalism," Jimmy Carter abandoned geometry altogether, taking a wholly disaggregated approach to foreign policy. Ultimately, where Kissinger saw regionalism as containment by other means—what Robert Litwak describes as "a differentiation of means within the prevailing bi-polar image of the international system"— Carter saw it as an end in itself.[54]

In the most general sense Carter and Kissinger were both forced to wrestle with the dilemma attributed to Carter by Michael Howard, that of achieving "a synthesis between the universalist liberal views" of the announced policy and the "framework of power politics" that he inherited.[55] Litwak explains the dilemma for Kissinger thus:

> ... the Nixon Administration came into office in 1969 with the avowed commitment to transform the theory and practice of American foreign policy. Yet, at the precise moment when the United States was psychologically prepared, as a result of the Vietnam debacle, to cast off an admittedly defective bipolar "image" of the international system in favor of one which reflected the implications of nascent multipolarity, the image was ostensibly being reconfirmed by events within this new context.... This had the effect of conferring an ostensibly new legitimacy to the "image" of bipolarity during the period in which its relevance across the spectrum of issues was already waning.[56]

The dilemma for Carter—in Litwak's words, "the challenge of reconciling the competitive demands of nascent multipolarity and revitalized bipolarity"—was even worse.[57] The idealistic, upbeat policy of the new administration was unveiled at the very moment when public and congressional concern with security issues was being rekindled by the achievement of nuclear equivalence by the Soviet Union, by the new capacity of the Soviets to project an effective military presence abroad, by the weakening of the Western alliance, by the growing vulnerability of energy supplies, by the weakening of the U.S. dollar, by the erosion of American preeminence in world affairs. Thus confronted with an even more glaring dysfunction between policy and circumstance than Kissinger, Carter faced enormous problems of reconciliation. From these problems would stem the difficulty of making an effective case for the opportunities inherent in the policy and of making individual initiatives such as the Panama treaties politically palatable.

What complicated public acceptance of Carter's new approach to foreign affairs was the inability to find some objective standard against which to measure it. For Kissinger the framework of policy, however much was said about legitimacy and the new demands of pluralism, had been the same. It still had its roots in containment, and even when the policy was conciliatory, as in the cases of detente and SALT, such initiatives were always comprehensible in terms of Kissinger's declared carrot-and-stick approach to dealing with the Soviets. For Carter there was no such obvious frame of reference. The very raison d'être of the new approach became a kind of tactical flexibility—indeed, so important was this flexibility, this *instrument* of policy, that it became nearly indistinguishable from the policy itself.

It was a point on which administration spokesmen where not apologetic. As one State Department official declared, "The problem does not lie so much in defining [foreign policy goals] as in managing complexity.... Our approach is to make constant, pragmatic, case-by-case decisions seeking the most constructive balance among our interests and adjusting our tactics as circumstances change."[58] Explained another: "There is no Carter Doctrine, or Vance Doctrine or Brown Doctrine because of the belief that the environment we are looking for is far too complex to be reduced to a doctrine in the tradition of post–World War II American foreign policy. Indeed, the Carter approach to foreign policy rests on a belief that not only is the world far too complex to be reduced to a doctrine, but that there is something inherently wrong in having a doctrine at all."[59] There was thus no obvious organizing principle in the new Carter foreign policy. The motif of "managing complexity," however appropriate to changing world circumstances, was not likely to provide a yardstick adequate for measuring the administration's ability to comprehend and respond to threats to national security. The entire policy was therefore highly susceptible to misinterpretation. In its tolerance of change, for example, it required delicate trade-offs (which heightened its vulnerability to charges of internal contradiction) between the iron equanimity that was often necessary to allow events to take their course and the need to make ad hoc judgments that in certain situations, where outcomes threated to impinge on U.S. security interests, events needed to be redirected. Likewise, in the absence of any simple, clear organizing principle such as "containment" itself, the emphasis on human rights—which *was* comprehensible—inevitably came to bear the burden of defining Carter's entire foreign policy. Because human rights came to epitomize a perceived lack of resolve to stick with allies and to impose order on world events, the entire policy was not long immune from serious criticism.

Thus in an effort to avoid losing touch with the world, the Carter administration began almost from the start to lose touch with the American electorate. In its attentiveness to matters of equity, the administration largely missed the incipient transformation of public opinion in the direction of renewed concern with matters of national security.[60] Just as the president was announcing at Notre Dame that Americans were "now free of [the] inordinate fear of communism," external events were newly arousing fears of Soviet power.[61] Just as the president was institutionalizing the disposition to adjust national goals to new international circumstances and to reduce America's role in the world from, in Richard Rosecrance's words, "manipulator" to "participant," a new wave of public anxiety was beginning to stir over the diminished capacity of the United States to shape the international environment to its own needs and interests.[62] In the absence of the easy reference points of containment policy, an almost inevitable gap developed between public comprehension and the administration's new prescription for dealing with a complex and dangerous world. As Thomas Hughes writes, "Above all, the public needs confidence that there is a firm, not a wavering hand at the helm. If it cannot know the mystery of the President's secret guiding purpose, it must have the conviction that he has one."[63]

It was into this atmosphere of uncertainty over the president's "secret guiding purpose" that the Panama treaties were introduced in the late summer of 1977. Under the circumstances it is not entirely surprising that what was intended as the set piece of an entirely new foreign policy became, instead, the catalyst that activated the misgivings in the public mind over the diminution of America's power and status in the world. In the end, therefore, the most formidable adversary Jimmy Carter had to face in his uphill effort to win public support for the Canal treaties may have been growing public opposition to the very foreign policy of which the treaties were the highest and most visible expression. As the *New Republic*'s TRB wrote:

In confronting his opponents over Panama, Carter suffers from a self-imposed weakness. His new foreign policy embodies all manner of virtues that make Americans feel good, but Carter has not made it clear how they also will be good for America in realistic self-interested terms. As Machiavelli noted, a prince must take great care to seem to be all mercy, faith, integrity, humanity and religion. At the same time, his people have to have confidence he is not naive. If a President of the United States is going to seem to play Daniel in the lion's den, his people want some confidence that he knows how to fight lions if he has to.[64]

Evidence was mounting by the end of Jimmy Carter's first year in the White House that such confidence was in increasingly short supply.

[3]

In this new era of complexity Latin America was in all respects a microcosm of the bewildering changes catalogued by the writers who stamped their influence on the Carter administration. It was, moreover, an ideal testing ground for policies refashioned to conform to the new requirements of international politics. The region was therefore a matter of special interest for Jimmy Carter from the outset. One catalyst that shaped his interest was yet another private study group, which did for Carter's perceptions of policy for the hemisphere what the Trilateralists had done to shape the future president's understanding of the larger arena of world affairs.

Like the Trilateral Commission, the Commission on United States–Latin American Relations was a creation of David Rockefeller. Founded in 1973 to survey the state of hemispheric relations after a decade of neglect during the Vietnam War, the commission was to make recommendations for the new administration that would take office in 1977. It was staffed by a group of prestigious Latin American experts whose views and whose membership, including scholars like Albert Fishlow of Yale, C. Fred Bergsten of Brookings, and George C. Lodge and Samuel Huntington of Harvard, overlapped with the Trilateral Commission. The commission on Latin America was chaired by Sol M. Linowitz, later to be conegotiator of the Panama treaties with Ellsworth Bunker. As Alan Howard writes, it was "not just another think tank"[65] but a body whose views Carter would grant the highest credibility, and whose members, like Linowitz and Robert Pastor (the commission's executive director and later the National Security Council's expert on Latin America), would have considerable influence on the evolution of Latin American policy. As Howard notes, Linowitz himself would have "more to say about the shape of our Latin America policy than anyone in the Administration except the President himself."[66]

The two reports issued by the commission, in 1974 and 1976,[67] were compendiums of the sweeping political and economic changes in Latin America during the decade of American preoccupation with

Vietnam and of recommendations for new policies toward the region—policies that would signal a radical break from the past. As the commission's first report summarized, old policies were being rapidly overtaken by events:

> Dramatic transformations within Latin America and the Caribbean, major developments in the wider international arena, and significant changes in the terms by which this hemisphere relates to the rest of the world, have all undermined the assumptions which governed U.S. policy in the Americas from the Monroe Doctrine through the Good Neighbor Policy to the Alliance for Progress and its successor, the Mature Partnership. We strongly believe that the policies which the U.S. has inherited from the past, including many of their most basic assumptions and goals, are inappropriate and irrelevant to the changed realities of the present and the trends of the future.[68]

Fundamentally, these "dramatic transformations" involved a new and growing ability of the nations of the hemisphere to act independently and energetically on the world stage. They were symbolized by the Cuban revolution—described by one consultant to the commission as "the most dramatic daily remainder that U.S. hegemony [in the region] has waned"[69]—and typified in the headlong rush to modernization that by the early 1970s was revolutionizing the face of hemispheric politics.

As the commission described the situation, all the signs by the early 1970s were pointing to a Latin American "coming of age." Economic development was for the first time beginning to produce reasonably steady rates of economic growth. Commodity positions were being strengthened in the aftermath of a wave of nationalizations that retrieved the production of raw materials from foreign control. Steady growth and cheap labor were making many Latin countries increasingly attractive to multinational corporations as sites for offshore production. In political terms individual nations (Brazil, Mexico, and Venezuela with its OPEC connection) were gaining new clout in regional and world affairs. Moreover, nearly all the nations in the region were demonstrating greater independence in world forums, finding strength in solidarity with other developing states around the globe and thus creating new pressures for reform within the international economic system. "What needs to be recognized," the first commission report noted in 1974, "is that a majority of Latin American and Caribbean states are preparing themselves to fulfill a global international role and not only an intra-hemispheric one."[70]

For the United States this new found independence was laden with policy implications. Historically a sphere of easy political access and economic influence, Latin America was suddenly economically stronger, politically more independent, more globally minded, and in general more outgoing in both its political and its economic contracts—less dependent in all respects on the colossus of the North. "One of the elements of Latin America's new strength," wrote Bergsten, "is its ability to go to different sources—and even play them off against each other—for imports once available only from the United States."[71] What was true for imports was true of investment capital as well. Competition from Europe and Japan for investment opportunities was for the first time making the region something close to a buyer's market. The Latin American governments were, moreover, becoming more aggressive in harnessing foreign investment to their domestic goals of lowering unemployment, increasing exports, diversifying local economies, and gaining access to advanced technology. Thus almost overnight the political passivity of Latin America and the exploitative aspect of "dollar diplomacy" were becoming the artifacts of a vanishing era. A decade earlier the "Latin American governments were, by and large, quiescent and generally content to follow the lead of the U.S.," as the commission wrote; but in the mid-1970s those countries "are moving out on their own on the world scene," demanding a larger share of the world's resources, fairer terms of trade, greater access to markets, a greater voice in international forums.[72] For the United States such changes were to make old policies for the hemisphere useless artifacts as well.

In prescribing new policies tailored to new circumstances, the commission laid down recommendations that were vintage Trilateral wine. The time had come, the commission urged, for the end of colonialism, for the end of "special relationships" of the kind implied in the Monroe Doctrine, for an end to the notion that considerations of military security have any continuing relevance in an age in which economic issues will be "the critical ones during the coming years."[73] "The historic U.S. presumption that Latin America is somehow our 'sphere of influence,' " the commission wrote, "is no longer appropriate in an increasingly interdependent world in which Latin American nations seek to be active and independent participants."[74]

In place of regional politics as usual, the commission argued, it was time to begin treating Latin America like the rest of the world. "The first step toward an improved Latin America policy," wrote commission consultant Abraham Lowenthal, "would be to realize that for most purposes we probably should not have a distinct Latin American policy at all."[75] New circumstances required new ways of relating to Latin America. One was to cooperate on a variety of such shared global concerns as food and energy shortages, population control, and human rights, the last even in countries with conservative regimes aligned with U.S. policy in opposition to communism.

Another, the "central" issue on the commission's agenda, was to attend to the task of equalizing the terms of competition in the international marketplace.[76] The United States was to take active measures to increase the access of Latin American countries to U.S. markets, resources, technology, and public and private capital, in effect defining a new set of ground rules "to govern the exchange of goods and services so that all countries developed and developing can realistically expect to benefit."[77]

A third way was to iron out problems in key bilateral relationships in the hemisphere, where possible through "policies which genuinely take the needs of Latin America into account, *by adjusting to nationalist aspirations rather than confronting them.*"[78] In the case of Cuba, the most tattered bilateral relationship in the region, the commission warned that a policy of isolation was counterproductive, as one by one, by the early 1970s, the other nations of the region began to reopen relations with Havana. American policy, the commission recommended, should aim to reintegrate Cuba into the "constructive pattern of inter-American and international relations, and to reduce Cuba's incentive to promote violent subversion elsewhere in the hemisphere."[79]

In the case of Panama resolution of the long-standing dispute over the status of the Canal was billed as the "most urgent issue" on the commission's agenda.[80] As the first commission report described it, the 1903 treaty represented the last vestige of American colonialism, of a "distasteful bygone era in American diplomacy." Unless the treaty were revised, the commission warned, it would be a perpetual source of friction in U.S. relations with Panama and a mortgage on good relations with the rest of the hemisphere.[81] Only by updating the old treaty relationship, by ceding control of the Zone to Panama and by expanding Panama's jurisdiction over the Canal itself, could a "potentially disastrous confrontation" be avoided.[82] Noting the diminishing commercial and military significance of the Canal, the commission argued that such interest as the United States retained in a neutral and accessible Canal would be best secured through arrangements that had the full support of the government and people of Panama. "The greatest threat to maintaining an open Canal," the commission wrote, "is likely to come from nationalist Panamanian resentment of U.S. attempts to continue to maintain a colonial enclave in Panama."[83] Still larger stakes in the new Panama policy were described by commission chairman Sol Linowitz:

> The Panama Canal issue involves far more than the relationship between the United States and Panama. It is an issue which affects all U.S.–Latin American relations, for all the countries of Latin America have joined with Panama in urging a new treaty with the United States. In their eyes, the Canal runs not just through the center of Panama, but through the center of the Western Hemisphere. Indeed, the problem significantly affects the relationship between this country and the entire Third World, since the nations of the Third World have made common cause on this issue—looking upon our position in the Canal as the last vestige of a colonial past which evokes bitter memories and deep animosities.[84]

The commission's sensitivity to the opinion of the Third World may be taken as a fair measure of the extent to which this new liberal internationalism represented a departure from past positions. It may, of course, be argued that the commission's view represented no real change in policy *objectives* toward the region. "The goal is the same," claimed one skeptic, "to maintain U.S. hegemony over the region and, indeed, to integrate [Latin America] even more closely into the U.S. sphere of influence and into the control of the trilateral powers."[85] Still, the commission's view did represent a significant shift in *tactics* for responding to changing conditions. Even if the new policy was less than disinterested, it called for extraordinary concessions as an index of newfound respect for Third World solidarity as a balance weight in world affairs (and indirectly, for the new primacy of economics in world affairs). It symbolized, for better or worse, a new taste for accommodation over confrontation as the surest route to security for American interests in the region. As the commission said in evaluating the alternative: "Unchanging policies in the face of rapidly changing conditions is a sure recipe for trouble."[86]

One result of the work of the commission was Jimmy Carter's early interest in Latin America. Abraham Lowenthal writes that "It took Kissinger years to discover Latin America. The Carter Administration *began* with an expressed concern for the region, stressed personally and often by the President himself."[87] The first year of the new administration witnessed the resurgence of active interest and new policy initiatives. Contacts with Latin America multiplied, beginning with an eight-nation goodwill tour led by First Lady Rosalyn Carter in June 1977 and culminating in individual Oval Office meetings with eighteen Latin heads of state during the signing ceremonies for the Panama treaties, which were held in Washington in September. As Lowenthal suggests, "Neglect, benign or otherwise, is no longer Washington's approach to the nations of the Western Hemisphere."[88]

The agenda that the new administration brought to the region was essentially the agenda spelled out in the 1974 and 1976 commission reports. In defining the goal of new U.S. policies for Latin America in April 1977, before the Organization of the American States in Washington, the president spoke in terms that faithfully reflected the Trilateral world view. "Our new approach," he told the OAS, "will be based on ... a high regard for the individuality and sovereignty of each Latin American and Caribbean nation," on "our respect for human rights," and "on our desire to press forward on the great issues which affect the relations between the developed and developing nations."[89]

In retrospect it is hardly surprising that, in dealing with the central interest of the developing countries for a "new international economic order" (NIEO), the administration could make only modest advances, principally in the form of marginal increases in multilateral and concessional assistance to the region. "The real name of the game," as Lowenthal describes the essence of the NIEO, was to be the "redistribution of power: of resources, income and status."[90] Such concessions, given the growing role of Congress in foreign policy, were never entirely Jimmy Carter's to make. Nevertheless, the heart of the Carter program for Latin America was a policy of righting old wrongs:[91] normalizing relations with Cuba and with such other leftist regimes in the hemisphere as Jamaica and Guyana, inaugurating long-needed human rights initiatives, and "treating the countries of the Western Hemisphere as they wish to be treated—as individual sovereign nations, each with interests of its own."[92]

The most obvious wrong in need of righting was the status of the Panama Canal, and it was an issue that came to the Carter team with just the right credentials. For one thing, as the product of three previous presidents the Canal negotiations were stamped with the imprimatur of bipartisanship, a fact that bode well to ease the political work of ratification once a draft treaty was in hand. For another, its resolution was now virtually the sine qua non of good hemispheric relations, as six Latin American presidents reminded Carter in a letter delivered just four days before his inauguration. For yet another, it was an issue that threatened at any moment to spark new violence in Panama, a point that doubtless figured prominently with Secretary of State Cyrus Vance, who as secretary of the army during the administration of Lyndon Johnson was a first-hand witness to the tragedy of the 1964 flag riots. Likewise, it had the appeal of being, in the words of Sol Linowitz, a "discrete event subject to definitive solution,"[93] an issue that could provide the occasion for a quick foreign-policy success, giving the administration the initiative in dealing with Congress and public opinion on such other issues as SALT.

Moreover, it was the ideal lead issue in announcing the new policy toward the hemisphere. It would do for this second "good neighbor policy" what the revocation of the Platt Amendment had done for the first, by serving as an unmistakable earnest of the administration's good intentions toward Latin America.[94] Finally, and in the largest sense, it was the key to the administration's entire new policy. By demonstrating the willingness to comprehend and to accomodate the legitimate aspirations of Panama, to act magnanimously in dealing with a small nation, the negotiation of new treaties would begin the process of revolutionizing American relations with the entire developing world. "If the Canal problem was solved," writes LaFeber, "Latin America could . . . act as the laboratory for United States policies in the developing nations."[95] As one White House lobbyist suggested, "Nothing would have worked without it."[96]

Thus the new Canal initiative promised at one stroke to defuse a growing crisis and to announce in the most dramatic way possible that the United States was fully alive to the opportunities that could accrue from placing U.S. policy squarely on the side of history. From Carter's first days in office, therefore, administration officials took up the Canal issue with a determination that destined the new round of negotiations, begun in February 1977, to ultimate success and that elevated the ratification effort thereafter to the highest possible priority.

In the end, however, this issue, which Linowitz later described as the "most explosive and urgent problem in the hemisphere"[97] and which was designed to inaugurate Jimmy Carter's entire new foreign-policy agenda, became the focal point of such controversy that it would compromise the very agenda it was supposed to inaugurate and would largely exhaust the pool of political capital necessary for its implementation. Through the negotiations, through the Senate debate on ratification, and through what Carter later described as the "extended nightmare"[98] of the sixteen months of debate over legislation to implement the treaties, the administration was forced to engage in a protracted war of attrition. Although the administration was finally successful with respect to the treaties themselves, its victory would compromise later efforts to marshal support on issues like SALT and the normalization of relations with Cuba. With an eye to the formidable price exacted by the treaties, one administration official would later conclude that the Panama fight was "the longest running legislative drama in the administration, and at every stage it cost us."[99]

CHAPTER 3

Organizing for Victory

The Panama negotiations—which were viewed by the Johnson, Nixon, and Ford administrations as an unfortunate necessity—were embraced by the Carter administration as the ideal starting point for a wholly new approach to foreign policy. The new administration's Latin America policy provided the incentive finally to close a deal with Panama. Thus the new round of negotiations begun by Jimmy Carter in February 1977 were favored from the start by circumstances that for the first time made the conclusion of new treaties a realistic possibility.

To give impetus to the negotiations the president designated Sol Linowitz as conegotiator with Ellsworth Bunker on a special six-month appointment beginning in February. Although the talks were expected to be at first largely exploratory, the deadline imposed by the Linowitz appointment may have provided the final prerequisite for success. "I think it put some pressure on the Panamanians, considerable pressure," commented Linowitz later. "It gave us both a date to shoot at."[1] Indeed, as that date approached, one seemingly intractable issue after another was resolved: joint administration and defense rights, payments to Panama, and legal protections for Americans working in the Zone.

The most important breakthrough came with agreement on the duration of a new treaty, which was central not only to U.S. relations with Panama but to relations between the U.S. State and Defense departments as well. From the outset of the talks State had expressed a willingness to settle for the year 2000 as a terminal date for both administration and defense rights, hoping, as Margaret Scranton writes, to use a generous exit date as a bargaining chip for broader prerogatives during the transition period to 2000.[2] At the Defense

71

Department, on the other hand, a lengthy extension of defense rights was the sine qua non of support for any new negotiations.

During the second Nixon round of talks Ellsworth Bunker had effected a tentative compromise, a single treaty with dual expiration dates for administration and defense. During the Carter round the issue was finally resolved with a formula, attributed to Linowitz, that provided for two treaties. One, to expire in the year 2000, provided for the gradual full assumption by Panama of the management, operation, and maintenance of the Canal (the "Panama Canal Treaty"); the other provided for the permanent neutrality of the Canal and for permanent U.S. rights to defend the Canal (the "Neutrality Treaty"). With this impasse broken, the most significant obstacle was cleared. As Linowitz recounted afterward, there was little chance, once agreement was reached on the two-treaty formula, that the process could be stopped to factor in domestic politics: "Once we had that, we knew we were on our way to moving toward a treaty. . . . It would have been virtually impossible for us to say we're going to stop the momentum now because we wonder about the political feasibility. We had to go forward with it; otherwise [new treaties] would have been impossible."[3]

Thus on 8 August President Carter was able to wire the 535 members of the House and Senate, home on recess, that a treaty was on the verge of being completed. Two days later, on 10 August, Ambassodors Bunker and Linowitz and their two Panamanian counterparts announced that, after thirteen years, negotiations on a new regime for the Panama Canal were finally successful.

With the work of diplomacy finished, the work of politics was now to begin. As the administration began to gear up for what would become one of the most extensive public relations offensives in American diplomatic history, the limits of salesmanship were about to be demonstrated. Although the Carter administration early acquired a reputation for being unskilled in the art of congressional relations, its ratification effort on Panama was, with only two major exceptions, managed with a generally high degree of competence.[4] In tending to the twin tasks of building public and congressional support for ratification, the administration demonstrated the kind of tactical flexibility and political sensitivity that were indispensable to success.

From the beginning, however, the issue stirred such controversy that efforts to shape the political environment, not only for the Canal treaties but for the entire Carter foreign-policy agenda, were to prove largely futile. In spite of an energetic lobbying effort on the part of the administration, and in spite of support from leading interest groups, the press, and the nation's foreign-policy elite, the treaties eventually became bogged down in a lengthy round of bartering. Individual senators were determined to exact compensation for the political risks of supporting ratification, demanding concessions that quickly depleted the administration's available pool of political capital. One such concession, made to Arizona's freshman senator Dennis DeConcini on the eve of the first Senate vote, nearly brought the thirteen years of effort on a new treaty to a premature end. As it was, the treaties were approved in the Senate not because of public acceptance of the rationale for ratification but in spite of it. What may have staved off defeat was, paradoxically, not the administration's appeal to a bold new policy for Latin American but the specter of a crippled president unable in the aftermath of defeat on the Panama treaties to conduct U.S. foreign policy effectively in the remaining years of his term.

[1]

"A treaty entering the Senate," Secretary of State John Hay once wrote, "is like a bull going into the arena: no one can say just when or how the blow will fall—but one thing is certain—it will never leave the arena alive."[5] If Hay's pessimism was extreme, the point can hardly be gainsaid that the Senate does not always provide a suitable environment for fledgling treaties. At least nineteen treaties submitted by U.S. presidents have failed to survive the ordeal of ratification politics.[6] As the Panama debate approached in 1977, there were more than a few reasons for the Carter administration to fear lest a similar fate might be in store for the new Canal treaties.

Most of the early indexes put the prospects for Senate ratification in some doubt. The first soundings of public opinion recorded lopsided majorities opposed to any agreement that would alter the historic circumstance of full American sovereignty over the Canal and the Zone, and even as the negotiations were winding to a conclusion, a renascent political Right was gearing up to translate such opinion into a tidal wave of public opposition to ratification.[7] In the House of Representatives there were renewed (though unsuccessful) efforts in June 1977 to delete funding from the State Department budget to implement any treaty written to transfer American jurisdiction over the Canal to Panama. In the Senate thirty-one of the original thirty-seven sponsors of the Thurmond Resolution of 1975 still held office, including Majority Leader Robert Byrd, whose support was understood by the administration to be indispensable. In May a survey of the entire Senate taken by the Washington-based Institute for Conflict and Policy Studies showed 25 members solidly opposed to a new treaty, only 37 (of 67 necessary for a two-thirds' majority) in favor, and a remaining bloc of "undecideds" with serious doubts about the economic and national security ramifications of any new agreement transferring sovereignty of the Canal to Panama.[8]

Adding to the administration's problems were changes in the institutional balance between the Congress and the executive branch, which had resulted from the Vietnam War. The long campaign to end U.S. involvement in Southeast Asia produced a Congress that was more assertive, less disposed to accept the conventional wisdom that the president knows best, and possessed of important new policy-making capabilities abetted by expanded, independent sources of research support.[9] Moreover, the breakdown of the congressional seniority system substantially decentralized power within the legislative branch, such that by the time of the Panama treaties it was no longer possible, as Thomas Franck and Edward Weisband write with reference to the bipartisan foreign policy of the Truman administration, to "keep Congress on a short leash by coopting a few Arthur Vandenbergs."[10]

To add to the weight of administration's task, it was becoming increasingly apparent that the ratification debate might become a referendum on the administration's whole approach to foreign policy, as human rights initiatives, new policies toward Rhodesia and South Africa, moves to normalize relations with Cuba and Vietnam and to reduce U.S. troop strength to South Korea, all began to draw conservative fires. Defeat on Panama would "gravely jeopardize the prospects for future foreign policy initiatives," noted the *New York Times*.[11] "It is as clear as anything can be," concurred columnist David Broder in the *Washington Post*,

> that failure to persuade the Senate to approve the treaties would finish Carter, prematurely, as a significant factor in international affairs for the balance of his term.
>
> If the judgment were rejected by a Senate of his own party, on an issue as important as the Panama Treaties, which he has asserted to be in the national interest of the United States, then no country would have any reason to negotiate seriously with his Administration on any issue of significance—not the Soviets on arms control, not the Japanese on trade, not the Arabs or Israelis on a Middle East agreement.[12]

Thus the administration was obliged to begin the struggle to secure ratification of the Panama treaties under the most difficult of all circumstances: lacking a clear-cut foreign-policy consensus, popularly or within the ranks of the traditional foreign-policy establishment; lacking the congressional acquiescence typical of the years before Vietnam; and lacking any ability to prevent the treaties from becoming a proxy issue both on Carter's foreign policy itself and on the larger issue of America's role in the post-Vietnam world. By the autumn of 1977 it was becoming apparent that the stakes in the pending contest over the treaties were to be, as Michael Mandelbaum suggested, not "so much the future of the Canal but the future of American foreign policy."[13] In short, what was shaping up was what the *Atlantic* called the "most bruising" and the *Washington Post* the "most wracking" foreign-policy debate since Vietnam.[14]

[2]

There were few illusions within the Carter administration about the magnitude of the task ahead. "Anyone familiar with this country," wrote Presidential Assistant Joseph Aragon to Hamilton Jordan, "knows that educating 230 million Americans on an issue, no matter how vital, is an enormous undertaking. In the case of the treaties, the problem is especially acute in that a great deal of misunderstanding has been produced through distorted rhetoric and demagoguery."[15] Nor was there any doubt that the central requirement for success would be strong presidential leadership.

Thus first attempts to formulate a strategy to win approval for new Canal treaties, attempts completed within the State Department in February 1977, called for energetic efforts to elicit expressions of both elite and grass roots support, to disperse administration speakers throughout the nation to explain why such treaties were needed, and to cultivate support among a wide range of organizations in the private sector. As the principal author of the strategy observed later, "The big issue in the memo was leadership."[16] When the definitive strategy for ratification was penned by Presidential Assistant Hamilton Jordan, it embodied the same formula for success: a "full-court press" with Congress,[17] liberal use of the president's time to shape public opinion, and an aggressive campaign to build constituency support throughout the country.

The Jordan memorandum reflected a healthy respect for the long odds the administration would have to face in its campaign to win public acceptance of the treaties. As Jordan wrote the president, conservative groups would try to use the Panama issue as an opportunity to embarrass the new administration. Duplicating tactics they had used in earlier congressional fights over the nomination of Paul Warnke to head the U.S. arms control agency and over common situs picketing legislation, they would marshal their resources for an all-out fight. For its part the administration, Jordan noted, was starting the ratification period without a carefully worked out public rationale, without the extensive public relations mechanisms and direct-mail capabilities possessed by opponents on the Right, and without strong, tested allies. In short, the administration had some serious catching up to do.

But if the odds were long, the ratification effort presented Jordan and his principal lieutenants with an almost irresistible challenge. And small wonder, since these were the very men and women who had only recently defied the longest possible political odds by making a relatively unknown former governor of Georgia president of the United States. If they could elect Jimmy Carter to the White House, they would only need to tailor their tactics to suit the new problem at hand. Starting again from scratch, or nearly so, they would sell the Panama Canal treaties just as they had sold Jimmy Carter—by creating the political environment that would make acceptance possible. One Carter aide drew the parallel with the principal issue on the administration's domestic agenda: "If the selling of the energy package demanded 'the moral equivalent of war,' then what this treaty demands is the moral equivalent of a political campaign. This is probably the biggest challenge we've had since we came to office, and we don't intend to lose it."[18]

Guiding both the congressional and the public relations components of the ratification effort were two simple—and to the administration self-evident—premises. The first was that the only reason public opinion was running against the treaties was because opponents had so far had the field to themselves. "It's a hysterical issue," said one administration official, "only because up until now the only information the American people have had has come from the ultraright."[19] The second was that given the time and opportunity, plus sufficient effort, the administration could make enough inroads on public opinion to make ratification possible. "We have the facts now," one aide explained, "and we can sell them."[20] As Jordan added, it was "a reversible issue.... It's not something that affects a lot of people's lives. That's why it's reversible—if we can just get the facts disseminated to enough people."[21] Confident that opinion was susceptible to persuasion, administration operatives in September set about the task of erecting an elaborate congressional and public mer-

chandising apparatus designed to make it possible for the large number of undecideds to climb aboard with the minimum of political risk.
The object was to "create an atmosphere in which we could make
our case on the merits, get our side of the story out, neutralize the
opposition, freeze public opinion, and dilute the venom," commented
one White House lobbyist later.[22] As the eight months of the ratification debate, beginning in September 1977, would amply demonstrate, however, the task of creating such an atmosphere would prove
formidable even for these talented strategists.

Confronted with solid opposition in the early public opinion polls,
the administration faced an uphill effort, and as White House and
State Department officials plunged into the work of reshaping the
political environment in time for the final Senate votes, they provided
a striking demonstration of the reach and uses of executive power.
Capitalizing on the reluctance of a majority in the Senate to take an
early position on the Canal pacts, administration operatives seized
the gift of time to try to work their miracle on public attitudes.

The administration's campaign to win public support for ratification
was inaugurated with the most ambitious public relations gambit of
all. A week of events in Washington in September 1977 centered
around a treaty-signing ceremony at the headquarters of the Organization of American States, which brought together the largest group
of visiting heads of state since the funeral of former president Dwight
Eisenhower. When it was over, one commentator would describe it
as "one of the greatest diplomatic extravaganzas in U.S. history,"
with all the "pomp and circumstance befitting a royal coronation."[23]
Even by Washington's high standards "Panama week," as it came to
be called, was a glittering, gaudy spectacle. It was a "production right
out of Cecil B. DeMille," wrote *Newsweek*,[24] all faultlessly orchestrated
by a twenty-person State Department team that worked around the
clock on the extraordinary logistical and protocol demands associated
with the presence of eighteen heads of state, and all carefully executed
to demonstrate the strength of hemispheric support for ratification.
For three days Washington was an endless round of parties and receptions and a tangle of motorcades, as government leaders and other
high dignitaries from every nation in the hemisphere except Cuba
shuttled between receptions, embassy parties, and "assembly-line"
summit conferences with President Carter at the White House. As
Time reported, there were "enough petit fours and napoleons" in
Washington during Panama week "to pave the inter-American
highway."[25]

On 7 September events converged on the OAS, where before two thousand guests and a national television audience Carter and Panama's "Maximum Chief" Omar Torrijos exchanged signatures, embraces, and compliments. "You have turned imperial force into moral force," Torrijos told his American counterpart.[26] The agreement, replied Carter, represented a "commitment of the United States to the belief that fairness, not force, should lie at the heart of our dealings with the nations of the world."[27]

Since the concluding weeks of the negotiations the question of where and how to sign the new treaties—or indeed, whether to hold formal signing ceremonies at all—had been the object of considerable debate within the administration. High officials at the State Department, including Ambassadors Linowitz and Bunker, voiced major reservations regarding the political risks associated with such highly visible proceedings. They would put the president's credibility squarely on the line, department officials argued, and unnecessarily expose the president to humiliation if the Senate were to disavow the treaties. Meanwhile, on Capitol Hill Senate minority leader Howard Baker cautioned that the president was "running a terrible risk. . . . I don't know what the Senate is going to do," said Baker, "and I don't believe he can know either."[28] Nevertheless, among the president's political operatives at the White House there was more attention to the opportunities than to the risks, and the chance to hold highly publicized signing ceremonies was seized as the best possible means of gaining the initiative in the early stages of the national debate.

Panama week drew predictably sharp opposition from the Right. Conservative Governor Meldrum Thompson ordered flags in New Hampshire to half-staff, proclaiming 7 September "a day of infamy," while one conservative organ ridiculed the ceremony as a "triumph of stagecraft over statecraft" designed to arrest the public's declining confidence in the president's leadership.[29] In *Human Events* columnist Morrie Ryskind reflected on the prevailing good temper of the week's events: "there hasn't been such harmony . . . since Munich, where Hitler declared himself fully satisfied and wanted no more territory, thank you; while Chamberlain returned to London with the umbrella—and damned little else—to receive the ovation of the cheering crowd."[30]

The ceremony drew fire from other quarters as well, as a transparent move to force the hand of the Senate. "The President has dared the Senate to withhold its consent," wrote one Capitol Hill correspondent. "If the Senate fails to take the dare, it will have surrendered to the President some of its constitutional powers."[31] One disgruntled

State Department official agreed: "The Georgia mafia, led by Hamilton Jordan, are handling the Panama Canal problem in the same way they got Jimmy Carter nominated and elected. By organizing this Latin American summit in Washington, they are pulling out all the stops in a blatant effort to support the treaties."[32]

But that was precisely the point. As conceived in the White House, the ratification effort was not for the fainthearted, and in retrospect it seems clear that the risks associated with the signing ceremony were warranted. Whatever territorial instincts the effort may have aroused in the Senate, however much it may have smacked of a "preemptive strike"—as one administration official suggested[33]—there was simply no missing the enormous consequences of rejection, as was demonstrated by the Latin American leaders who attended the signing and who themselves became signatories of the protocol (the so-called Declaration of Washington) that endorsed the treaties. Nor was the publicity value of the ceremony inconsequential to the administration. Through the entire first week of September Panama virtually dominated the news, and this time, unlike in the 1976 Republican primary campaign, the coverage was entirely on the administration's terms. As a publicist for the opposition later conceded, the White House handled the signing "very, very well.... We had nothing to counter with. We scheduled a breakfast on the Hill for opposition senators and there was press coverage. The press probably couldn't afford not to come because of the attention lavished on the administration all week. Even so, the real story was with them and not us. Our efforts to compete with it were largely ineffectual."[34] Thus in the short space of a week the administration made the Panama treaties a national issue again and in the process regained at least some of the valuable ground lost during the negotiations. By mid-September there were clear indications that the administration, as a result of its bold gamble, had won an impressive victory in the first round of the crucial contest for public opinion.

[3]

Through the months of the negotiations the administration had kept a low profile on the treaties, careful not to jeopardize the work of the negotiators by prematurely politicizing the issue. Most of what little public relations activity preceded the September signing had been managed at the State Department. With the signing ceremony the initiative passed to the White House and to a task force managed by Hamilton Jordan that became a model for nearly every subsequent legislative initiative during the Carter administration. Under the direction of the Jordan steering group administration officials executed a three-tiered strategy designed to create an environment conducive to ratification.[35]

At one level the effort was directed toward building mass support nationwide. Major responsibility for the task was assigned to a speakers' bureau at the State Department; between June 1977 and April 1978 it all but saturated the market for public forums across the country. Operated from the department's Office of Public Affairs and drawing on a stable of over thirty mid-to-high-level department officials, including Ambassadors Linowitz and Bunker, the speakers' program provided an impressive demonstration of the government's outreach capabilities. All carefully monitored in a weekly tracking report (described by the *Washington Post* as "one of the most closely held limited circulation documents in the State Department"[36]) and working out of a map-laden command center that invariably invited comparisons with the Pentagon War Room, the campaign was organized by department operatives who placed the "highest priority" on unearthing "every available opportunity . . . to get the message across on the Canal issue."[37]

Several criteria governed the allocation of speakers. Highest priority was given to the states where at least one senator's vote was undecided.[38] In some cases speakers were made available to provide a show of support for senators already committed to ratification. Little or no attention was given to states where both senators were firmly opposed. Planning decisions were routinely based on political information from friendly Senate staffers and the State and White House congressional offices.

One department official said that "this was the first time we had such a big effort on a single issue. Normally, we just respond to requests when they come in. On Panama we solicited events. We plugged into even the most marginal events."[39] And wherever speakers were scheduled, so were a host of ancillary events, including meetings with local newspapers' editorial boards and appearances on radio and television talk shows. Within a month State's Office of Public Affairs had "already amassed as many invitations . . . as have already taken place in the past year."[40] By the time the Senate finally disposed of the Canal issue, no fewer than fifteen hundred separate events had originated with State—in size and scope an effort unprecedented in the department's history.

A second level involved focusing public relations efforts on fifteen states singled out by White House and State Department lobbyists as the key theaters in the battle for public support. Here the Jordan task force orchestrated a multifaceted strategy of cultivating allies, organizing town meetings, tracking opponents, building interest-group support, briefing citizens' groups, organizing a citizens' committee to duplicate the direct-mail and grass roots capabilities of opponents on the Right, and briefing editors and legislators. At every point in the process the State, Defense, and Commerce Departments, plus the Democratic National Committee and state party functionaries, were harnessed to the task of getting the administration's arguments across. It was a controlled, carefully orchestrated outpouring of activity that culminated in a round of speaking tours led by Secretary of State Cyrus Vance and other high-ranking administration officials—the so-called January offensive[41]—and a fireside chat delivered by the president to a national television audience on the eve of the Senate floor debate on 2 February.

But if the administration was eager to cultivate mass support for the treaties, both nationally and in key states, the primary target of its public relations campaign was a select group of local and national opinion leaders. In a remarkable reversal of roles the "liberal" Democratic administration of Jimmy Carter came to base its hopes for ratification on the support of key business and foreign-policy establishment elites, while treaty opponents on the "conservative" Right adopted a strategy of mass-based opposition that drew on the extensive use of direct mail. By cultivating elite support the administration in effect sought to legitimize the case for ratification by associating protreaty sentiment with the broadest possible cross section of respected opinion. Given the long postwar history of bipartisan support for new treaties, the task of building an elite consensus was destined to be at once the administration's easiest and its most noteworthy success.

The most influential national opinion leaders were courted early by the administration. The president himself met with former president Gerald Ford, lunched with Henry Kissinger, and made personal appeals for support to various high-ranking business and labor officials and foreign-policy experts. But the bulk of the president's personal time on the treaties (apart from conferences with individual senators) was invested in a series of briefings held at the White House. The briefings represented a major effort, as Presidential Assistant Landon Butler later explained, to "keep the elite consensus together and transfer it to the local level."[42] The outgrowth of planning in the Jordan steering group, the briefings were conceived as an effective means of reaching carefully chosen community leaders—attorneys, business-people, state officials, civic and religious leaders, educators, and publishers—from states with at least one undecided senator. Names were typically drawn from lists supplied by the appropriate senators themselves, an arrangement designed, as the president later noted, to help "convince an acceptable number of key political leaders in each important state to give their Senators some 'running room.' "[43]

There were in all ten sessions for opinion leaders from thirty states, and they represented the ultimate in low-key, high-prestige salesmanship. They became a model that the Carter administration would follow in building public support for many later legislative initiatives including the Strategic Arms Limitation Treaty, the outcome of which Panama did so much to influence. At each of the sessions the administration produced its ranking officials: Ambassador Linowitz or Bunker, one member of the Joint Chiefs, Secretary Vance and Brown or National Security Advisor Brzezinski, and the vice-president. The concluding speaker at each session was the president himself who, in such intimate settings, was by all accounts the master of the "soft sell." Indeed, few who attended the White House briefings left unconvinced. A druggist from Wilmington came with "total animosity" and left "completely turned around," while a real-estate developer came with "an open mind" and left "100 percent in favor."[44] A Panama City, Florida, auto dealer came "adamantly opposed" and departed "100 percent sold on it."[45] An editor from Kentucky reflected that, sitting "in the stately grandeur of the State Dining Room, beneath a somber portrait of Honest Abe," he was persuaded that "though Panama would eventually operate the locks, we would come ı and beat up or throw out anyone who tried to stop us from using as we need it."[46] Summarized one reporter: "What . . . everyone aw was a masterful selling job."[47]

Eventually the format was duplicated to encompass a variety of interest groups including out-of-town editors, state legislators, Jaycees, senior citizens, business groups, and religious leaders. The State Department packaged a slightly altered format and took it on the road to twenty-four cities in states with undecided senators and major media markets.

Perhaps the most visible expression of elite support was a citizens' committee, belatedly formed under White House direction in November 1977. The committee represented the resurrection of an old idea, whose colorful antecedents included the influential William Allen White Committee to Defend America by Aiding the Allies.[48] The proposal for a citizens' committee was first raised in the Ford administration with such antecedents consciously in mind, but it was abandoned, along with the negotiations themselves, under the constraints of the 1976 campaign. Hamilton Jordan revived the idea in the April 1977 strategy memorandum as a means of linking the issue to previous administrations and as a vehicle for dramatizing the existing bipartisan support for the treaties. The committee was officially the outgrowth of a White House breakfast held on the morning of the signing ceremony, 7 September, for seventy members of the nation's corporate, foreign-policy, and institutional elite, including the chairmen and chief executive officers of over twenty major corporations, former government officials including Clark Clifford, Douglas Dillon, Melvin Laird, and John McCloy, labor leaders, black leaders, educators, and prominent retired military officers. As Jordan noted beforehand to the president, this group was not likely to require a "hard sell" on the treaties.[49] At the breakfast Father Theodore Hesburgh of the University of Notre Dame recommended the formation of the committee to develop a nationwide campaign in support of the treaties. Under the direction of former diplomat and New York governor W. Averell Harriman, former Senate minority leader Hugh Scott of Pennsylvania, former congressman and Ford White House counselor John O. Marsh, Jr., and former Democratic National Committee finance chairman S. Lee Kling, the committee came into formal existence two months later.

In his seminal article on the "American Establishment" Richard Rovere writes that "*ad hoc* committee rosters serve the Establishmentologists in the same way that May Day photographs of the reviewing stand above Lenin's tomb serve the Kremlinologists."[50] From Harriman on down, the names that appeared in newspaper advertisements announcing the formation of the Panama committee were enough to delight the most ambitious Establishment watchers.[51] As White House aide Landon Butler observed, the White House had "to recreate the foreign policy establishment to get the treaties ratified," and for one brief moment all of the blue-chip names on the roster of the nation's ruling elite were brought together again.[52] Fleetingly, and perhaps for the only time between the shattering impact of Vietnam and the divisive debate over SALT, the Establishment reappeared, as the remnants of Europe's old regime had gathered one last time at the funeral of Edward VII on the eve of World War I. As the *Boston Phoenix* noted, the faces on the committee roster were "three decades worth of *Time Magazine* covers and evening news broadcasts:"[53] prominent Republicans like former president Ford, Nelson Rockefeller, and Henry Cabot Lodge; retired military officers Matthew Ridgeway, William

Westmoreland, Maxwell Taylor, Elmo Zumwalt, and Lauris Norstad; Democratic hawks including Paul Nitze, Walt Rostow, and Ben Wattenberg, who even then were constructing the political apparatus to defeat Carter on SALT; NSC advisors Brent Scowcroft and McGeorge Bundy; and the architects of thirty years of Democratic foreign policy including Dean Rusk and George Ball, John McCloy and Douglas Dillon. There were union chiefs including George Meany of the AFL-CIO and Douglas Fraser of the United Auto Workers, corporate executives including Tom Watson of IBM, Max Fisher of United Brands, oil czar Armand Hammer, and Irving Shapiro of DuPont—and, inevitably, the indispensable David Rockefeller of Chase Manhattan Bank, without whose presence no roster of the nation's ruling elite would be complete.[54]

The committee was set up to abet the administration's public relations offensive, but it never had a chance to become an effective vehicle for direct political action. For one thing, its small, mostly corporate-supplied budget of $350,000 (of a hoped-for $1 million) precluded anything like the media or direct-mail capabilities of the antitreaty organizations on the Right.[55] For another, even though the committee was top-heavy with influential names, it never had a broad public base. Three or four local chapters worked well with important senators in such states as Delaware and New Hampshire, but the committee never became a rallying point for treaty supporters to resemble, for example, the William Allen White Committee with its 300-odd local chapters, four regional offices, and 10,000 local members.[56] Moreover, from the beginning the committee was largely a creature of the White House; it therefore lacked some of the independence and spontaneity prevalent in the citizens' committees of the 1930s or within the organizations on the Right that were working to defeat ratification. At all events, the committee was formed much too late to be significant in the ratification debate. Nevertheless, to the extent that it gave expression to a mood prevalent within the nation's elite, the committee may warrant the judgment passed by historian Mark Chadwin on another leading citizens' effort during the 1930s, the Fight for Freedom Committee: while it had little direct influence on the outcome of the debate in the Senate, it may by counterbalancing the outpourings of the antitreaty organizations have helped free the Senate, to some degree, to decide the issue on its merits rather than because of external pressure.[57] As an articulate, if small, voice for treaty supporters, it doubtless played a role in the process whereby the case for ratification was "legitimized." As such it was a significant expression of the third tier of the administration's public relations strategy of building credibility by association.

[4]

As the significance of the public relations offensive lay in the sheer size and scope of the administration's effort to mobilize public and elite opinion, so the noteworthy feature of the campaign to win congressional approval was its careful attention to the political needs of uncommitted senators. Notwithstanding the generally low estimate that commentators have given to the administration's overall management of relations with Congress, the work of ratification in the special case of Panama was accomplished, for the most part, through smart, flexible, accommodationist policies that were a model of effective executive-congressional relations.

The public relations campaign itself was one component of a strategy designed ultimately to insulate senators from the strong antitreaty sentiment reflected in almost unprecedented amounts of congressional mail. A second part of the strategy was an effort to saturate the Senate with information favorable to ratification. The president initially entreated senators to keep an open mind until the issues were fully debated. What followed was a determined effort to fill those open minds with as much solid, protreaty information as possible, a strategy that I. M. Destler writes was "premised on the view that most Senators wanted to support the treaty if they could and that the more they knew the facts, the more favorable they would become."[58]

This information offensive was actually started during the last months of the negotiations, as administration officials engaged in what Senate minority leader Howard Baker approvingly described as an "unprecedented amount of prior consultation."[59] For weeks treaty negotiators Linowitz and Bunker and other State Department officials routinely briefed senators on the progress of the negotiations and solicited advice on the remaining military and economic issues under negotiation. Once the treaties were formally submitted to the Senate, the enterprise was significantly expanded, as White House and State Department lobbyists became the conduit for a flood of information—fat briefing books, question-and-answer packets, draft speeches, articles, oral briefings—all of which, as one official at State noted, "surfeited the Senators with information they could defend themselves with."[60] Much of the effort was defensive in nature, as administration operatives labored to keep up with the outpouring of arguments and allegations from opposition senators on such sensitive issues as treaty economics, sovereignty, defense rights, and in one notable instance charges of Torrijos family involvement in drug trafficking. Still, the work of the administration's lobbyists was an efficient servicing operation, which kept sympathetic senators armed with arguments necessary to ward off opponents and skeptical constituents, and which bought time as the battle for public opinion was being waged outside.

An adjunct to the information campaign was a series of congressional trips between August and January. Providing forty-five senators with first-hand exposure to the potential volatility of the Panama situation, these visits gave the administration's case a substantial boost. Most of the trips were arranged by the State Department, and though nominally impartial—visiting senators, for example, routinely met with Canal Zone residents opposed to ratification—for the most part they provided exposure to parties already sympathetic to ratification: representatives of the U.S. military command who detailed the problems of containing terrorism in the wake of rejection; American businessmen in Panama concerned with the financial implications of rejection; Panama's articulate Roman Catholic archbishop, Marcos G. McGrath, who elucidated the moral dimensions of the new Panama policy. In Panama the senators "learned first hand," the president later wrote, "the same facts that had been faced for fourteen years by American Presidents and negotiators in devising an acceptable solution to the Panama problem."[61]

One Panamanian complained after the long parade of American senators had finally ended that "We . . . have developed a complex of being in a zoo."[62] But if being on display for six months was an imposition, it was also the most persuasive part of the work of convincing wavering senators of the probable consequences of rejection. One senator, Spark Matsunaga of Hawaii, told a rally of treaty supporters in November 1977 that when he surveyed from his helicopter the dense tropical forest that grows down to the Canal, he understood for the first time just how vulnerable the waterway would be to terrorist attacks: "When I flew over the Canal, I almost wished I was the commander of a company of infantry with the mission of putting it out of order. Why, there'd be nothing to it. Nobody could stop me. I could put a mine in here, and then slip out of the jungle at another point and drop a mine in there, and I could put satchel charges on different locks, and really tie things up. And the ships would be like sitting ducks—I could knock 'em off with bazookas. The Canal'd be paralyzed."[63] If other senators were more restrained, few returned without deeper insights into what White House lobbyist Robert Beckel describes as "the intensity of Panamanian support for the treaty" and the hazards of ignoring it.[64]

After the treaties went to the floor of the Senate in early February, the congressional effort took on yet a third aspect, as administration lobbyists began to search for ways to help individual senators find the political cover necessary to make a vote for ratification as easy and free of cost as possible. The effort in part represented a patient search for collegiality, as in countless individual meetings with senators and staffs and in one important collective setting—a staff group on Panama representing forty undecided senators—congressional and administration officials "got to know each other's world of rewards and punishments" and gained "mutual confidence and respect."[65]

Administration officials also demonstrated a willingness to adjust their strategy to the limits faced by individual senators. Many senators made it clear that they would be able to justify a vote in favor of ratification only if they could be seen to force the administration into some kind of compromise. Administration strategists eventually conceded the general point, and they developed a carefully controlled strategy that was designed to give as many senators as possible the opportunity to exact at least pro forma concessions.

The strategy began with an agreement with the Senate leadership that the Foreign Relations Committee would report the treaties out with as few amendments as possible, to preserve opportunities for changes on the floor. Once the treaties were before the entire Senate, the administration took the lead in drafting numerous amendments (or in sanitizing the wording of proposed amendments), which it then publicly opposed to give credibility to a vote "against" the administration. Senators were thus able to tell their constituents that although they had voted for the treaties, they had first guaranteed that their terms were tougher and more protective of the national interest than the original version.

The strategy was the ultimate in responding sensitively and sensibly to the legitimate political needs of senators under mounting pressure to oppose ratification. Instead of ignoring the need for credit sharing the administration dealt openly with it and at least until the final days of debate successfully channeled it in constructive directions so that no amendment materially altered any provision of the proposed treaties.

The most significant evidence of the administration's willingness to make compromises and to share credit with the Senate came in the form of two "leadership amendments" added to the Neutrality Treaty in February 1978. The amendments were the product of concerns first voiced in Congress during the summer of 1977 and which for eight months thereafter posed a constant threat to ratification. Throughout the ratification debate they posed for the Carter administration the perpetual challenge of finding ground for concessions at home without compromising the integrity of the draft treaty in the eyes of the Panamanians.[66]

At issue were two highly ambiguous, and thus controversial, provisions of the Neutrality Treaty. One, in Article IV, specified that the United States and Panama would "agree to maintain the regime of neutrality established in this defense treaty;" the other, in Article VI, guaranteed the right of "expeditious" transit for American warships in time of emergency.[67] The necessity of clarifying the meaning of these residual rights forced the administration into a prolonged two-front war—or more aptly, perhaps, into a suspenseful high-wire act, as White House and State Department officials searched for ways to expand the definition of these rights far enough to satisfy the Senate but not so far as to force Panama to reject the treaties. The search for just the right formula constituted the central drama of the ratification contest, and down to the last hours of the Senate debate the almost impossibly limited latitude for maneuver was matched only by the height of the risks and the delicacy of the sensitivities involved on both sides. The situation demanded the utmost diplomatic and political finesse, and until the last weeks of the ratification debate the administration demonstrated a large measure of both.

The Article IV provision was a magnet for controversy, for the question of just how far the United States could go in maintaining the "regime of neutrality" after the year 2000 spoke directly to the matter of sovereignty, which had prompted the negotiations in the first place. From the outset the issue was clouded with uncertainty, both inside and outside the administration.

In impromptu hearings called by the House Merchant Marine Committee in August 1977 the administration stated its position on the issue in unequivocal terms. The United States, explained conegotiator Sol Linowitz, would never use the words "intervene" or "intervention" to describe U.S. rights to restore order in the Canal after the year 2000.[68] Still, under repeated questioning both inside and outside Congress administration spokesmen gradually liberalized their position, eventually arguing that intervention rights were, in effect, to be taken as understood in the language of Article VI. By the time of the first round of hearings before the Senate Foreign Relations Committee such rights were being construed more generously than ever. Responding to a question during those hearings regarding the distinction between "our right to intervene as opposed to our power to do it," Secretary of State Cyrus Vance all but abandoned the administration's earlier reluctance on the point: "I think our right to do so is clear, and there can be no question about it."[69]

As the administration's construction of these controversial provisions grew looser, reactions in Panama grew predictably hotter. No matter how necessary the interpretations offered by administration spokesmen might be for the American political process, warned one Panamanian official in a widely noted statement, "there were some things no Panamanian government could accept."[70] "It is sad to see highly responsible officials in the United States say that this Neutrality Treaty grants the rights of intervention. It is sad to note this inconsistency, not only because there is nothing in this treaty to serve as a basis for such a claim, but also because the term 'intervention' has been left out of international diplomatic jargon since World War II." He then added, speaking of the controversy over Article VI: "Let us state very clearly that expeditious does not mean priority or preferential treatment. . . . From where does this interpretation come, when the history of the negotiations reveals that every notion of preferential treatment was rejected?"[71]

Thus even before the signing ceremony administration officials were caught in the incipient stages of what Margaret Scranton depicts as a "prolonged transnational debate."[72] As the autumn progressed, and especially as the Senate Foreign Relations Committee hearings continued through late September and early October, it became clear that such differences of interpretation would have to be reconciled as a precondition to ratification.

The point was underscored for the president by a six-man delegation from the Foreign Relations Committee, which visited the White House on 11 October.[73] Without some clarifying language, they explained, the treaties had little chance of surviving a full debate in the Senate. The point was reinforced on 15 October, when Republican member Robert Dole of Kansas released the transcript of a classified State Department cable containing excerpts from a speech delivered by Panamanian negotiator Romulo Bethancourt Escobar, in which Escobar challenged the State Department's interpretation of Articles IV and VI. The statements proved "beyond a doubt," Dole explained to his colleagues, that the treaty meant different things to the two parties and that the differences impinged on "the most important part of these treaties—the portion which bears directly on our vital national defense interests." The conclusion, warned Dole, was inescapable: the Senate would have to "clarify our defense rights by *Amendment*, not by weak 'understandings' that have no legal and binding effect.' "[74]

The evidence suggests that by early October administration officials had become reconciled to the need for concessions to allay growing concerns in the Senate. Of three possible courses of action, one was a simple declaration of force majeure, though at the Pentagon, in particular, there was strong sentiment in favor of some more specific provision that would clarify the circumstances which would warrant intervention and that would thus put the Soviet Union and Cuba on notice.[75] A second was some unilateral declaration, perhaps in the form of a letter from Carter to Panamanian leader Torrijos, though with a plebiscite to ratify the treaties in Panama scheduled for 23 October, some more definitive (meaning *bilateral*) measure seemed necessary. From State issued warnings that if the points were left unclarified before the plebiscite, opponents could charge that the two countries were ratifying two different treaties. "I fear such an argument . . . could be highly effective with Senators desiring unconditional assurance that the U.S. understandings/reservations are a binding element of the treaty relationship," wrote the department's legal advisor to Deputy Secretary Warren Christopher. "The most effective counter" to probable right-wing charges "would be pre-plebiscite publicizing of an agreed interpretation of the key Treaty issues that have emerged since September 7, in a form suited to the political needs of both countries."[76]

The administration accordingly seized this third option, made hasty arrangements for a White House meeting between Carter and Torrijos, and produced a Joint Statement of Understanding to resolve conflicting interpretations of the Article IV and VI provisions. The statement specified that

> the correct interpretation [of the principle of U.S. intervention rights] is that each of the two countries shall, in accordance with their respective constitutional processes, defend the Canal against any threat to the regime of neutrality, and consequently shall have the right to act against any aggression or threat directed against the Canal or against peaceful transit of vessels through the Canal. This does not mean, nor shall it be interpreted as, a right of intervention of the United States in the internal affairs of Panama.[77]

Although the joint statement was little more than a skillful rephrasing of an ambiguity essential to the diplomatic purposes of both countries, it received the strong endorsement of key senators, including Majority Leader Byrd, who pronounced it "more than I had expected to achieve."[78] In response to pressures growing within and outside the Senate, Carter thus made the first of three important concessions to the Senate's moderates and began the process by which he would help drive a wedge between the moderates and the chamber's small but powerful group of irreconcilables. Summarizing the import of the joint statement Destler writes that treaty supporters needed to "devise means whereby Senators could move to support the treaties without appearing to rubber-stamp them. Senators needed to be able to argue that they had improved the treaties, strengthened the protection given American interests; yet amendments needed to be severely limited. The Carter-Torrijos understanding proved a godsend for helping square this particular circle."[79]

In January the administration made its second concession on the point, once again in response to the prescient warnings of Senate moderates. The Carter-Torrijos understanding, almost before the ink was dry, began to draw heavy opposition fire as an inadequate guarantee of residual intervention rights. The statement was, in fact, unsigned, and its status in international law was left unclear. Since it was not formally a part of the treaty, it would arguably lapse on the passing of the government of either signatory. The Carter administration reluctantly accepted the wisdom of upgrading the status of the understanding, and it consented to a proposal to incorporate the substance of the understanding into the treaty itself. "It seems to me," Senator Frank Church described the logic of the move, "that the American people would be better satisfied if this understanding were formalized in some way. I see nothing to be lost by that, and I think the people would be reassured to know that both countries understand the meaning of the treaty the same way."[80]

By an agreement worked out between Senators Baker and Byrd and Foreign Relations Committee chairman John Sparkman, the treaties were to be reported out of the Foreign Relations Committee with the recommendation that amendments paraphrasing the joint statement would be introduced on the floor. This strategy would allow, in Sparkman's words, "maximum participation in the shaping of the Senate's activities on these treaties."[81] As the report of the committee later noted, "This procedure was proposed to allow a large number of Senators who were not members of the Foreign Relations Committee to co-sponsor amendments and reservations to the treaties, particularly the incorporation of the October Statement of Understanding and to share credit for the amendments."[82]

Thus not only were the objections of Senate moderates and conservatives met and the status of the October understanding clarified, but credit for strengthening the treaty was shared by no fewer than eighty-seven senators, who eventually enlisted as cosponsors. On 7 February, by a vote of 87 to 5, the Carter-Torrijos language was formally incorporated into the text of the treaty, and another important safety valve was added to relieve opposition pressure. By February it appeared that the Carter administration's strategy—retaining just the right amount of tactical flexibility in adjusting the controversial provisions of the Neutrality Treaty—might assure the moderate support necessary to the final success of the ratification effort.

[5]

The final votes on the two Canal pacts were eventually postponed until March and April 1978. By the time the treaties actually moved to the Senate floor in early February, however, administration officials could take satisfaction in a convincing display of the uses of presidential power. Under the general direction of the Jordan task force scarcely a stone had been left unturned. Within four months the administration had successfully mobilized the relevant actors in the executive branch. It actively intervened in the congressional process, beginning with briefings even before the treaties were signed and continuing after the signing with a massive information effort designed to shore up support and to counteract conservative arguments. It initiated one of the largest public relations campaigns in history. It worked skillfully to cultivate elite opinion at the national and local levels, thus trading on the built-in advantage of support inherited from past Republican administrations. It actively solicited expressions of support from hundreds of newspapers across the country through editorial briefings at the State Department and the White House, and through meetings with editorial boards held by traveling administration officials. It aggressively culled expressions of support from leading national interest groups. Moreover, in responding to mounting pressures for amendments to the treaties, the administration demonstrated a high degree of adaptability and thus solidified the important moderate support without which ratification would have been impossible.

By February there seemed to be clear indications that the ambitious work of the administration's treaty managers was beginning to pay off. One significant index was growing evidence that the public relations campaign was starting to bear fruit.[83] Results published by the principal national polling organizations after September 1977 showed much closer margins than polls taken in 1975 and 1976 and during the first eight months of 1977. By October 1977 the Gallup and Caddell polls were actually recording pluralities and in some cases real majorities in favor of ratification, in a turnabout one administration official termed an "unexpected success."[84] Meanwhile, by the Christmas break a broad constellation of business, labor, ethnic, minority, religious, and civic groups—plus a majority of daily and weekly newspapers across the country—had gone on record in support of the new treaties.

In Congress there were significant breakthroughs as well. Even though the administration had some distance to go to secure the sixty-seven votes needed for ratification, an initial core group of mostly liberal supporters had by November grown to include some important Republicans and conservative Democrats.[85] Among them were Democrats Ernest Hollings of South Carolina, Robert Morgan of North Carolina, and Walter Huddleston of Kentucky, and Republicans Samuel Hayakawa of California and John Chaffee of Rhode Island. In January the administration officially received the support of Senate majority leader Robert Byrd and minority leader Howard Baker, as well as that of another key Southern conservative, Democrat Lloyd Bentsen of Texas.[86] Administration leaders were thus assured of full cooperation from the bipartisan Senate leadership and from key conservatives whose support would presumably carry weight with important fence-sitting moderates. Moreover, on 2 February the Senate Foreign Relations Committee reported the treaties out by a 13 to 1 vote, a margin that was significant not only because of the near unanimity it represented but also because among the thirteen votes in favor were four important, hitherto undeclared, Republican moderates.[87] Among the remaining undecideds in the Senate there were indications that the congressional delegations to Panama and the gradually shifting polls were having the desired effect.

Thus congressional, elite, institutional, and press opinion appeared to be tending unmistakably in the administration's direction in response to the long campaign of patient, persistent persuasion. By February there seemed every reason to believe that the impetuous self-confidence of Jimmy Carter's political operatives in the White House had not been misplaced. The only problem was that by February there was no way of knowing the high price that would have to be paid to round up the remaining votes necessary for ratification. Nor, significantly, was it yet entirely apparent that forces existed which sheer hard work, even smart work, would be incapable of overcoming.

[6]

Just when confidence that the ratification effort was on the right course began to give way within the administration is difficult to pinpoint. Through the autumn and into January the gradual but growing indications of support for the treaties both inside and outside Congress kept spirits high, even though hopes of having the issue settled by the Christmas break had long since been abandoned. Through the first weeks of the new year there was still ample reason to be confident that the careful, patient strategy of cultivating public and elite opinion, and of carefully tending to the needs of individual senators, was the most promising approach to the difficult task at hand.

As the treaties went to the floor of the Senate in early February, however, the limits of the strategy were gradually to become more apparent. By March the sense of momentum began to dissipate, as the ratification effort became mired in the repetitious rhetoric of the protracted floor debate. By the eve of the first Senate vote both hopes and patience were worn down to the bone. The debate had "almost everything bogged down," the president complained in his memoirs; it "continues on and on."[88]

What concerned administration officials most was that by early February the sixty-seven votes necessary for ratification were still nowhere in sight. An administration count taken on 1 February showed only forty-eight solid votes in favor of the treaties, up only three from two months before and still fully nineteen shy of the mark.[89] Worse yet, by February the strategy that had guided five months of intensive work on behalf of ratification was largely exhausted. With no more elite groups to cultivate, no more editors to brief, every conceivable protreaty argument and antitreaty rebuttal conveyed to the Senate, there was no obvious means of securing the remaining twenty votes. As the time for the final Senate votes grew closer, the president was thus obliged to relinquish the high ground and to demonstrate a more active interest in the individual needs of undecided senators. The administration, increasingly desperate for the remaining votes necessary to secure ratification, was belatedly forced into a series of concessions, until, as we shall see, the president made a concession on the eve of the first Senate vote that almost brought thirteen years of effort to naught.

James Reston described the interaction of politics and policy at work in the final weeks of the ratification debate in these words: "Senators have their own ways of reminding the White House that they also have problems in their states that they hope the President will not forget. It is a very subtle process, a little more than friendly persuasion and a lot short of blackmail."[90] For the most part, concessions were not directly treaty-related. In March, for example, the administration suddenly dropped its long-standing opposition to a $2.3 billion emergency farm bill sought by Senator Herman Talmadge of Georgia, which would pay farmers for not growing crops on 31 million acres of land. In the same month the United States agreed to the purchase of $250 million worth of Arizona copper for the already surfeited strategic stockpile, a move championed by the state's junior senator, Dennis DeConcini. The reputed asking price for Samuel Hayakawa of California was a larger voice in administration defense policy. The cancellation of the neutron bomb and the ongoing SALT negotiations made the United States "look like a weak nation," Hayakawa told the president in a White House meeting held prior to the Senate vote on the Panama pacts.[91] One day after the final vote Hayakawa issued a press release announcing that the president had agreed to invite the senator to discuss foreign-policy and defense issues before final decisions were made in the White House.

Other concessions, while treaty-related, were largely perfunctory, as the case of Florida senator Richard Stone illustrates. Stone, a first-term Democrat, faced some of the stiffest opposition to ratification in the country. "I would say that if there were a referendum," Stone explained to a reporter, "Florida voters would come down so heavily against the treaties they would lead the United States."[92] Under the weight of constituent pressure, Stone announced in January that the price for his vote for ratification would be a modern reaffirmation of the Monroe Doctrine. "The United States," he said, "must tell the world clearly and unequivocally that no Soviet military installations will be tolerated in the Western Hemisphere." The administration accordingly prepared and sent a letter that Stone described to his constituents as a "major" policy statement.[93] In it the president cited his determination to "oppose any efforts, direct or indirect, by the Soviet Union to establish military bases in Latin America" and pledged to "maintain our bases in the Caribbean necessary to the defense of the Panama Canal and the security of the United States."[94] As John Goshko of the *Washington Post* summarized the significance of this wholly pro forma statement, "When the shouting is all over, Stone will have shown himself to be an Administration loyalist. But he will also be able to tell the voters in Florida how his vigilance had helped force Torrijos and Carter into the changes and clarifications that turned the Canal agreement into a 'good deal' for the U.S."[95]

Equally meaningless were an "understanding" exacted by Texas senator Lloyd Bentsen that the Neutrality Treaty would not obligate the United States to provide foreign aid to Panama and a "reservation" sponsored by Georgia senators Talmadge and Sam Nunn that nothing in the Neutrality Treaty would preclude the United States and Panama from reaching further agreement to station forces in Panama.[96] The administration allowed in all six reservations and seven understandings to the two treaties, in addition to the two leadership amendments. With the indispensable help of the Senate leadership, the Administration was able to ward off each of a series of "killer amendments," sponsored by treaty opponents who sought to make substantive changes that would force the Panamanians to repudiate the treaties. But in dealing with the nongermane concessions and reservations allowed to the likes of Nunn, Bentsen, and Talmadge, the administration signaled a willingness to compromise, to make whatever trade-offs were necessary to ensure against critical defections. Under the unique pressures of the Canal issue, as *Newsweek* noted in a retrospective on the Panama treaties in April, by the end "the aloof and didactic technocrat had been forced to demonstrate that he could scratch and bargain for votes like any other mortal politician."[97]

[7]

Through the eight weeks of the floor debate the administration survived repeated attempts by conservative opponents to defeat the treaties by adding amendments unacceptable to Panama. Unexpectedly, the one "killer amendment" that did survive came not from a treaty opponent on the Right but from Dennis DeConcini of Arizona, a relatively obscure freshman senator from the president's own party. Nor was his amendment introduced with the purpose of sinking the ratification effort but rather of buying support back home to make possible a vote in favor of ratification. This "killer amendment" was in fact not an amendment at all but a short, tersely worded "condition" that very nearly provoked a repudiation of the entire treaty by the Panamanian government. In the most dramatic episode of the entire ratification debate it forced the administration into the very crisis that months of solicitous attention to the needs of Congress had been designed to avoid. Ironically, Senator DeConcini's amendment raised the very issue of U.S. intervention rights in Panama, which had presumably been settled once and for all in the October joint statement and in the leadership amendments attached to the Neutrality Treaty in February. In March DeConcini reopened the question and for a brief moment, on the eve of the first Senate vote, he brought thirteen years of effort to the edge of disaster. With the help of the Senate leadership the situation was retrieved, but not before the president's position was seriously compromised and not without throwing into sharp relief the extent to which the effort to create an environment conducive to ratification had fallen short.

The circumstances that momentarily propelled Dennis DeConcini into national prominence were not dissimilar to those that numerous other moderates faced. DeConcini represented a conservative state where, despite the administration's best efforts, opposition to the new pacts ran high. There had been indications in the early fall that Arizona's senior senator, conservative Republican Barry Goldwater, might declare for ratification and thereby take some pressure off the politically more vulnerable DeConcini. Responding to the blandishments of conservative friends and associates, however, Goldwater recanted, and in February he publicly declared in opposition to the treaties.

This reversal came just as an official delegation to Panama of which DeConcini was a member first raised serious questions about the adequacy of the intervention right defined in the modified language of the leadership amendments. As DeConcini later recounted, probes of Torrijos's tolerance for the veiled intervention rights retained by the United States in the amendment to Article IV produced growing doubts. "What if there is a strike in your country and the Canal is closed?" he asked Torrijos. "This will never happen," Torrijos responded. "I then asked about revolution and if as part of that revolution the Canal was closed. Do we have the right to intervene?" "Only if you come in at my request on our side," came the artless reply.[98] Vexed with substantive misgivings and perhaps an understandable measure of political timidity, DeConcini, on 27 February, introduced a new amendment to the treaty designed to strengthen U.S. intervention rights. As one correspondent for the *New York Times* suggested, it was a move that reflected "a real belief that his reservations are needed and a canny understanding that the conservatism they displayed cannot harm him with Arizona voters."[99]

Within the administration and the Senate there was no missing the implications of DeConcini's wrestlings and the probable consequences of reopening the sensitive question of intervention rights after the 23 October plebiscite. DeConcini was accordingly included in a series of luncheons in the majority leader's office the week of 6 March, held to assist key undecided Democrats to find political cover in reservations or understandings that would be acceptable to the Panamanians.[100] At the luncheon on Friday, 10 March, the vice-president and Deputy Secretary of State Warren Christopher negotiated what was in effect a quid pro quo with DeConcini. In return for a promise of administration support for his proposed changes, DeConcini agreed to downgrade the amending language from an amendment per se, as introduced on 27 February, to a "condition." Christopher then took the DeConcini draft back to the State Department to revise the language in a way that would preserve the substance of DeConcini's proposal but in words that would be less likely to ruffle Panamanian sensibilities.

Over the weekend Christopher revised the wording and on Monday gave the draft back to DeConcini with the offending words "in Panama" deleted from the critical section regarding the use of U.S. military force to keep the Canal open. But DeConcini, persuaded by his staff that Christopher's change had "gutted" the proposal, reinserted the controversial wording to "assure that we can get back in without being branded as outlaws and international bandits."[101]

Notwithstanding the provisions of Article V or any other provision of the treaty, if the Canal is closed, or its operations are interfered with, the United States of America and the Republic of Panama shall each independently have the right to take such steps as it deems necessary in accordance with its constitutional processes, *including the use of military force in Panama*, to reopen the Canal or restore the operations of the Canal, as the case may be.[102]

Early on 14 March Christopher returned to Capitol Hill to make a second unsuccessful attempt to persuade DeConcini to moderate the language of the reservation.[103] Before leaving, Christopher agreed to a request from DeConcini for a meeting with the president the next day, Wednesday the 15th, just twenty-four hours before the final Senate vote on the Neutrality Treaty. The meeting was nominally scheduled to secure the president's personal consent for the wording of DeConcini's condition to the Neutrality Treaty, but for the junior senator from Arizona the meeting clearly offered enormous public relations possibilities as well.

In the meantime pressure was building on a different front, as the

Panamanians issued first warnings of the probable consequences of tampering with the fragile compromise struck on intervention rights in the leadership amendments. At the White House on Monday morning, 12 March, before Hamilton Jordan, Vice-President Mondale, Congressional Liaison Robert Beckel, and Robert Pastor of the National Security Council, Panamanian Ambassador Gabriel Lewis expressed grave reservations about the trend of events and warned of the dangers posed by DeConcini's last-minute intervention.[104] Jordan, alerted to the seriousness of the situation, dispatched Linowitz aide Ambler Moss on a hasty overnight trip to Panama to try to soothe ruffled nerves. What Moss found when he arrived was a full-blown crisis. He learned, as Lewis had warned, that the language of the DeConcini reservation expanding U.S. intervention rights in the internal affairs of Panama was wholly unacceptable and that an angry Torrijos had only hours earlier requested national television time to denounce the treaties publicly, a move that was almost certain to trigger widespread anti-American violence in Panama. Moss and U.S. ambassador William Jordan quickly relayed the information back to Washington, and after spirited entreaties from the Panamanian negotiators and lengthy personal calls from the president and Hamilton Jordan, Torrijos was finally persuaded to let the ratification process run its full course before taking any definitive action. In a letter to Carter dated 15 March, however, Torrijos issued an explicit warning that "It will be unacceptable for Panama any reservations [sic] staining the national dignity" or "addressed to impeding the effective exercise of Panama's sovereignty over all its territory." He nevertheless pledged that "Panama would reserve judgment until the Senate completed action on both Treaties."[105] In retrospect it seems clear that the planned television address would have brought thirteen years of effort to an irrevocable and bitter end.[106]

When Dennis DeConcini came calling at the White House on the morning of the 15th, the president was caught in an awkward dilemma. Only a week earlier senior administration officials had concluded that the vote count was too close for comfort and that the situation was on the verge of deteriorating. The most optimistic estimates at the White House showed no more than sixty-seven votes, including DeConcini's. On the very day of the final vote Senate leaders could count on only 62 of the 67 votes necessary, with only one sure vote in reserve.[107] The president was therefore faced with an unenviable set of choices. On the one hand he could reject the reservation and risk losing DeConcini's vote, and with it the entire treaty. On the other he could accept the reservation and thereby

ensure ratification of a treaty that, as recent events had made unmistakably clear, the Panamanians would reject. Among the president's top political advisers, Jordan, Beckel, and congressional liaison
chief Frank Moore, the recommendation to accede to DeConcini's
request was unanimous. One deciding consideration was a warning
from Montana Democrat Paul Hatfield that his vote for ratification
would be contingent on approval of the DeConcini reservation. Thus,
by the 15th, the decision had been made to go for the necessary votes
first and to worry about the reaction in Panama later. By DeConcini's
retelling, the president was unaccountably casual when the crucial
meeting finally took place. When DeConcini asked for the administration's consent, the president simply deferred to Christopher. "Is
this o.k.?" asked Carter. "This will give us a bit of the problem,"
replied Christopher, "but nothing we can't handle."[108] The president
conceded later that he "had no idea that the meeting would create
the single biggest threat to the treaties."[109]

In Jordan's office that evening Gabriel Lewis underscored the dangers involved in ratifying the Neutrality Treaty with DeConcini's condition. It was agreed that the only possible way to control the damage
at this eleventh hour was some type of corrective language, presumably in the form of a leadership-sponsored reservation. On Thursday
morning, the day of the vote, administration lobbyists, including the
vice-president and Christopher, approached Senator Frank Church
to ask for his floor time to introduce such language prior to the Senate
vote, while last minute amendments were being debated. But both
Church and cofloor leader Paul Sarbanes recommended against such
a course, on the grounds that it was not advisable to rock the boat at
such a late hour. The recommendation was reported back to the president at 3:00 P.M. just minutes before the vote, and with the president's
concurrence the decision was made to abandon efforts for compromise. Moments earlier DeConcini told his collegues on the floor of
the Senate that "I have assured the President that if my [reservation]
is accepted by the Senate that I will vote in favor of the Neutrality
Treaty. In turn, the President assured me yesterday in a meeting at
the White House that he would accept and support my amendment."[110] Thus, at 3:50 P.M., the Senate approved the Neutrality Treaty,
replete with the language penned by DeConcini.

If DeConcini failed to "see gunboat lurking behind those words,"
as the *Wall Street Journal* characterized the import of his reservation,
others did not.[111] In Panama reactions were swift and predictable.
News of Senate approval of the DeConcini language catalyzed every

stratum of Panamanian society, including Panama's conservative, pro-American business community. Angry mobs burned copies of the treaty outside the U.S. Embassy in Panama City. Panamanian Foreign Minister Aquilino Boyd denounced the new treaty as "immoral," an example that "the strong once again are trying to wield excessive power over the weak."[112] Torrijos, *Time* reported, was "furious" at the insult imposed by the reservation. "Listening to DeConcini, I ask myself the question: Have we by any chance lost a war? The U.S. didn't demand as much from Japan."[113] On 6 April, Torrijos wired United Nations secretary general Kurt Waldheim that the reservation constituted a violation of the UN Charter by giving "the U.S. the unilateral and perpetual right to take military action on Panamanian soil without the consent of the Panamanian government. . . ."[114] In a separate letter to the 151 members of the United Nations he denounced the reservation as a contravention of provisions of the UN Charter respecting the sanctity of national sovereignty.

On Capitol Hill the reaction was a mixture of surprise and indignation. Though Panamanian feelings about the proposed wording of the DeConcini reservation were well known at the White House and State Department through the warnings of Gabriel Lewis, the reports of Moss and William Jordan, and through the president's and Hamilton Jordan's own conversations with Torrijos, the reaction in Panama to the ratification vote caught the Senate completely by surprise. An angered Minority Leader Howard Baker complained that the Senate was "not advised" by the administration of the "acute concerns that the Panamanians apparently had about the DeConcini amendment until well after the fact."[115] From the chamber's erstwhile liberals, meanwhile, came protests that the sweeping intervention rights prescribed in the DeConcini reservation were tantamount to resurrecting the Platt Amendment. The reservation "has the ring of military interventionism," declaimed Massachusetts senator Edward Kennedy. It is a "political and diplomatic disaster," echoed South Dakota's George McGovern, a "killer amendment humiliating to Panama."[116]

In the *Washington Post* DeConcini was vilified as "ludicrous and irresponsible and hopelessly out of his depth. . . . Whether Mr. DeConcini can comprehend the dimension of the mischief he has wrought is not altogether clear," editorialized the *Post*. "In any event, it is up to Carter to impress on him that if he persists in his ways, the wreckage will be on his hands and on the hands of those other Senators so cynically playing his game."[117]

The sudden outpouring of criticism in the aftermath of the Senate's approval of the Neutrality Treaty underscored for treaty supporters the urgent necessity of undoing the damage caused by DeConcini and of ensuring that the Arizona senator would not have the last word in the effort to resolve the Panama problem. Inexplicably, however, no major initiative came from the White House. Instead of speedy efforts to draft remedial language for a leadership reservation that could be attached to the second treaty, scheduled to be voted within the month, there was only silence. On 27 March an impatient Gabriel Lewis warned negotiator Ellsworth Bunker that unless something were done before the second vote to counter the DeConcini reservation, Panama would be forced to reject the treaties out of hand. On 5 April an exasperated Lewis explained to chief White House lobbyist Frank Moore that "I think that at this time it is necessary that you act more quickly and take into account the reactions in Panama. We have been patient until now, but everything has its limits...." The Panamanian government was "very worried," continued Lewis, because Congress is "not aware of the Panama reality, and [Americans] think, especially at the Capitol, that everything is running smoothly and that General Torrijos and our Government are not facing serious problems as a result of what the Senators are doing here."[118]

The administration's response to the crisis consisted for the most part of largely ineffective efforts to persuade DeConcini to modify the language of yet another proposed reservation, for the purpose of making it a vehicle for the reiteration of the principle of nonintervention.[119] Panamanian officials, meanwhile, began their own initiative to ensure that the final Senate vote would not leave the DeConcini challenge unanswered. Moved by the "massive concern" over the DeConcini reservation in Panama,[120] Lewis, on 28 March, turned to a long-time friend of Latin America, Washington attorney and former Alliance for Progress administrator William D. Rogers, for help in breaking the impasse over the DeConcini wording. With the concurrence of Christopher and—at Rogers's insistence—without any White House participation, Rogers assumed responsibility for the delicate task of negotiating compromise language with the Panamanians. On 8 and 9 April, at a secret Florida location provided by the U.S. government, Rogers, Gabriel Lewis, and Panamanian negotiator Aristides Royo agreed on the first draft of a compromise reservation. With this draft in hand, the Senate leadership took over the job of putting the language in a form acceptable to a majority of the Senate—and to DeConcini, without whose support no compromise reservation would be credible to the Panamanians.

As *Newsweek* commented, the purpose of the new reservation was to "both preserve DeConcini's language and modify it."[121] Idaho's

Frank Church explained the process thus: "What we can do and must do is reassure the people of Panama what we have done. . . . We must state categorically that we neither sought nor obtained a right to intervene in their internal affairs nor do we have any intention of doing so. In this way we can show not only that we insist on preserving the legitimate rights of the United States to protect the Canal, but also that we are prepared to respect the legitimate rights of the Panamanian people to independence and national dignity."[122]

On Sunday night, just two days before the final Senate vote on the second treaty, Rogers, Lewis, Christopher, Byrd, Church, and cofloor leader Sarbanes met in Church's Capitol Hill office to put the final touches on the compromise resolution. In its final form it was a straightforward statement of the extent—and the limits—of U.S. intervention rights in the Canal. "Pursuant to its adherence to the principle of non-intervention, any action taken by the United States of America in the exercise of its rights to assure that the Panama Canal shall remain open, neutral, secure and accessible, shall not have as its purpose or be interpreted as a right of intevention in the internal affairs of Panama or interference with its political independence or sovereign integrity."[123] According to the majority leader, Lewis pressed at the meeting for more explicit assurances that the United States would not use the Canal as a pretext for intervention in the domestic affairs of Panama. "I told him that this was all he could hope to get and all I could get for him," said Byrd.[124] Lewis accordingly, relayed the draft text to Torrijos on Sunday night. Torrijos responded with approbation, saying it was "a dignified solution to a difficult problem."[125]

The next day the leadership took the draft text to Senator De-Concini. After meeting with Paul Hatfield (D.-Mont.) and Kaneaster Hodges (D.-Ark.), DeConcini proposed several minor changes, and the language was finalized on the evening of the 17th. The next day, Tuesday 18 April, Byrd and DeConcini cosponsored and introduced the final version of the leadership reservation. After three procedural challenges it was approved, 73 to 27, and the way was cleared for final approval of the resolution of ratification.

It seems apparent in retrospect that in nearly every respect the handling of the DeConcini affair represented a net loss to the administration. It was arguably an avoidable loss. To negotiator Linowitz it "muddied up" the ratification effort in a way that was unnecessary; it was a "regrettable chapter. . . . I would have discouraged [the president] from going forward with it."[126] To Bunker the Panamanians were correct in perceiving that the language of the DeConcini reservation represented a threat to their territorial and political integrity. The reservation, said Bunker, "clearly went beyond what Panama could have accepted."[127] To one Senate staff aide the administration's performance reflected a larger failure to play its longest suit effectively. The administration should have made clear to the Senate, and to individual mavericks like DeConcini, that they would be made to bear the onus if rejection were to lead, as there was every reason to believe it would, to political complications in Panama and to the possible closure of the Canal by terrorism. The administration, he suggests, "should have been more forthright in saying 'you guys bear the responsibility.' "[128] It was a potentially effective trump card, but, curiously, it never left the administration's hand.

More to the point, it was a trump card that should have been left in the first place to the Senate leadership to play. As Destler writes, the principal strategic mistake in the handling of the DeConcini affair was the assumption that the outcome was solely the administration's problem. Byrd and Baker had at least comparable stakes in the outcome: "It was *their* first foreign policy test as Senate leaders, and what DeConcini was attacking was the cornerstone of *their* 'leadership amendment' strategy."[129] Indeed, all the available evidence suggests that the DeConcini problem was one the Senate could have handled by itself. It was, after all, the Senate that applied the strategy of isolation which ultimately forced DeConcini to accept the compromise language finalized on the evening of 16 April. With the information the White House had available the week of the first Senate vote, there is little reason to doubt that Democratic leaders in the Senate could have found a way to dissuade DeConcini from introducing the resolution in the first place, at least not with the wording that Christopher had tried unsuccessfully to change. If he had known, said Byrd later, "I would have taken care of it."

> The Department of State and White House should have known much earlier what needed to be done, and then come to me. They can't expect to achieve much when they negotiate with a single Senator. On the other hand, I can. I know a lot of things they don't know and can pull a whole lot of levers that aren't available to them. I know who is close to whom, who owes whom, all that sort of thing, and I can work on individuals indirectly.[130]

White House lobbyists shared a firm conviction that they had done what needed to be done under a difficult set of circumstances. Ac-

cording to chief White House Panama lobbyist Beckel, the president
was fully informed of the possible consequences of acceding to the
DeConcini proposal but for domestic political considerations he had
no choice but to give the administration's consent:

> The president was not only not isolated, he was perfectly well aware of
> the Panama problem. The president talked to Torrijos. Hamilton talked
> to Torrijos. But you have to understand the context. Tuesday we had
> only 64 votes—*including* DeConcini and Hatfield, plus one other. We
> simply didn't know where we were getting the votes. We had good
> news with Bellmon who broke on Tuesday. We knew Brooke looked
> good by then. And Randolph said he'd be with us in a pinch. Long was
> 66 and DeConcini was 65. It was all a very interesting math game. We
> had an absolute, firm belief it was impossible to ratify without De-
> Concini. We knew what the political situation was on both fronts. Tues-
> day night we really did think it was lost.[131]

Beckel elaborates that at the White House there was no missing the
difficult options as the president made his final decision to support
the DeConcini reservation. Without the treaty there would be "terrible
riots in Panama." With the treaty and DeConcini, "it would be rough—
but [the Panamanians] could ultimately live with the treaties.... The
fact is we knew there would be a problem, but [the president] also
knew there would be a bigger problem without the treaties. He made
exactly the right decision." The key administration lobbyists, concludes Beckel, "will go to our graves absolutely convinced that without the DeConcini amendment the first treaty would not have been
passed."[132]

But hindsight also brought a recognition that the administration
should never have gotten itself into such a winless situation in the
first place. As Beckel concedes, "We should have turned over the key
votes ... to the leadership. After a while, all the pressure was coming
from us and they were saying 'who are you guys to be telling us.'
They needed to hear it from their own more and less from us."[133]
Beckel concludes, "If we were doing the whole thing over, we'd
probably not try to negotiate with DeConcini directly but have the
Senate leadership take him on.... We now realize there's no ticket
to publicity quite like saying 'no' to the president. We just wouldn't
stick the president's head in the noose again."[134]

That the administration committed a tactical error of such consequence may have been a function of panic as much as anything else.
With time running short and with the treaties hanging in the balance,
there was a reflexive disposition to deal with the DeConcini threat

directly at the White House. In one sense that reaction was the logical outgrowth of highly centralized White House control of the ratification effort. So long as the work of ratification lay in building a public constituency and in keeping senators informed, the arrangement doubtless maximized the administration's advantage. But once ratification came to hinge on one-on-one negotiations with the remaining handful of undecideds, greater responsibility should have been entrusted to the Senate leadership—who, as Byrd suggests, had considerably greater leverage in such situations.

The administration should at the very least have conveyed to the Senate a more accurate picture of the sensitivity of the Panamanians to the DeConcini language, though in this instance the problem may have been caused by the failure of the administration itself fully to comprehend the threat. As Carter later conceded, he "had seriously underestimated the concern of the Panamanians."[135] Even so, Senate leaders were fully aware of the closeness of the vote count, and they should have been called on earlier to help resolve a delicate situation.

In the end, dealing with Dennis DeConcini proved unnecessarily costly to the administration. The DeConcini affair never jeopardized the bloc of sixty-six votes (including that of Kaneaster Hodges) already secured by mid-March. But it did damage the administration's *reputation*, nullifying the careful, patient work that characterized the administration's overall effort. As Destler concludes, "Despite what was, on balance, a competent and impressive Congressional relations effort, one critical misreading ... led to events that created a very different impression politically."[136] As a result, the opportunity to gain credit for and to build on a solid legislative victory was lost.

[8]

The administration was finally able to come up with the sixty-seven votes necessary for ratification. But how, having done so much right in the process, did it come so perilously close to losing? How, in Destler's words, "on an issue where the President and the bipartisan leadership were both aligned and deeply engaged ... [did] 'victory' [become] so compromised in its pursuit that it was reduced to the avoidance of defeat?"[137]

When Carter administration officials sized up the approaching ratification debate during the summer of 1977, they entertained confident hopes that the treaties would serve to accomplish two major objectives. The first was policy-related: Panama would be the set piece of a more flexible approach to foreign affairs and an earnest of the president's determination to adjust U.S. policy to changing world circumstances. The second objective was political. Using the treaties, the administration would have its showdown with the Right and thereafter use the impetus gained from a major Senate victory to set the stage for other initiatives: the normalization of relations with Peking, Hanoi, and Havana; the new human rights policy; measures to curb conventional arms transfers; and, in particular, a new strategic arms treaty with the Soviet Union for which the Panama ratification debate was invariably understood as a "dry run." As the *New Republic's* TRB wrote, "Carter would like to make a battleground of the new Panama Canal Treaty, in hopes of trouncing his forces quickly and using the victory as momentum for tougher tests yet to come."[138]

Reviewing the ratification effort in retrospect, what stands out is the extraordinary determination and energy with which administration officials set about the task of reshaping the political environment in time for the final Senate votes. In selling the new Panama pacts to Congress and the public, the administration demonstrated the kind of "energy in the executive" of which Hamilton wrote with approbation in the *Federalist* and without which the treaties would never have survived the rigors of the long Senate debate.[139] As one White House aide said later, "It was the largest lobbying effort I'm familiar with in twelve years in Washington and perhaps in modern times."[140]

Still, measured against what the administration hoped to gain from the treaties, the debate was assuredly *not* a success. Even though the treaties were finally ratified, the administration was not able to generate any discernible sympathy for its guiding world view, so perfectly epitomized in the new treaty relationship with Panama. Nor did success on the treaties translate into the kind of political leverage that administration officials had hoped to gain as a means of ensuring legislative success on later policy initiatives. Indeed, despite the virtually universal international acclaim that greeted ratification, the domestic legacy of eight months of political warfare was a treasury exhausted of political capital and a reputation for political competence seriously damaged in the aftermath of the DeConcini affair. It is in these respects that the treaties came to represent for the Carter administration a Pyrrhic victory.

The question remains why an essentially sound political strategy failed to produce the desired political results. One answer may be that the president was not forceful enough in making clear to individual senators and to opponents on the Right that they, and not the administration, would be made to bear responsibility if violence or closure of the Canal were to follow in the wake of rejection.

Another may be that the administration lost precious time at the outset by not gearing up its formidable ratification machinery before the treaties were concluded and signed in August and September 1977. Although State Department officials did undertake some prior consultation on the Hill, the administration could have taken other measures to lay the groundwork for ratification without exposing the negotiations to unwarranted risk. For example, planning could have been completed for the citizens' committee, but the committee was not fully organized until mid-November, much too late to be of significant help to the administration. The waiting time before the end of the negotiations might have been used to develop themes, to draft speeches, to refine plans for the Congressional strategy, perhaps even to schedule a presidential address to explain the history and purpose of the negotiations and to place them in the context of a decade of bipartisan foreign-policy culminating in the Kissinger-Tack Agreement of a previous, Republican administration. As it was, valuable time was lost as the apparatus for selling the treaties was put in place, and some of the initiative gained from the attention-grabbing signing ceremony was forfeited as the administration scrambled to get the long-awaited ratification offensive off the ground.

But problems of leadership and timing notwithstanding, the most basic reason the administration had to bid so high for support on the treaties may have been that the "climate of opinion"[141] was much too restrictive to make an easy victory possible. Jimmy Carter's problem was in this respect not unlike that faced by Woodrow Wilson and Franklin D. Roosevelt who, under different circumstances, were forced to row upstream in efforts to win public and congressional support for internationalist foreign policies in times of deepening isolationism.

Earlier political decisions made by Carter—notably proposed unilateral troop withdrawals from Korea and the sudden cancellation of the B-1 bomber project—apparently raised first doubts, fairly or unfairly, about the president's reliability as custodian of the nation's security interests. But it was the full-dress debate over Panama that effectively catalyzed latent public fears of retreat and withdrawal and created the environment that compromised a ratification effort managed, for the most part, with a high degree of skill. Under the circumstances even a flawlessly executed political strategy may have been destined to founder. As presidential aide Hamilton Jordan noted later: "It really didn't matter if we started several days or several months late. Public opinion was set before we got into this. We were behind the curve the day Carter was elected. There was never much we could do."[142]

One specific casualty of the shifting public mood was that the administration was never given a full opportunity to present the strong case it had for ratification. Through the entire ratification period the burden of every administration speech, every article, every government publication urging ratification was to demonstrate that the treaties would *not* do what critics claimed they *would* do, namely, weaken U.S. defense, strengthen Communist influence in the hemisphere, deprive Americans of access to the Canal in an emergency, and impose heavy costs on U.S. taxpayers. As one Senate staffer reflected later, the administration was "forced to fight with one hand tied behind its back. It couldn't use the argument from idealism—that is, that in the face of an historical inequity it was the right thing to do—and was therefore forced to emphasize the negative themes."[143]

Another casualty was the effective use of the personal prestige of the president in making direct appeals for public support for ratification. From the beginning there were repeated calls, from inside and outside the administration, for the president to take to the electronic hustings to make the case for the treaties. "The President is going to have to take the lead in informing the public," the majority leader urged in October.[144] From State Department spokesman Hodding Carter, and from Hamilton Jordan and presidential press secretary Jody Powell, [145] came warnings that the president's low visibility was creating the impression that he was not wholly committed to the issue and that he was leaving congressional supporters exposed and without the reinforcement only a forceful presidential statement would bring.[146]

The original plan was to have the president address the nation at the beginning of the ratification campaign, perhaps as a logical follow-up to the signing ceremony. But as opposition to the treaties forced the floor debate past the Christmas recess, the administration was obliged to postpone arrangements for a presidential address, concerned that whatever momentum might have been generated in the autumn would be lost over the holidays. When the speech, a "fireside chat" from the White House library on 2 February, was finally delivered, it proved too little and too late. CBS refused to carry it live, and without a captive audience it became, as one media commentator later wrote, "probably the least watched of any President's address to the nation in the last two decades."[147] Thus, to a president who, in the words of the *New Republic's* TRB, had the luxury of reaching the nation to discuss Panama "in less time than it took Woodrow Wilson to pack his trunk," the advantage of the "bully pulpit" was largely lost, and the political support it might have generated went unrealized.[148]

Thus, even though the administration's ambitious, mostly skillful efforts were indispensable to the final Senate victory, administration lobbyists were forced to operate in a political environment they could never quite control. Even mistakes in handling the DeConcini situation came after all but two votes for ratification were secured, as noted above, and therefore do not explain the enormous difficulty in rounding up the first sixty-six votes. What started as an effort to inaugurate a new policy and to undermine the political capabilities of the Right thus became something the administration never expected or intended. The issue "caught fire in a way we simply didn't anticipate," remarked State's congressional chief, Douglas Bennet.[149] "We knew it would be tough," adds the White House's Beckel, "but I don't think any of us expected the intensity of the guerrilla warfare on the Right, and we didn't expect many of the issues which would be raised—the drug issue, the money...." Continues Beckel:

> The treaties just took on a life of their own. They became something so much bigger. No one could quite grasp it. No one really realized how politically explosive this would be. It seemed like such a reasonable thing to do, we really didn't grasp what was about to happen. It became such a lightning rod.... It was enormous in terms of what we had to concede.... It was like borrowing a guy's last fifty bucks and then asking for another ten. We simply wore out our welcome on the issue.[150]

The administration was consequently forced into a high-risk gamble it never intended to take. By the time the risks were apparent, there was no choice but to pay whatever price was necessary for ratification in the Senate. Seeing the potential damage that defeat in the Senate would have inflicted on Carter's young presidency, enough undecided senators supported the administration to rescue the president from his unintended dilemma. Their concern, together with bipartisan elite support and some political horse trading at the top, finally made ratification possible. But it would not become apparent until later just how issue-specific the winning coalition was.[151] Nor was it immediately apparent what a costly mortgage the Canal treaties would impose on later foreign-policy initiatives. "The administration lost untold political leverage in terms of other initiatives," commented White House lobbyist Dan Tate later: "Virtually everything that was controversial, that would pit one significant segment of the Senate against another, was compromised. I can't tell you how many times we went for support on other issues and heard 'I gave at the office.' Even when you factor in the normal ducking and dodging, this was significant."[152] Adds Beckel: "We paid the price so many ways: in the president's time; in the deals we had to cut; in compromises on the energy debate. The whole legislative agenda would have been different without Panama."[153]

The final irony was that the effort to use the Panama treaties to produce a new foreign-policy consensus ended by exacerbating the deep divisions inherited from Vietnam. As we shall see, eight months of intensive work by the administration managed to produce no visible public appreciation of the need, or of the national-security implications, of revising the 1903 treaty. As a result the administration was obliged to pay a debilitatingly high cost for ratification; for the balance of his presidency Jimmy Carter was forced to live on borrowed time. As columnist James Reston concluded, "This was not a vote of confidence for Mr. Carter.... It was a suspended sentence."[154]

CHAPTER 4

Panama and Public Opinion

Year's end 1977 marked the conclusion of a long and, in some respects, disappointing season for the administration of Jimmy Carter in its efforts to secure ratification of the Panama Canal treaties. Hopes had run high through the year, and even into the ratification period, that this controversial item could be cleared from the legislative calendar by the end of 1977, relieving anxieties within the administration and among treaty supporters on Capitol Hill over the prospect of extending the debate into an election year. "When we mapped out a timetable on Panama at the very beginning," National Security Council staffer Robert Pastor said later, "we started with the fact of an election year and worked back from there."[1] But as Senate hearings grew long and congressional delegations to Panama more frequent, hopes for an early vote in the Senate began to wane. As early as September Senate majority leader Robert Byrd began to lay the administration's hopes to rest. "Anyone who thinks I will bring [the treaties] up before January is living in a dream world," he told his regular Saturday press conference on Capitol Hill. To bring them up in the autumn of 1977 "would ensure...rejection."[2] Thus, as Jimmy Carter prepared for his first Christmas in the White House, his timetable, if not his overall strategy, became a casualty of the slow, deliberate process of ratification politics.

If the delay was good news for Jimmy Carter's opponents, however, the White House found some genuine cause for optimism as well. To offset the misfortune of resuming the debate in the new year, White House staffers could look back with satisfaction on what they had accomplished through the autumn struggles now concluded. Taking stock in December, Hamilton Jordan wrote to the president: "Administration efforts to build public support for the Panama Canal treaties are starting to bear fruit. A poll released only a few days ago indicates that opposition to the treaties has dropped from 87% in mid-August to 55% in mid-November, a 32% drop. Those favoring the Treaties have climbed to 38% from a low of 13%.... A favorable trend is being established."[3] The administration's pollster, Patrick Caddell, agreed. Reflecting on the events of the fall, he reported that two points stood out: "(1) Until recently, all surveys [on Panama] have shown more Americans opposed to the treaties than in favor; and (2) almost all the polls show major increases in support since September. As the Panama campaigns have begun, the proponents seem to be gaining the momentum.[4]

More satisfying yet, public opinion had shifted even before the president made his long-awaited "fireside chat" to the nation and before senior officials took to the road in January to carry the administration's message directly to the people. "There is a shift and there is a trend," Jordan noted, "and the trend has taken place before we've used our big guns."[5] Presidential Assistant Joseph Aragon wrote in November that "the Administration's efforts to build public support" are "remarkable" and an "unexpected success."[6] The administration's performance, said Presidential Press Secretary Jody Powell after the final Senate vote, was "an effort that really turned the country around in three or four months."[7]

The impression that opinion was shifting was not confined to the corridors of the West Wing. Appearing in Washington just before Christmas, the president's late political adversary now become leading Republican supporter on the issue, former president Gerald R. Ford, sensed that "the mood of the nation has changed significantly over the past six weeks."[8] On Capitol Hill in January Senator George McGovern described with approbation the "solid consensus on these treaties that are now before us.... By margins of 2-to-1 the American public supports these two treaties as we now propose to modify them."[9] In the pages of the *New Republic* veteran British journalist Henry Fairlie wrote that while the "first popular reaction to the Panama Canal treaties was extremely hostile...President Carter, and also many senators and representatives, chose to take the lead on the question. The result has been a dramatic decline in opposition to the treaties.[10]

Meanwhile, the *New York Times* noted the achievement of "a political climate in which the required two-thirds of the Senate will find it possible to vote for the treaties."[11] *Foreign Affairs* judged the administration's "vigorous campaign to correct public misconceptions" a success "in reducing the lopsided 2-to-1 public opposition to the treaties to something like a standoff—enough public support to sustain the Senate approval."[12] In the *Washington Post* political correspondent David Broder wrote that Panama showed the administration to be good at two things: "One is education—or persuasion—of the public. . . . [The administration] has significantly changed public opinion, not by the bravura of the President's speeches, but by a patient, well-plotted and continuous series of briefings, meetings and grass-roots conferences, involving leaders of business, labor and civic opinion, Republicans as well as Democrats."[13]

By March even the president himself indulged in a bit of optimism. "Public opinion polls are slowly turning in our direction," he noted cautiously.[14] "Our campaign was paying off," he wrote later in his memoirs; "it was becoming more fashionable to support the treaties."[15]

It is easy to see how much the administration's confidence was buoyed by polling results. For an issue on which such an inordinately high premium was placed on visible expressions of public support,[16] the polls appeared to provide the critical margin of safety for undecided senators hard-pressed by vocal opponents of ratification at home. As Senator McGovern noted before the Senate Foreign Relations Committee, the major obstacle on the road to ratification was that the Senate could not "make a foreign policy commitment that does not have broad political support here at home."[17] By Christmas it seemed apparent that, as a result of its intensive public relations efforts, the administration was solving that problem by creating an environment more and more conducive to ratification; and poll after poll seemed to verify the point. In the exhaustive search for trends that accompanied the entire course of the ratification debate, the beneficiary of every trend in sight was the Carter administration. The only trouble was that every trend in sight was wholly illusory.

[1]

Although attempts to gauge public attitudes on the transfer of the Canal to Panamanian control date back as far as 1964, the first polling questions that came to national attention were fielded in 1977 by a Princeton, New Jersey, firm, Opinion Research Corporation. The first ORC poll was commissioned by the American Council for World Freedom, a member of the powerful coalition that formed in opposition to ratification, and it asked the following question: "Do you favor the U.S. continuing its ownership and control of the Panama Canal or do you favor turning ownership and control of the Panama

Canal to the Republic of Panama?"[18] The ORC question was posed on four different occasions, but it was the May 1977 asking that garnered the most attention, in part because of the efforts of antitreaty groups to give the results wide exposure. The May results showed a mere 8 percent undecided, and these figures quickly became the standard reference point in the analysis of polling trends. "It was ORC's figures," wrote the State Department's Roshco, "that became the benchmark" against which to measure subsequent trends.[19]

For leading conservative opponents the ORC poll was proof that the nation would not countenance any change in the status of the canal. "The vast majority of Americans are not fooled," wrote Senator Paul Laxalt (R-Nev.) in October 1977. "They do not want and are not willing to accept the Canal giveaway. Recent polls show that an overwhelming majority of Americans resent efforts to blackmail America into giving away the Panama Canal under threats of violence."[20] Grasping the essence of the ORC figures, Senate Majority Leader Robert Byrd declared that "public opinion is very, very, very much against the treaties."[21] Translating its political significance, he said that "the polls indicated that about 75 percent of the American public are opposed to giving up the Canal, and you're not going to get two-thirds of the Senate to ratify that treaty until there's a substantial change in the polls."[22]

The ORC figure took on a more ominous aspect when its 78 percent opposition mysteriously became 87 percent, first in the Jordan memorandum to the president in December and later in news accounts of polling trends. "Last May," the *New York Times* wrote in February, "according to public opinion surveys conducted for the White House by pollster Patrick Caddell, an overwhelming 87 percent [of all Americans] opposed the treaties."[23] Caddell's office denied any knowledge of the 87 percent figure,[24] but whether the error was intentional or typographical, the ORC figure presented the administration with significant possibilities. Whatever mileage the results may initially have provided the opponents of ratification, they became in the end far more important politically to the *proponents* of ratification. And they did so for good reason: juxtaposed against the results of virtually every other sampling of opinion made during the ratification period[25] the result was the appearance of a major trend, the very trend, in fact, that had brought such satisfaction to the White House and that became the jumping-off point for nearly every news assessment of the administration's ratification efforts. Such a juxtaposition made the administration's strategy look like a textbook example of the efficacy of presidential power to influence public opinion. The most seasoned veterans were drawn to its apparent logic. As the *Christian Science Monitor*'s Washington correspondent Richard Strout noted, "The Carter Administration is trying to lead public opinion—and is succeeding on at least one front. With formal Senate debate to begin on the Panama Canal treaties February 6, popular opposition to yielding the Canal has diminished markedly, according to opinion polls. . . . During his eight month campaign public opposition to the treaties has dropped from 87 percent to 55 percent, White House polls indicate, with a faster decline in Congress."[26] The source of the latter figure (55 percent against ratification) was actually a Caddell poll taken in October 1977. But by February the *Times* and the *Monitor*, and anyone else for that matter, could have cited numerous other polls that showed dramatically different and more favorable responses than the benchmark ORC question.

Time's pollster, Daniel Yankelovich, writing two years after Senate ratification, offered the obvious interpretation:

> Thanks to the surveys that followed [the public relations efforts of the Administration], the Senate realized that many of the original public attitudes toward the treaties had not been settled judgments but rather off-the-cuff reactions to questions about a perceived American foreign policy "loss." Even today, three years [*sic*] later, an ardent core of opposition to the treaties remains. Still, when the Senate finally acted, it had been shown the true dimensions of public opposition, not an exaggerated and misleading picture.[27]

Nevertheless, if the ORC data were misleading, as their skewed opposition to treaty modification suggests they were, so also was the prevalent assumption of a positive trend in opinion toward the administration's position. The available data suggest that the administration, far from succeeding, singularly failed in its expansive efforts to produce a sea change in public attitudes. The fact is that throughout the ratification period, and extending well before and after, public opinion on the Panama Canal treaties remained almost completely static. Despite one of the most extensive public relations efforts undertaken on any foreign-policy issue in American history, public attitudes never budged. That the contrary perception was so universally held makes Panama a near-perfect example of the hazards of pegging complex public issues to perceived public attitudes.

[2]

The evidence on the point is abundant and persuasive. In methodological terms the most reliable way to gauge the trend of public

Table 1. Responses to Roper question on Canal treaty (percentages)

	June 1976	Jan. 1977	Aug. 1977	Sept. 1977	Nov. 1977
Modify	26	24	28	27	31
Keep as is	46	53	44	53	50
No opinion	28	24	28	20	19

opinion is to look at the responses to similar polling questions posed over time to comparable samples. Fortunately, such long-term trend analysis is possible with the polling data on Panama, and it readily confirms the *absence* of a trend. The point can be verified two ways. The first is to examine comparable questions asked by each polling organization individually; the second is to compare questions asked by the different polling organizations, grouped according to information content.

Of the ten national polling organizations that sampled opinion on the treaties, the Roper Organization, CBS, NBC, and the Harris survey provide the best test of the first method. The most convincing indication of the absence of a trend comes from data produced by questions asked by Roper beginning in June 1976—fourteen months before the treaties were signed—and ending in November 1977. Roper's question was: "There has been a good deal of discussion recently as to whether or not the United States should negotiate a new treaty with Panama concerning the Panama Canal. Do you think the time has come for us to modify our 1903 Panama Canal treaty or that we should insist on keeping the treaty as originally signed."[28] The similarity of the "marginals" is strikingly apparent in Table 1. By November, well into the ratification period and at a time when the White House was seeing the first hints of a trend, respondents were registering the same proportions of support and opposition as they did before Jimmy Carter was even a candidate for President. There was in all a shift of 9 percent from the undecided column, with partisans and opponents effectively splitting the difference. In June 1978, two months after the final Senate vote and seven months after the last comparable Roper question, Roper solicited views on the Panama treaty one last time: "Do you think the Senate *should* have approved the Panama Canal treaties or should *not* have approved them?" The results were indistinguishable from the earlier round of questions: 30 percent approved, 52 percent opposed, and 18 percent remained uncommitted. In short, there was no real ground swell one way or the other. After the longest and hardest-fought treaty contest in half a

Table 2. Responses to CBS question on Canal treaty (percentages)

	June 1976	Oct. 1977	Jan. 1978	Apr. 1978
Approve	24	29	29	30
Disapprove	52	49	51	53
No opinion	24	22	20	17

century, the proportion of responses pro and con stood roughly where it had two months before and two years before.

The results of polling done by CBS were essentially the same. CBS asked four comparable questions between June 1976 and April 1978 and got an identical proportion of affirmative and negative responses. The basic CBS question was: "The Senate now has to debate the treaties that President Carter signed granting control of the Panama Canal to the Republic of Panama in the year 2000. Do you approve or disapprove of those treaties?"[29] The responses show the same, roughly five-to-three, level of opposition as Roper (see Table 2). "On the issue of the Panama Canal treaties," the *New York Times* reported on the eve of the second vote, "the [April] poll showed participants still opposed to them...as the Senate vote on the second pact, due next Tuesday, approaches. That margin has remained constant for six months."[30]

The two other organizations that asked comparably worded questions through the ratification period drew similar results. NBC asked three such questions, beginning in August 1977. The August poll asked, "Do you think the U.S. should sign a treaty which would eventually return control of the Panama Canal Zone to the government of Panama or don't you think so?" In October and January, NBC asked this question: "The new treaty between the United States and Panama calls for the United States to turn over ownership of the Canal to Panama at the end of this century. However, this treaty still has to be approved by the Senate. Do you favor or oppose approval of this treaty by the Senate?"[31] Once again the opposition held, and by somewhat larger margins (see Table 3).

The wording of two questions posed by the Harris Survey at the beginning and end of the ratification debate evoked the same response (see Table 4).[32] Once again the same trend—or absence of a trend—is borne out, and once again by the same relatively constant percentages. In each case—Roper, CBS, NBC, and Harris—a slightly higher percentage of respondents shifted to the "disapprove" column, at least during the ratification period itself. In June Harris asked

Table 3. Responses to NBC question on Canal treaty (percentages)

	Aug. 1977	Oct. 1977	Jan. 1978
Approve	27	30	28
Disapprove	55	61	62
No opinion	18	9	10

one last question about the Panama treaties: "Now that the Panama Canal treaties have passed in Congress, do you feel that all in all it will be a good thing for the United States or don't you feel that way?" The percentages had by now shifted upward: 37 percent answered in the affirmative, 44 percent were opposed, and 19 percent were unsure. But the results still speak to the central fact that after six months of intensive efforts to condition public attitudes on the treaties, the opinions of a majority of Americans were unchanged.

The stability in the results of the Roper, CBS, NBC, and Harris polls is striking. Whatever small statistical significance may be attributed to the difference in these results, there is clearly no political significance to these differences—at least not with respect to demonstrating the movement of opinion in one direction or the other.[33] Through the entire ratification debate public opinion was impervious both to the best efforts of the administration and to well-financed, well-publicized efforts to oppose ratification. From beginning to end the polls, by virtue of posing roughly the same question to roughly comparable samples through most or all of the ratification period, give an accurate impression of the inelasticity of opinion. "When it was all over," noted Roshco later, "the basic finding of approximately five-to-three opposed that had emerged when the issue of the treaty became salient seemed to have reemerged. The trend that was confirmed most strongly could have been graphed with a straight horizontal line."[34]

Exactly why a divergence came to exist between the real and the perceived meanings of the polling data on Panama almost entirely concerns the problem that confounded public polling from the beginning, namely, the near-total absence of an informed public. Gone

Table 4. Responses to Harris question on Canal treaty (percentages)

	Oct. 1977	Apr. 1978
Approve	26	29
Disapprove	51	60
No Opinion	23	11

by the time of the Panama debate was liberal America's sanguine belief in the existence of a rational, informed citizenry as the source of enlightened government. American Progressivism of the early twentieth century was probably the last paean to such a notion. After Walter Lippmann's seminal works on public opinion, published in the 1920s, faith in the virtue and rationality of popular opinion all but vanished.[35] Lippmann's mass men labored in vain against a perpetual inability to distinguish between "the world outside and the pictures in our heads," between the "fictions" of the popular mind and "the world that we have to deal with politically."[36] They suffered from "anemia, from lack of appetite and curiosity of the human scene," and as Leo Bogart later described it, the polls that gauged their opinions came to be regarded as little more than a "magnifying mirror of our collective ignorance and perplexities."[37]

As Bogart suggests, such ignorance calls into question the very raison d'être of survey research: "Public opinion is commonly measured for and against various causes, with the undecided as the residue. Often it may be more revealing to measure the degree of apathy, indecision, or conflict on the part of the great majority and consider the opinionated as the residue. The first question a pollster should ask is: 'Have you thought about this at all? Do you *have* an opinion?'[38] Little in the extensive polling on the Panama treaties challenges these skeptical assessments of popular understanding of public issues. The available evidence suggests that, for all the political emotion generated by the Panama controversy, political knowledge, either of the history or of the terms of the Canal debate, remained at an extraordinarily low level. As we shall see, this anomaly had a direct and fundamental bearing on diverging assessments of Panama polling data.

Although the major national polling organizations asked nearly fifty opinion questions during the ratification debate, there were only two reliable measures of the public's *knowledge* of the Panama issue. The first was a pair of questions posed by Opinion Research Corporation in its first polling on Panama, in June 1975. ORC's first question asked respondents about the location of the Panama Canal: "As you may know, the Panama Canal is the waterway in Central America that connects the Atlantic and Pacific Oceans. As far as you know, what country owns the Panama Canal and the Canal Zone surrounding it?"[39] Responses ranged across the lot, from Arabs to Israelis, from Cubans to communists to Panama itself. The correct answer, the United States, was supplied by only one-third of the respondents.

The second question asked if respondents were aware of the negotiations that had begun eleven years earlier: "The United States secured full ownership and control of the Canal Zone by way of a treaty signed with the Republic of Panama in 1903. How much, if anything, have you heard or read about the possibility of negotiations on a new Panama Canal Treaty: a great deal, a fair amount, very little, or nothing at all." Fully 82 percent knew little or nothing of the negotiations. When the question was asked again in April 1976, nearly 70 percent confessed such ignorance despite the fact that the Canal had become an issue in the Republican presidential primary campaign of 1976. Even as late as May 1977, with the negotiations winding to a conclusion, 62 percent of the public had little or no knowledge of the negotiations, suggesting that not least among the administration's ratification troubles was a near-total lack of preparation for the proposal to give up the Canal.[40]

The second knowledge test was administered in October 1977 and February 1978 by the Gallup Organization. On both occasions this trilogy of questions was asked:

(1) As far as you know, in what year is the Panama Canal to be turned over completely to the Republic of Panama by the terms of the treaty?

(2) As far as you know, will the U.S. have the right to defend the Panama Canal against third nation attacks after Panama takes full control?

(3) To the best of your knowledge, how much do the biggest U.S. aircraft carriers and supertankers now use the Panama Canal: A great deal, quite a lot, not very much, or not at all?[41]

In October only 7 percent of respondents could answer all three factual questions about the treaties correctly. In February, the results were only marginally higher. As Gallup comments:

Analysis of the survey reveals that Americans have very little knowledge of the treaties' particulars considering the amount of media attention given them.

Even when the results are computed on the basis of those who have heard or read about the debate surrounding the treaties, only 35% know when the U.S. will turn over the Canal and Canal Zone to Panama; 58% know that the U.S. retains the right to defend the Canal against third-nation attacks; and 19% know that the largest warships and supertankers currently do not use the Canal at all. . . . When the results are based on the total sample, the percentages are even smaller.[42]

The figures offer striking evidence on the difference between being "aware" and being "informed," and they vividly illustrate the nature of the raw material the pollsters had to work with.

The specific implications on the Panama polling concern the important inverse relationship that existed between the level of information held by respondents and the influence that the exact wording of the pollsters' questions had on the direction of opinion. "The paradox of the scientific method," Bogart writes, "is that we can change phenomena by measuring them."

> An interview acts as a catalyst. The confrontation of interviewer and respondent forces the crystallization and expression of opinions where there were no more than chaotic swirls of thought. The respondent's statements themselves represent a form of behavior; they are commitments. A question asked by an interviewer changes an abstract and perhaps irrelevant matter into a genuine subject of action.... The conventional poll forces expression into predetermined channels, representing clear-cut and mutually exclusive choices. To accommodate one's thought to these channels represents for the respondent an arousal of interest, an affirmative act.[43]

The mechanism of "arousal" was clearly the pollster himself—or, more specifically, the wording devised by the pollster to elicit a response on the issue. The less respondents knew of the issue to begin with (and the evidence makes it abundantly clear that most knew very little) the more their opinions were influenced by the exact wording of the polling questions, whether they were biased, consciously or unconsciously, for or against ratification. The correspondence between wording and response in the case of the Panama treaties was, given the low levels of public understanding, all but exact. Through months of poll taking on the treaties nothing altered this basic cause-effect relationship.

As it happened, the wording of many of the later questions on the treaties contained more justification for supporting ratification, especially after reference was made to the leadership amendments, reflecting the progress of the debate in the Senate. By the rule just elucidated, such questions drew responses more favorable to the administration's position. This change undoubtedly provided political refuge for many senators who could now argue the presence of a favorable trend. Still, such responses cannot accurately be interpreted as an index of growing popular support for the transfer of jurisdiction over the Canal to Panama. Closer examination makes it clear that what appeared to be a trend toward public approval of ratification was nothing more than a trend toward wording in the polling questions themselves more likely to draw favorable responses.

As previously noted, the second way to demonstrate the absence of a trend, that is, the persistence of public opposition to ratification, is to categorize poll questions on the treaties according to their informational content and then to compare responses. In fact the nearly fifty questions asked by the major national polling organizations fall easily into four such categories, as shown in Appendix A.

One type, asked only by Opinion Research Corporation, dealt exclusively with the matter of ownership and control of the Canal, without reference to the treaties and without qualifications pertaining either to the possible length of a transition period or to residual rights actually defined in the 1977 treaty. A second type, which includes the Roper, NBC, CBS, and Harris questions quoted earlier, contained less evocative wording. The questions in this category either made no reference to the sensitive issue of the transfer of ownership and control of the Canal to Panama (for example, Roper's question simply referred to a modification of the old treaty arrangement) or, where such reference was made, appended some qualifying language (for example, "until the year 2000" or "by the end of the century") that altered the perception of immediacy. A third category includes questions that contain more specific information about rights which the United States would retain under the treaty but without specific reference to the so-called leadership amendments.[44] Questions in the final category include the actual details of the leadership amendments.

The data shown in Appendix A intimate the presence of an internal trend in only two polls. One was Gallup's, culled from surveys done in September and October 1977 and January 1978, which showed a 6 percent overall increase in support for ratification. The other was Caddell's, which between August 1977 and February 1978 purports to show a 12 percent increase in support and a simultaneous 12 percent decrease in opposition to ratification.[45] But like the 87 to 55 percent drop that the *Times* and *Monitor* reported in February (based on a comparison of ORC and Caddell figures), these trends reported by Gallup and Caddell must also be discounted. In both cases the presumed movement was situationally induced under controlled conditions created by the asking of questions that included more information on the treaties.

That such conditions did not obtain outside such laboratory settings is demonstrated by another set of Caddell's own polls taken in May, September, and December 1977. On these occasions Caddell asked the neutral questions (shown in Category II in Appendix A), and each time he came up with the very five-to-three opposition shown in response to every such question asked by the national polling organizations between May 1975 and June 1978.[46] In other words, at the very time one set of Caddell questions was producing a trend, the other was not. Had there been a *real* trend, it would have been visible in both Caddell polls and in the Roper, CBS, and other data as well. Instead, all spoke unanswerably to the resistance of opinion to movement in any direction.

The treaty period is punctuated by examples of even more remarkable instant shifts in "public opinion" based on the addition of follow-up questions. For example, NBC's January 1978 question produced a negative response by a margin of 62 percent to 28 percent, but appending a second question elucidating rights promised in the leadership amendments reversed the results with 65 percent in favor and only 25 percent opposed.[47] When CBS asked its own set of comparable back-to-back questions, public opinion shifted from 49 percent opposed and 29 percent in favor to 63 percent in favor and 24 percent opposed. Even in a statewide poll in Texas, where Opinion Research drew an overwhelming 79 percent to 11 percent negative response with its "ownership and control" question, the addition of a question about the leadership amendment guarantees produced 49 percent in favor of ratification with only 33 percent opposed.[48] Caddell cited the obvious implications: "Most people always argue that those who oppose [the treaties] do so from ignorance; in this case it just happens to be true. Giving the people knowledge about the treaties has to be a high priority item."[49]

As suggested above, the appearance of a trend based on more favorable responses to questions citing the leadership amendments doubtless had its uses for the administration. It made it possible for senators to argue that they could now support the treaties because the public now supported the treaties. Although the influence of the polling results cannot be isolated with any precision, it may well have been an important factor in gaining or retaining some swing votes in the Senate. Still, the "trend" that provided such political refuge was essentially illusory.

In its purest form the prevailing misconception on the point grew from a universal misreading of conclusions announced by George Gallup in October 1977, based on a poll fielded between 30 September and 3 October. "The more Americans know about the Panama Canal treaties," he reported, "the more likely they are to favor Senate ratification of the pact, lending support to President Jimmy Carter's thesis."[50] The press release describing Gallup's data and findings was widely circulated by the White House and the State Department and

through the various private-sector organizations that abetted the ratification effort.

Technically, Gallup's observation was correct. When respondents
were given more information in polling questions—or when they
brought to the question a more detailed knowledge of the issue—
their disposition to favor ratification was verifiably higher.[51] But the
problem was never the causal relationship between information and
support. The problem was that no one had the information in the
first place—no one, that is, except Gallup's 7 percent "better informed" plus those very few who were actually privy, as respondents,
to the pollsters' questions.

The most extreme failure to comprehend the implied caveat in Gallup's statement appeared in the April issue of *More* magazine, under
the by-line of historian Walter LaFeber. LaFeber used the February
New York Times article, quoted earlier, as his straw man. "The treaties
have yet to win the approval of a majority of Americans," LaFeber
quoted the *Times* as saying, "although a change in opinion since last
summer has produced a political climate more favorable to ratification." Observed LaFeber:

> The White House profited handsomely from such early reports. The *New
> York Times* story used Administration sources to detail how the Presi-
> dent's efforts had supposedly reduced the 87% opposed in May 1977,
> to only 55% in early 1978. The figures were those of a White House
> pollster, Patrick Caddell, and the *Times* did not question them.
>
> Readers not able to keep up with the public opinion shell game must
> have been impressed with the power of the President and pro-treaty
> pressure groups to sway feelings on the agreements. As the *Times* wrote
> on March 27, the "turnabout" in the polls was an accomplishment "for
> which the Administration can claim substantial credit."
>
> In reality, there was no turnabout.

So far, so good. But LaFeber then concludes that

> the press simply never consistently understood that a majority of Amer-
> icans favored treaties that included the two amendments sponsored by
> the Senate leaders, Democrat Robert Byrd of West Virginia and Repub-
> lican Howard Baker of Tennessee.[52]

In fact a majority of Americans did *not* favor ratification. All that can
be said with confidence is that they would have supported ratification
if they had been aware that the leadership amendments existed and
were part of the treaty. But clearly they were not. LaFeber's mistake,

duplicated by others who misread Gallup, was a failure to couch such conclusions in the conditional case.

This point is central to an understanding of the Panama polls and illustrates one of the basic idiosyncracies of public polling generally. The "public opinion" that was so assiduously courted, and whose presumed movements were so anxiously scrutinized by opponents and partisans alike, proves, on a closer look, to have been nothing more than a collection of responses all but predetermined by the information imparted in the questions asked.

The striking thing is thus the degree to which the public opinion polls actually became a *factor* in the process of political education on the treaties, rather than merely an *account* of it. For those who heard the pollsters' descriptions of guarantees provided in the leadership amendments, the logic of ratification was demonstrably more apparent. The fallacy in most commentary on public opinion lay in the assumption that what happened under the controlled conditions of a polling query would happen—or, indeed, *did* happen—among the public at large. What could have happened in theory did not happen in fact, despite the best efforts of a presidential administration and various powerful allies to make it so.

Whatever gain the administration may have enjoyed by the prevalence of the contrary assumption is an open question. What the evidence makes indisputably clear, however, is that no interpretation, whether juxtaposing the results of different questions, relying on the internal trends cited by Gallup and Caddell, or a leap of faith that the public always supported ratification with the key amendments, can disguise the basic truth: when it was all over, nothing had changed. After six months virtually no inroads had been made in what one State Department official described two months after ratification as "the American public's unrelenting distaste for the Panama treaties."[53] There is a "wide gap between the people and the politicians," concluded Jude Wanniski in April 1978. "Who doubts that if there were provision in the Constitution for a national referendum, and one were held on the Canal treaties, that the voters would bury them?"[54]

[3]

The story of public opinion on the Panama treaties is not entirely told in the nearly universal misattribution of trends, both inside and outside the government. It also involves the reasons why the administration was unable to produce such a trend, in spite of the almost unprecedented size of its "all hands on deck" effort to win public acceptance for the new pacts.

The White House and the State Department undertook the task of building public support for the treaties with a special sense of urgency. Organized opposition groups always had the luxury of operating successfully without the need for public support.[55] But inside the Carter administration there was a frank recognition that the burden of proof in the coming debate would rest with those who supported rather than with those who opposed ratification. As we have already seen, the failure actually to win such support was partially mitigated by the *appearance* that opinion was slowly shifting in the administration's direction. As we shall now see, the inability to create a *real* ground swell did not reflect any major strategic miscalculation at the White House. Rather, it was the product of a variety of circumstances over which the administration had no control and which effectively doomed the public relations campaign to futility.

As the ratification debate began in August 1977, both the administration and leaders of the two principal conservative coalitions formed to defeat ratification, felt considerable confidence in the prospects for influencing public attitudes on the treaties. Both camps reasonably assumed that there existed substantial latent opinion which, when coaxed out of inattentiveness and undecidedness, would tip the balance in the national polls and provide the requisite environment either for ratification or for rejection. The administration, in particular, placed a special premium on the undecideds, since from the beginning polls showed that the intensity factor among opponents was more than double that among supporters of ratification.[56] Its hope and expectation was that as the issue became more important to more people, there would be some movement in opinion, like a dormant "giant"— to use Thomas Bailey's analogy[57]—awakened to dictate the course of events. In fact the available polling data strongly suggest that the assumption was unfounded. Contrary to all expectations, it appears that there was no appreciable amount of convertible opinion for either side to mobilize.

As it happened, part of the administration's hope was realized. As the ratification debate progressed, the issue did indeed become more important to larger numbers of Americans. The best indication on the point comes from Roper, who between May 1976 and March 1978 asked comparable samples on six occasions how closely they followed the issue. The trend is clearly visible in Roper's published results[58] (see Table 5). The responses show a significant increase—from a low

127

Table 5. Responses to Roper's question on public interest in treaty ratification (percentages)

	May 1976	June 1976	July 1976	Nov. 1977	Feb. 1978	Mar. 1978
Following closely	25	27	19	45	43	45
Following casually	36	38	35	36	36	38
Not following	40	35	46	19	21	16

of 54 percent in July 1976 to a high of 83 percent in March 1978—of those who followed the issue, and a 29 percent decrease in inattentiveness between the same high and low months. The polls constitute a crude but suggestive measure of salience: briefly, the treaty issue came to occupy a relatively high place in the hierarchy of public concerns. Significantly, however, this increase did nothing to alter the ratio of opposition to support, which, as we have seen, remained unchanged through the entire ratification period.

The most accurate gauge of the relationship between salience and the direction of opinion also comes from Roper. In June 1976 and November 1977 Roper posed back-to-back salience and opinion questions to identically sized samples. The opinion question, cited earlier, was: "Do you think the time has come for the U.S. to modify our 1903 Panama Canal treaty, or that we should insist on keeping the treaty as originally signed?" In June 1976, 26 percent favored modification, 46 percent opposed modification, and 28 percent were undecided. In November 1977 the results were 31 percent for modification, 50 percent against, and 19 percent undecided.

A statistical analysis of the Roper data (Table 6) verifies that salience increased significantly between June 1976 and November 1977. It appears that lobbying efforts on both sides, therefore, had the effect of drawing more respondents into attentiveness. Nevertheless, the increase effected no significant change in the balance of aggregate opinion—indeed, the balance of opinion pro and con was surprisingly impervious to the rise in salience. The data indicate that as salience increased, it drew all groups into opinion.[59] Moreover, among those "closely" following the Panama issue there was a statistically significant shift in opinion from opposition to support of ratification (although the majority—55.5 percent—still remained in opposition in November 1977). This shift, however, was offset by movement in the "casually following" group. As a result the overall movement was sufficiently small that it had no political significance whatever (from 47 percent opposed and 26 percent favoring in 1976 to 50 percent opposed and 30 percent favoring in 1977). Indeed, even if all those

Table 6. Cross-tabulation of polling data published in June 1976 and November 1977

June 1976	Liberalize	Keep	Don't Know	Total
Closely	31.5%*	36.0%	9.5%	
	29.7%**	61.2%	9.1%	27.8%
	82***	169	25	276
Casually	46.5%	34.3%	32.7%	
	32.9%	43.8%	23.4%	37.1%
	121	161	86	368
No Attn	21.9%	29.8%	57.8%	
	16.3%	40.1%	43.6%	35.1%
	57	140	152	349
Total	26.2%	47.3%	26.5%	100.0%
	260	470	263	993

November 1977	Liberalize	Keep	Don't Know	Total
Closely	51.6%	50.2%	22.9%	
	35.0%	55.5%	9.5%	45.5%
	158	251	43	452
Casually	38.6%	33.6%	30.9%	
	34.3%	48.8%	16.9%	34.8%
	118	168	58	344
No Attn	9.8%	16.2%	46.3%	
	15.2%	40.9%	43.9%	19.9%
	30	81	87	198
Total	30.8%	50.3%	18.9%	100.0%
	306	500	188	994

Source: The Roper Center, Office of Archival Development and User Services, Storrs, Conn. Cross-Tabulation Ref. no. 05-RS-172, 21 December 1981.
*Percentage of vertical column.
**Percentage of horizontal column.
***Total number of correspondents in each category

who moved out of the "no opinion" category had shifted in favor of ratification, the political difference would still have been insignificant.

One factor accounting for the apparent failure of higher salience to alter the direction of opinion may have been that the efforts of the administration and opposition groups had offsetting effects. As Herbert Hyman and Paul Sheatsley have noted in connection with research conducted in the 1940s on the obstacles facing public information campaigns, "people tend to expose themselves to information which is congenial with their prior attitudes, and to avoid exposure to information which is not congenial.''[60] It may well have been the case that information was assimilated only selectively and that many of the newly attentive actually "heard," and were therefore influenced by, only one side of the debate. Paul Lazarsfeld, reporting on the exposure of a control group to political campaign propaganda, noted that "even those who had not made a decision [on how to vote] exposed themselves to propaganda which fit their not-yet-conscious political predispositions.''[61] To the extent that people on both sides of the issue demonstrated this tendency, they may well have neutralized the efforts of partisans pro and con.

A second factor may be the apparently disproportionate influence of demographics on public attitudes toward ratification. The Gallup, Roper, Caddell, Harris, CBS, and Opinion Research organizations all describe a close correspondence between certain key demographic characteristics and the disposition either to support or to oppose ratification. Predictably, status (defined by occupation and income) and education were the most reliable indicators, while age, party affiliation, and region had a secondary influence. George Gallup profiled the supporters of ratification in this way:

> Analysis of the attitudes of the "informed" segment of the population (those who have followed the debate concerning the treaties) indicates that support for the treaties is highest among the college-educated, young people under the age of 30, those in the upper-income brackets ($20,000 per year and more), those in the professions and business, as well as people living in the East, primarily in non-rural areas. Democrats, not surprisingly, are more inclined to support the treaties than are Republicans and Independents.[62]

Summarizing treaty opponents, Pat Caddell wrote that " 'give away' sentiment is highest among lower-income groups, the poor, blue collar workers, and old citizens. Residents of the Central states moreover are much more likely to see giving up of the Canal Zone as a loss of U.S. property than other areas.''[63] These conclusions are corroborated by virtually all of the other national polling organizations.

One advantage the Carter administration enjoyed during the ratification debate was the support of the more politically involved and influential segments of the "attentive" public described by Gallup.[64] As noted in chapters 3 and 5, efforts were successfully mounted both inside and outside the White House to harness various groups of elites to the work of ratification; such support was undoubtedly influential in holding several Senate votes, in particular those of a few moderate Republicans.

But even with this built-in advantage the administration had no success in transforming the the overall political environment, primarily because of the particular influence demographics had on its efforts to arouse and direct opinion. The phenomenon at work is described by Bauer, Pool, and Dexter in their landmark study of the politics of the foreign-trade legislation of the 1950s and 1960s:

> We found that, among the general population, liberalism on foreign trade was highly correlated with education and social status. The lower in the social spectrum one looked, the more latent protectionists one found and also the more people unaware of the foreign-trade issue. Under such conditions, any propaganda campaign which increased popular attention to the issue would probably thereby increase manifest protectionist sentiment by bringing otherwise apathetic persons who tend to have a disproportionate number of latent protectionists among them, into the area of discourse. . . . The direction of the stimulus in such a situation matters little. What matters is that the reservoir of uninformed protectionism at the bottom of the cultural ladder is apt to be tapped by any campaign sufficiently vigorous to catch the attention of the whole public. Any sort of popular propaganda on foreign-trade matters could trigger the protectionist potential.[65]

In short, it proved easier to arouse opinion than to direct it, and the parallel with the Panama treaties appears to be nearly exact. While the organized public information campaigns were successful in stimulating interest, they retained only a marginal capacity to condition actual responses (save, presumably, among those already favorably disposed). Once moved to attentiveness, the public generally found its own reasons to support or oppose ratification.

The dissociation of stimulus and response doubtless worked to the greater disadvantage of the Carter administration. The simple mathematics involved suggests the appreciably smaller number of people likely, by virtue of education and experience, to have been conversant with the external circumstances that administration lobbyists argued gave logic to their position. In the process of trying to tap this potential pool, already smaller to begin with, the administration, like the Truman and Kennedy administrations during the trade debates, may well have triggered the rejectionist sentiment that neutralized its own gains. Whatever hope existed of mobilizing an apparently promising reservoir of potential support was thus doomed from the outset to be counterproductive. As long as opinions were influenced more by predisposition than by newly assimilated information, there was always a certain risk involved in trying to heighten public awareness

131

of the treaties. Indeed, had the number of potential converts been significantly larger, the administration might well have run the risk of sizable *losses* in support. As it was, the damage was contained, and both sides ended up purchasing one of the most expensive public relations standoffs in history.

[4]

The steadfast resistance of public opinion in the face of reported increases in salience suggests the essential futility of administration efforts to win acceptance for its case with anything like a majority of public opinion. This conclusion is underscored in a different way by the fact that through the entire eight months of the ratification campaign the administration was never able to find a way to "position" the issue effectively,[66] that is, to explain and defend it in terms relevant to prevailing public concerns. Ironically, Roper, Mervin Field, Caddell, Harris, and Gallup produced an abundance of data (principally tests of public reactions to arguments used by both sides) that, as Louis Harris said, "lay bare the pressure points," and that, in theory at least, should have made it possible for the administration to tailor its defense in some broadly acceptable manner.[67] But even with this information in hand, the administration was never able to marshal arguments capable of convincing any sizable portion of the public that ratification was worth supporting.

While arguments tests have only marginal statistical reliability, they provide further evidence of the insurmountable obstacles that the administration faced in its efforts to generate popular support for the treaties. At one level, for example, administration estimates of the consequences of nonratification were rejected out of hand by large majorities. Sixty-three percent of Harris respondents disagreed that passage of the treaties would improve relations with Latin America.[68] Fifty-seven percent in a Caddell poll disagreed that Communists would gain a propaganda victory in the wake of rejection.[69] When the administration pleaded that rejection could trigger outbreaks of anti-American violence in Panama, the argument completely backfired.

In this last instance the problem was not that the warning was discounted. Mervin Field reported that both supporters and opponents of ratification in California (by margins of 65 percent and 58 percent, respectively) agreed with the proposition that rejection would increase the likelihood of terrorism.[70] But the majority opposed, took that greater likelihood as an argument *against* rather than *for* ratification. Roger Seasonwein Associates, which sampled opinion for ABC in October 1977, reported that the prospect of retreat under pressure was the most frequently cited reason for opposition.[71] Field himself drew the largest positive response with this statement: "We should not let the threat of mob action or sabotage from a little country like Panama force us to give up what is ours."[72] Sixty-five percent of all respondents concurred, including many who favored ratification.

At another level the argument for ratification was simply consigned to irrelevance. When the administration endeavored to make its case on the basis of national security, it offered what may have been its best defense, backed up by an unusual display of open unanimity by the Joint Chiefs of Staff. The problem was that the issue stirred hardly a ripple of public concern. Where Pat Caddell found nearly 60 percent of respondents in one poll concerned with the principle of relinquishing American territory, only 5 percent mentioned the implications of such a transfer for national security.[73] Gallup's October 1977 poll cited national security next to last in a list of antitreaty arguments.[74]

When the argument was made from idealism, it likewise met with little or no response. Harris showed overwhelming opposition from all respondents to the idea that "it is wrong for the U.S. to own the Panama Canal, which goes right through the middle of another country, Panama."[75] When Caddell suggested to his own sample that "it is only fair and just and a sign that we are a great Nation, that we return [the Canal] to Panama," nearly 60 percent disagreed.[76]

At yet another level the administration was obliged to deal with concerns for which no airtight response existed. Harris, Field, Caddell, and Gallup, for example, all noted widespread concern over the prospect that the government of Panama might someday repudiate the treaties or renege on its obligations. "Panama may not stick to terms of treaties" and "They will soon keep us from using the Canal at all" were reported by Gallup to be high-ranking concerns.[77] Sixty-four percent agreed with Field's statement that, "If we turn over the Canal to Panama, we run the risk of some future Panamanian strongman discarding the treaty and taking it over completely, with no strings attached."[78] Here the problem for the administration was that repudiation was not completely out of the question, and doubts on the issue were scarcely assuaged by administration protests of Panamanian good faith.

But the administration faced its major challenge in couching an acceptable justification for relinquishing American property. Soundings by Caddell, Harris, and Field suggest this was the most basic issue in the ratification debate and the issue that touched the most sensitive public nerves.[79] Writes Caddell, "the sharpest polarity of viewpoints is evidenced by the statement that the treaty is a giveaway of American property. The pattern overall is that those who oppose the treaty can see no good reason to give up the Canal and, since they feel it is rightfully ours, believe we should keep it. Those who favor the treaty feel that the Canal is rightfully the property of Panama and because they see no good reason for keeping it, we should give it up."[80]

Clearly it was the former and not the latter which typified the attitude of most Americans—and for reasons that are not difficult to understand. The Canal was not just any territory, but territory weighted with a unique symbolic significance inculcated from childhood. As David McCullough, author of a best-selling history of the building of the Canal, wrote to President Carter:

> To say that the opposition [to ratification] springs from some vague or naive nostalgia for a simple past is really to miss the point. There is a grandeur about the Panama Canal and a grandeur of a kind we like to think of as particularly American. The Canal is a triumph of an era we remember fondly for its confidence and energy, youth and sense of purpose. The Canal is something we made and have looked after these many years; it's "ours" in that sense, which is very different from just ownership.[81]

The point is significant, for in the face of this deep, proprietary attachment to the Canal, administration arguments that U.S. control over Panamanian territory was somehow unjust were ineffectual at best, irrelevant at worst.

More than anything else, this one issue epitomized the administration's ratification troubles. No issue threw into sharper relief the contrary frames of reference that underlay the arguments for and against the treaties. No issue better illustrated the extent to which proponents and opponents talked past each other through much of the heated debate inside and outside the Senate. At whatever level of rationality a fight could be waged over the technical aspects of economics and national security, the issue, at the level of ownership and of "giving away" this prized American accomplishment, as in an argument over religious faith, fell largely beyond the pale of meaningful debate. The only way out for the administration was, in effect, an "end run," a campaign that emphasized the gradual pace of the turnover and the residual rights to be retained. But as we have seen, the effort to convey the point was largely in vain, even though the treaties were finally approved by the Senate. In the end ratification came not because of but in spite of the arguments the administration used to make its case.

[5]

Under the best of circumstances the capacity to educate is finite. In the case of Panama it appears to have been almost nonexistent. Pollsters gauged opinion on the transfer of the Canal for nearly three years, concentrating their soundings during the eight-month ratification campaign, and for nearly three years opinion remained stable. A graph of the polling results between 1976 and 1978 would betray virtually nothing of the timing or intensity of the efforts mounted on both sides to change public attitudes. As we have seen, this failure was in part because there may have been no sizable pool of potential converts to be tapped in the first place; because among those whose opinions were malleable there was no automatic connection between the source of the stimulus and the actual formation of opinion; because public information campaigns pro and con doubtless had offsetting influences; and because, at all events, no arguments in the administration's arsenal were capable of bridging the wide attitudinal gap that separated supporters and opponents of ratification.

What exacerbated nearly all of these problems for the administration, and what may in the last analysis have proved the most formidable obstacle of all facing the public campaign to sell the treaties, was the ratification timetable. Working against sizable odds, the administration had a meager eight months to make its case for ratification and to produce a seachange in public attitudes. Under the best of circumstances the task would have been an uphill effort. Given the almost total absence of preconditioning, that is, of prior awareness of the issue on the part of a sizable majority of the public, it became all but impossible.

The polls verify that until the eve of the ratification debate only the smallest percentage of respondents was ever even aware of the negotiations, much less, presumably, of the circumstances that made revision of the 1903 treaty such a pressing matter for four successive presidential administrations.[82] Thus what doubtless made education the leading factor in conditioning individual attitudes was the awareness, most prevalent among the college-educated, of the history of the negotiations and of the international pressure to which they responded. But most people had no such awareness. As a result, when the treaties were announced, they were greeted by millions of Americans with surprise and consternation. In much of the public mind there was no apparent logic to the fact that after seventy-five years of American ownership the Carter administration was suddenly lobbying to give away this important national asset, much less to a left-leaning dictator with questionable loyalties to the United States. Lacking any familiarity with the predisposing circumstances, the public found the reasoning behind the administration's move all but incomprehensible.

Part of the blame for the misunderstanding, if blame is to be apportioned, doubtless lies with Jimmy Carter's predecessors who actively sought revision without ever explaining the reasons why. But part of the blame was Carter's as well, for his administration made a deliberate, perhaps unavoidable, decision to postpone its public information campaign until the start of the ratification debate, understandably careful lest it arouse the latent antagonism exposed in the 1976 Republican primary campaign during the last sensitive stages of the negotiations. As a result, when the treaties were finally signed in the carefully staged ceremonies at the Pan American Union in Washington, and when the administration suddenly began to press upon Congress and public the importance of relinquishing the Canal, most Americans had no obvious frame of reference to make an objective evaluation of the administration's case. Try as it did, the administration was never able to impart to the public the sense of urgency about treaty reform that prevailed in policy-making circles.

The surprising thing, as we have seen, is that given the right laboratory setting, such as a favorably worded polling question or a White House briefing, given the chance to explain the context of the decision to push for ratification and the actual terms of the treaties, the administration did demonstrate the capacity to win converts. As meager a diet as it was, that capacity fed the hopes of administration lobbyists through the eight months of the ratification campaign. In the end, however, the countervailing forces at work were too formidable, and for reasons that theorists and practitioners of public relations could have explained thirty years earlier.[83] In spite of the unparalleled size and scope of the administration's public outreach effort, the barriers to communication—the inability to hear, the unwillingness to hear, the disposition to draw different conclusions from the same evidence, the phenomenon of selective hearing, the absence of prior conditioning—all proved too much to overcome. As a result the treaty campaign became an object lesson in the limits of public education.

Even in retrospect it is difficult to see what additional measures the administration could have taken to alter opinion on the treaties. The outpouring of activity in support of ratification may arguably have offset the massive drive spearheaded by the Right in opposition to the treaties. Still, the effort actually to win support was probably destined to failure from the beginning, since the apparatus to reshape *attitudes* was forced to work on attachments to the Canal that existed largely at the level of *values*. If in the short run the widespread mis-impression that the administration's campaign for public support was succeeding may have helped make the slim Senate victory possible, in the long run the administration was never able to escape the consequences of the fact that it *was* a misimpression. In spite of the confidence displayed by administration officials in the wake of ratification, two and a half years later, as Jimmy Carter left the White House, there was still little or no public understanding of the rationale behind the foreign policy of accommodation, of which Panama was the first and highest expression. As for the treaties themselves, the truth remains that after eight months of intensive effort a solid public constituency for ratification remained as elusive as ever. After one of the longest public relations campaigns in history, Americans remained as unconvinced of the need to give away the Panama Canal as they were before Jimmy Carter even became president.

CHAPTER 5

Interest Groups, I:
A Policy without a Constituency

One reason for the high cost of ratification was the administration's inability, despite an aggressive public relations campaign, to fashion a public consensus either behind the Panama policy itself or more generally behind the president's foreign-policy assumptions. We now turn to another explanation for this central anomaly of the ratification debate: the failure of the administration to gain effective interest-group support to shore up its lobby in the Senate.

The Panama debate was the object of considerable interest among a wide range of national lobbying groups; for the purposes of this study we may divide them into three general categories. The first includes organizations on the Left and various church groups, all of which were highly interested in and supportive of ratification but had little effective leverage in the Senate. The second was a group of multinational corporate and banking interests, which had leverage but an insufficient stake in the outcome of the debate to translate sympathy for ratification into an active lobby. The third was a coalition of groups on the political Right that had both an interest—in this case, an interest in defeating the new treaties—and effective political leverage, the latter derived from the scope and intensity of nationwide grass roots organizing.[1]

In simple quantitative terms, at least, the administration drew from a considerably broader base of support than treaty opponents on the Right. Big business, labor, most of the Protestant church denominations, Catholics, Jewish organizations, civic groups, minority and ethnic associations, all were on record in favor of the new treaties. Moreover, it appeared that such support—especially among the banks and corporations—was one key to the administration's final success in the Senate. The appearance of a causal relationship was deceptive, however, for at no point during the ratification debate did such support run deep enough to be politically significant. It was thus never translated into a counterweight effective against the massive lobby mounted by right-wing organizations opposed to ratification. Within the antitreaty lobby, on the other hand, intensity more than compensated for a narrow political base, consistent with the rule of thumb defined by one White House lobbyist that "one activist against you is as good as ten people who support you and who sit home."[2]

Thus the administration had, in effect, everything and nothing. While the treaties attracted one of the broadest expressions of interest-group support in recent memory, in the end the administration was left almost entirely on its own in the long, uphill struggle to win the sixty-seven votes needed for ratification. As Senate majority leader Howard Baker summarized the administration's plight, "the Canal has a constituency and the treaty has no constituency."[3]

[1]

Among many liberal groups there was wide support for the Canal treaties as a symbol of international justice. Such groups included the United Nations Association, the World Federalists, Americans for Democratic Action, and the National Women's Political Caucus. They were joined by ethnic and minority organizations that concurred with the National Association for the Advancement of Colored People in the view that "colonialism has long been a threat to international peace, to freedom and the liberty of people of color."[4]

Cold War liberals in the labor movement, whose foreign-policy views have traditionally been more hawkish, also supported the treaties once the rights of U.S. workers in the Zone were guaranteed. One of the first public endorsements of ratification came from AFL-CIO president George Meany. "We are convinced," Meany wrote in the organization's monthly, the *American Federationist*, "that the treaties serve as the basis for the rational conduct of Hemispheric relations."[5]

Detroit's United Auto Workers union declared for the treaties soon after, calling the new pacts a "long overdue diplomatic effort."[6] Behind the AFL-CIO and the UAW was an impressive, nearly unanimous array of labor support from the AFL's member trades as well

139

as the major independent unions representing steelworkers, communications workers, and government employees.

The labor unions mounted a fairly concerted lobbying effort. Like many of the churches, the unions had close ties to their Latin counterparts and were thus sensitive to the symbolic importance attached to the treaties throughout Latin America. "We believed in it very strongly," one union official commented, describing labor's commitment to the Canal pacts. "This wasn't Labor Law Reform, but this wasn't a minor issue for us."[7] Still, it was not a major issue either, and one result was that the unions, like other groups on the Left, were unable to generate the grass roots support the administration so badly needed.

The principal collective vehicle for the expression of liberal support for ratification was New Directions, the foreign-policy counterpart to John Gardner's Common Cause, whose leading principals included such luminaries in the liberal foreign-policy community as Norman Cousins and Harlan Cleveland. This recently formed, Washington-based organization seized the Canal treaties as one of its maiden issues, and with the primary financial backing of organized labor dispatched field organizers to key states. New Directions also sent out the largest single protreaty mailing (1.1 million letters), an appeal signed by anthropologist Margaret Mead rallying opposition to the "gigantic well-financed campaign" on the Right that "threatened to scuttle ratification."[8]

The effort to use Panama to put New Directions on the political map backfired completely. The huge financial burden of the mailing and the failure to galvanize either new support for ratification or new memberships were probably instrumental in hastening the early demise of the organization. As one outsider familiar with its work comments: "They thought they could capitalize on the [Panama] issue to create the organization. They overestimated the ability of Panama to build a public base. It was a serious miscalculation."[9]

Undoubtedly the most fervent support for ratification came from a broad cross section of major Protestant, Catholic, and Jewish religious organizations. Among the churches the Panama treaties presented an issue of obvious moral significance. A resolution passed by the United Methodist Church declared that the "rectification of this unjust relationship" was demanded by the "ethical imperatives of the Christian gospel for equality, restitution, reconciliation and self-determination of peoples."[10] The Southern Baptist Convention—one notable exception to the general influence of sectionalism on ratification preferences—condemned the 1903 treaty as a "symbol of colonial exploitation which cripples our witness as American Christians in the Third World."[11] For the National Council of Churches, representing thirty-two denominations, the treaties epitomized "the understanding that true security for our nation rests on the power of respect for justice rather than on the power of armed might."[12] To the Synagogue Council of America, as for other major Jewish organizations, the treaties were a simple matter of justice. "Equity between nations," wrote the council, "demands that what one country would not wish for itself, it ought not to inflict on another country."[13]

The principal contribution made by the churches to the process of treaty reform came before the end of the negotiations. In 1975 they played an important, almost exclusive, role in helping to mobilize Senate opposition to an effort to stop funding for the ongoing treaty talks. At a period when no other organized constituency was supporting the negotiations, the churches filled a critical vacuum to help keep the treaty process alive.[14]

After the White House assumed direction of the ratification effort, however, the role of the churches diminished to near-insignificance. Through the months of the debate support came principally through education rather than lobbying. It was spearheaded by the individual denominational organizations and by such cross-denominational groups as the Washington Interreligious Staff Council, the church-based Coalition for a New Foreign and Military Policy, and the National Council of Churches. Close to half the members of the Panama task group at New Directions were religious organizations. But apart from its saving efforts in 1975, the contribution of the churches on Panama largely conforms to the conclusion of political scientist Alfred Hero, that religious groups traditionally suffer from the inability to gain serious consideration of their views both in the high councils of government and among their own congregants.[15] Unable to communicate effectively either up or down, church leaders of nearly all persuasions thus had only marginal political value to the Administration.

[2]

To these generalizations about limited influence, the activities of the Roman Catholic church on behalf of ratification may be taken as at least a partial exception. The participation of key Catholic clerics is a significant story that has its roots in a historic change, first evident in the early 1960s, in church attitudes toward the developing world.

In Latin America a general decline in church fortunes, exacerbated by the twin challenges of the Cuban revolution and the growing appeal of evangelical Protestantism among the urban working classes, prompted church leaders to loosen their embrace of the status quo and to become more attentive to social change. Beginning with two encyclicals issued by Pope John XXIII, *Mater et Magistra* in 1961 and *Pacem in Terris* in 1963, and continuing with the Second Vatican Council, which ended in 1965, the church began setting its relations with the developing world on a fundamentally different course. It placed itself, if belatedly, on the side of decolonization, human rights, and economic development.[16]

The shift in church policy culminated in a conference at Medellín, Colombia, in 1968, described by one writer as a "watershed in Latin American Catholicism,"[17] where Catholic bishops "analyzed the reality of Latin America" and "assessed the temporal dimensions of the church's evangelizing task."[18]

As a result, many church leaders gradually abandoned their strident opposition to communism and came to embrace, even to preempt, the Marxist agenda in organizing the poor and in legitimizing social change. Moreover, the church began to reason publicly, as Alfred Hero notes, that "national sovereignty should be increasingly limited" and "that powerful states should cease pursuing their 'one-sided interests' at the expense of the weaker ones."[19] Whatever their larger implications, the changes set in motion in Rome in 1961 were destined to bear significantly on the politics of the Canal debate. They would make of the Catholic church one of the most committed forces in the effort to secure ratification.

The new era in church politics was aptly represented by a Catholic cleric who would come to play a major role in the treaty debate, Panamanian archbishop Marcos G. McGrath. In *Foreign Affairs*, McGrath, a child of American parents residing in the Canal Zone, described one of his formative political experiences when, as head of the theology department at the Catholic University in Santiago, Chile, in 1958, he felt the shock waves of Salvador Allende's near-victory over Christian Democrat Eduardo Frei.[20] This event impelled McGrath and other Catholic clergy to work for social change in an effort to forestall further socialist advances. Later, as a bishop in an impoverished rural diocese in Panama, his efforts at organizing the local campesinos typified the attention to the imperatives of social justice that became the "new" church's raison d'être. Under the circumstances it was an easy, natural step for McGrath to embrace Panamanian aspirations for the end of American colonialism in the Zone.

Reflecting on McGrath's participation after the treaties were ratified, one American priest judged that "he was as good a spokesman as [the Panamanians] had."[21] Throughout the final years of negotiation and ratification McGrath was a peripatetic advocate. In 1974 he convened the Conference of Catholic Bishops in Panama and successfully pressed a resolution, opposing the 1903 treaty, that was quickly endorsed by the U.S. Bishops Conference. "Our perspective in the treaty negotiation," the U.S. bishops resolved,

> is set by a text from Pope John XXIII's *Pacem in Terris*. In his discussion of relations between states, the Pope said: "Each of them, accordingly, is vested with the right to existence, to self-development and the means fitting to its attainment, and to be the one primarily responsible for this self-development." It is this principle which is at stake in the treaty negotiations.... We support a new treaty because we see it as a requirement of justice between our nations.[22]

In March 1975, during the Security Council meeting in Panama, it was McGrath who played the leading role in helping bring the weight of the church to bear on the passage of a United Nations resolution urging a new treaty. Describing the 1903 treaty as "morally unacceptable" and citing John XXIII's admonition that "no country may unjustly oppress others or unduly meddle in their affairs," he argued before the Security Council that circumstances "legitimately called for the abrogation of the present treaty."[23]

Once the ratification debate began the American church, operating primarily through the U.S. Catholic Conference, plunged into the work of ratification, issuing public statements, activating local bishops, and for only the third time in a decade calling on the services of a cardinal (John Krol of Philadelphia) to represent the conference's interests before the Senate Foreign Relations Committee. Through the entire ratification debate McGrath was a frequent presence, meeting with individual senators both in Washington and Panama. In sessions with nearly every congressional delegation visiting Panama, McGrath and other church leaders underscored the moral dimensions of the new treaties. As McGrath later wrote, "Undoubtedly, as some of the senators told me themselves, this moral influence played a great role in voting for the treaties...."[24]

Undoubtedly McGrath's most important contribution to the administration's efforts resulted from conversations with a conservative Catholic journalist, William F. Buckley, Jr., whose switch on the Panama treaties played a major role in keeping Canal treaties from becoming a party issue in the United States. As McGrath recounts, he read one of Buckley's columns in 1977 in which Buckley expressed "the simplistic view being repeated by the then governor Ronald Reagan." McGrath wrote Buckley in response, suggesting that "in this particular column he showed himself not to be sufficiently informed." The letter elicited an invitation to meet with Buckley in New York and resulted, in turn, in a week-long visit by Buckley to Panama. "Afterward," says McGrath, Buckley "wrote several columns, and . . . had a formal TV debate . . . with Ronald Reagan. In all of these he had come full around to supporting the treaties, basically on moral grounds as a logical effect of Patriotism among Panamanians."

The Catholic church may or may not have played the "great role" that McGrath suggests. But as the major religious, social, and political force in Latin America, with a sensitive finger on the pulse of the region, the church and the views of McGrath and the American bishops doubtless lent significant weight to the rationale invoked by the administration. Such support helped, at the very least, to offset opposition charges that the treaties were a product of Marxist influence. Writes McGrath, "It was not the role of the church to enter into details of political settlements within the treaties, but to insist upon Panama's right to new treaties recognizing effectively its sovereignty. The result of this was to assist many people to overcome the very dangerous notion that any support to the treaties was a sign of communist or anti-yanki spirit."[25]

On the other hand, with respect to mobilizing any visible expression of grass roots sentiment in favor of ratification, the Catholic hierarchy was as unsuccessful as its Protestant and Jewish counterparts. Two years later events in El Salvador—the assassination of Salvadoran archbishop Oscar Romero in March 1980 and the killing of four missionary nuns in December 1980—would catalyze a flurry of lay activity, local organizing, and letter writing, which made the church a powerful force in opposition to continued U.S. military aid to the Salvadoran junta. But there was no comparable response among the Catholic rank and file on behalf of the Panama treaties. In the end the main burden of Catholic support was borne by the U.S. Catholic Conference and the Bishops Conference themselves, with help from Panama's McGrath, while the administration was left without the evidence of public support it so badly needed.

[3]

The nation's leading multinational banks and corporations comprised the second category of interest groups engaged in the ratification debate. The conventional wisdom among observers from across the political spectrum was that, because of fears that treaty rejection would threaten hemispheric investments, the multinationals became the administration's most powerful and committed allies. Some writers on the Left, arguing that external U.S. investment has historically dictated U.S. foreign policy, assumed a one-for-one correspondence between the size of corporate investment in Latin America (and in Panama, specifically) and the extent of the business lobby on behalf of the new treaties: the greater the exposure, the more U.S. firms would stand to lose, and thus the greater the pressure for ratification. On the Right many critics of ratification argued that the Canal treaties were but the latest example of a powerful clique of corporate and banking leaders subordinating the national interest to their own financial interests and forcing an unpopular policy on the American public.

In fact an abundance of circumstantial evidence lent plausibility to the notion of active corporate involvement in the ratification campaign. As we have seen in discussing the Trilateral and Linowitz commissions, changes in the international environment bearing on trade and investment opportunities in Latin America made corporate leaders among the leading exponents of the more accommodationist Third World policies of the Carter administration. In addition corporate and banking executives were among the most prominent advocates of a new treaty, while corporate endorsements and contributions helped sustain efforts within the private sector to garner public support for ratification once the new treaties had been drafted[26] (see Table 7).

Among the nation's leading corporations and banks, moreover, the move to mobilize support for a revised treaty arrangement with Panama substantially predated Carter's election. Two years before the Carter administration began gearing up for the ratification debate in the Senate, the U.S. Chamber of Commerce threw its support behind a new Canal treaty based on the Kissinger-Tack principles. Meanwhile, corporations were organizing through the prestigious Council of the Americas and the ad hoc Business and Professional Committee for a New Panama Canal Treaty to fend off efforts in Congress to throw the negotiations off track. They also led a broadly based public relations campaign in support of revised treaties. The council later described the proprietary motive at work: "The business community has a responsibility to assume a leadership role on matters such as this which are not clearly understood by the American people but which have serious adverse consequences for U.S. foreign policy and the U.S. presence abroad."[27] Underlying these expressions of cor-

Table 7. Corporate members of the Committee of Americans for the Canal Treaties, Inc.

Robert O. Anderson	Chairman, Atlantic Richfield
Thomas Ayer	Chairman, Commonwealth Edison
George Ball	Senior Partner, Lehman Brothers
Barry Bingham, Sr.	Chairman, (Louisville) Courier-Journal/Times
W. Boeschenstein	President, Owen-Corning Fiberglass
Col. Frank Borman	President and CEO, Eastern Airlines
Edgar Bronfman	Chairman, Seagrams Distillers
Howard Clark	Chairman and CEO, American Express Co.
John T. Conner	Chairman and CEO, Allied Chemical
John DeButts	Chairman, AT&T
C. Douglas Dillon	Managing Director, Dillon, Read and Co.
James H. Evans	Chairman, Union Pacific
Max M. Fisher	Chairman, United Brands
Peter Flanigan	Vice President, Dillon, Read and Co.
J. Wayne Fredericks	Vice President, Ford Motor Co.
Richard M. Furland	Chairman, Squibb
John D. Gray	Chairman, Hart, Schaffner and Marx
Armand Hammer	Chairman, Occidental International
Ben Heineman	President, Northwest Industries
Andrew Heiskell	Chairman, Time
Arthur B. Krim	Chairman, United Artists
R. Heath Larry	President, National Association of Manufacturers
Harding Lawrence	Chairman of the Board, Braniff Airlines
Helen Meyer	Chairman, Dell Publishing Co.
G. William Miller	Chairman, Textron
J. Irwin Miller	Chairman, Cummins Engine Co.
Roger Moreley	President, American Express
Peter G. Peterson	Chairman, Lehman Brothers
Jane Cahill Pfeiffer	Chairman, NBC
David Reynolds	Chairman and CEO, Reynolds Metal Co.
David Rockefeller	Chairman of the Board, Chase Manhattan Bank
Robert Roosa	Partner, Brown Brothers Harriman and Co.
Theodore Roosevelt IV	Vice President, Lehman Brothers Kuhn Loeb
Irving Shapiro	Chairman, DuPont
George P. Shultz	President, Bechtel
Norton Simon	Chairman, Norton Simon
Alexander Trowbridge	Vice Chairman, Allied Chemical
Lew Wasserman	Chairman, MCA
Thomas Watson	President, United Brands

Source: COACT: The Bi-Partisan Citizens Committee of Americans for the Canal Treaties (Washington, D.C., 1977).

porate interest was an enormous trade and investment stake in Latin America; by the time of the ratification debate it totaled close to $50 billion. As one critic of the new treaties wrote, summarizing the role of the multinationals,

Focusing on the money enables us to ponder the seemingly curious phenomenon that American big business, unlike our conservative ideologues, is overwhelmingly in favor of the Panama treaty. One general reason for this support is that these sophisticated business groups understand and welcome the treaty as a more subtle and acceptable form of American imperialism. A more specific reason is the effect the treaty will have on those firms with trade and investment in Latin America. Rejection of the treaties might mean anti-U.S. unrest throughout the region and might have a destabilizing effect on American investments there. . . . As John M. Goshko reported in the . . . *Washington Post*: "These economic factors could produce some startling surprises about where different interest groups line up in the battle. There is the strong likelihood that the normally conservative, Republican-leaning business establishment will be solidly on the side of a Democratic president."[28]

As it happened, U.S. businesses never did play a major role, either in the formulation or in the ratification of the new Panama policy. Throughout the ratification debate the companies remained politically passive, even in the face of serious prospects that the Senate might reject the treaties. When business leaders did speak out, they almost always justified ratification in terms of the need to preempt terrorism directed at the Canal itself and to avoid political trouble in Panama and Latin America that, in the wake of rejection, would strengthen the hand of local Marxists and their foreign sponsors. Contrary to the conventional wisdom, the extent of investment exposure never provided a reliable guide to the level of corporate lobbying. To be sure, the moral support of the business community was of indirect help to the administration. It served to legitimize the case for ratification among an important group of moderate Republicans. In the final analysis, however, the administration was obliged to toil in the Senate in the near-absence of active corporate lobbying support.

[4]

As the record of labor and church interest illustrates, one significant variable bearing on the disposition to support ratification was the existence of counterpart organizations in Latin America—for example, the Panamanian Bishops Conference—which transmitted an appreciation of the urgency of the treaty issue in Latin America. For the multinational banks and corporations such sensitivity was the product of more direct exposure to local circumstances in Latin America, and it suggests again a correspondence between familiarity with the international environment and receptivity to the case for ratification. In particular, growing investment and trade ties,[29] along with the presence of hundreds of American subsidiaries throughout the region, made the companies highly sensitive bellwethers of changes in hemispheric relations.[30] Their sensitivity largely accounts for the high level of corporate interest in the work of the Trilateral and Linowitz commissions. It also underscores the counterintuitive fact that for four years the most natural constituency Jimmy Carter had for his new policies in the Third World were the banks and corporations. By virtue of long exposure in the developing world they were the first to comprehend the significance of the changing milieu to which the treaties themselves were a direct response.

In the most general sense business support for ratification was the product of a "quiet revolution" that, by the time of the treaty debate, was gradually transforming corporate relations with the entire Third World.[31] This revolution was occasioned in part by growing international competition for the sale of capital and technology to the developing world. By the 1970s West European and Japanese enterprises were beginning to make significant inroads into the Latin American market, once an exclusive preserve for U.S. companies. It was also a response to the necessity imposed on multinationals to relocate production facilities "offshore," that is, in the cheaper labor markets of underdeveloped countries, to sustain global market positions.[32] In a larger sense the revolution was a reflection of a shifting balance of power between corporations and host governments. Host countries were learning through experience to be more selective in dealing with the multinationals—more adept at harnessing foreign investment to domestic economic goals, more alive, in Isaiah Frank's words, to the recognition that relations with the multinationals need not be "of the zero-sum variety."[33]

By the time of the treaty debate events were thus producing, in U.S. corporate and government circles alike, a major reassessment of how best to preserve American interests in a rapidly changing international setting. It was not surprising, therefore, that when the Carter administration moved to defuse the troublesome Canal issue, corporate officials responded positively, eager to remove an aggravation in hemispheric relations that threatened to jeopardize their competitive positions throughout the region. Shifting ground rules governing the international movement of capital made business leaders in the United States "keenly aware," one State Department official noted, "that our stakes in the outcome of the ratification debate go far beyond our immediate interests in the Canal itself."[34] Elaborated one corporate official: "All of the challenges and the opportunities for multinationals stem from the new realities reflected in the Panama Canal treaties.... We must evaluate our goals, improve our behavior and be more attentive to the political and economic trends that affect the corporate environment. Without that kind of sensitivity today, no international company is going to do very well in *any* host country."[35]

By the time of the treaty debate events were producing a rare coincidence of idealism and economic self-interest that brought political liberals and corporate conservatives under one political umbrella. Under the circumstances it was not unreasonable to expect that the administration would have the leverage to recruit some important allies in the coming contest against Senate conservatives.

[5]

While the multinational corporations were adjusting to one set of changes, the banks were caught up in a two-pronged revolution of their own. By the mid-1970s that revolution had produced a remarkable and wholly unexpected alliance of interests between the "Marxist" dictator of Panama, Omar Torrijos, and the gray-suited capitalists of Wall Street. The first half of this revolution was an important transformation in the destination of commercial bank lending, from investment capital for private corporations to balance-of-payments financing for foreign governments; the second was the decentralization of the so-called Eurodollar market to offshore locations, to accommodate loans both to foreign governments and to multinational corporations. The first heightened the interest of the banks in the Third World generally.[36] The second had more direct implications, for it apparently disposed the banks to support the transfer of the Canal as a reward to Torrijos for creating lucrative offshore privileges in Panama itself.

The changing distribution of commercial bank lending had its remote origins in the recession of the early 1970s. As the recession produced a sharp downturn in the demand for investment capital on the part of prime domestic customers, the banks located eager new customers in the capital-hungry developing world. The banks were highly liquid and prepared to offer large loans to Third World customers at low interest rates for long terms. Significantly, many of the bankers' new customers were the governments themselves, which found the absence of conditions and strings a welcome alternative to

IMF, World Bank, and regional development bank lending. Such loans were typically used to finance resource development for the purpose of shoring up flagging trade balances. Thus, between 1970 and 1973 there occurred what the Senate Foreign Relations Committee characterized as a "mini-boom" in commercial bank lending to the Third World.[37]

The miniboom was translated into a full-scale revolution by OPEC. The shocks produced by the quadrupling of oil prices after 1973 were seismic in the developing world, and they created a major new demand for international credit, principally among governments seeking to finance burgeoning trade deficits.[38] The pressures imposed on the international financial system were more than the multilateral lending institutions were capitalized to handle. Within two short years the private banks, spurred by what the Foreign Relations Committee described as "a spectacular expansion of international lending," replaced the multilateral banks as the principal source of worldwide balance-of-payments financing.[39] Suddenly, almost overnight it seemed, the banks came to dominate a market they had only just entered. By the time of the Panama debate, therefore, important new links were being forged between the banks and the developing world, and with this increased exposure came heightened sensitivity to those political problems in the Third World which had the potential to jeopardize new investments.[40]

The second half of the banking revolution involved the rapid decentralization of the Eurodollar market and the growth of offshore banking centers in such locations as the Cayman Islands, Singapore, Nassau—and, after 1970, Panama.[41]

The refinement of offshore banking was brought to Latin America by Torrijos. His Cabinet Decree no. 238 made Panama a major thoroughfare for "passthrough" capital, that is, for foreign currencies being held for foreign or "offshore," rather than domestic, loans and investments. Panama was a natural candidate for such offshore services. The combined advantages of location, good transportation, and communications, the presence of an active private-sector economy, a local currency fixed to the U.S. dollar, and domestic political stability were duplicated nowhere else in Latin America.[42] The real key, however, was the legal environment defined in Torrijo's banking decree. It provided total freedom to carry on intermediary business in foreign currencies with no central bank regulations, no controls on the movement of capital, no bookkeeping requirements, no access to records for foreign authorities, no reserve or liquidity requirements, and, best of all, no taxes. In short, Decree 238 created for American and other foreign banks a virtually constraint-free environment, and at the very moment they were suddenly inundated with petrodollars.[43] The result of the decree was a surge of new American banking activity in Panama, which by 1977 brought U.S. investment to $1.8 billion.[44]

Under the circumstances it hardly seems remarkable that many contemporary observers saw an apparent cause-effect relationship at work in the politics of ratification. In addition to a growing investment stake in the region, American banking and corporate officials now appeared to have a demonstrable interest in the political longevity of Omar Torrijos himself.[45] The conclusion seemed almost inescapable: as a reward for lucrative financial and commercial privileges extended by the Torrijos regime, American business executives supported the Carter administration's efforts to turn the Canal over to Panama. "Many Americans, including Members of Congress, suspect the banking interests may be behind the Canal giveaway," declared one congressman whose subcommittee held hearings to investigate the connection.[46]

And if the apparent object of ratification was to stabilize the Torrijos regime, then the potential consequences of rejection—the revocation of banking privileges; the repudiation of commercial bank loans in Panama and elsewhere in Latin America; the possible loss of future investment opportunities; outright nationalization; terrorist activity directed at American production, retail, or banking facilities in the region; or the more general fear expressed by the *Nation*'s Penny Lernoux that behind the political solidarity in Latin America on behalf of the treaties could lie some form of economic solidarity directed against American corporate and banking interests[47]—all these potential consequences seemed to lend credibility to the notion that enormous stakes weighed in the balance as the Senate debated the new pacts. With chief executives of the very banks and corporations that stood to profit among the most visible spokesmen for ratification, the corporate-government relationship looked almost incestuous. "Given what is at stake for U.S. banks," concluded one observer, "their support for the treaties is hardly remarkable.... It makes one wonder."[48]

In fact the record clearly demonstrates that business and banking interests in Panama and the hemisphere did *not* translate into the kind of powerful political support that administration officials worked so energetically to cultivate. Had such support been forthcoming, it might well have eased the burden of ratification in the Senate.

[6]

The first formal manifestation of business interest was the founding of the frequently noted Business and Professional Committee for a New Panama Canal Treaty. Press accounts invariably described the committee as a comprehensive, well-oiled lobbying apparatus, the product of skillful efforts at the State Department to harness the energies of important allies in the private sector.[49]

In fact the impetus for the committee originated not with the State Department but with Senator Gale McGee (D.-Wy.), a specialist in Latin American affairs and long-time advocate of treaty reform, and with a retired Commerce Department trade expert named Richard Eisenmann. With the permission (though not at the instigation) of Assistant Secretary of State William D. Rogers, an exploratory meeting was held at the State Department on 30 October 1975 for two dozen corporate representatives. Its purpose was to create a counterweight to previously unanswered conservative attacks on efforts to revise the 1903 treaty. The move reflected growing fears among a variety of groups with interests in Latin America that, because no broad-based organizing was being sponsored on behalf of a new treaty, efforts by the Right to subvert the negotiations might win by default. As Eisenmann, the committee's temporary chairman, wrote, "To date, religious . . . organizations have sustained the major effort in favor of the treaty. However, business and professional knowledge of the problem is unique and would be very influential if disseminated and shared."[50]

The forty or so, mostly corporate, representatives who attended the October meeting agreed on the urgency of the task. They made tentative plans to assume the leadership of a corporate-based lobbying and public relations offensive, "using the personnel of members as much as possible."[51] A steering committee of twelve members was formed to lay out an agenda and to set a budget (estimated by outsiders at between $100,000 and $500,000), while subsequent meetings were scheduled for November and December.[52] After the December meeting, however, the committee suddenly disbanded. Not a dollar was spent; not a congressman was lobbied; not a single salvo of protreaty propaganda was lobbed into the nascent debate over the Panama question. The details of the committee's sudden death are fuzzy, but its status was apparently complicated by personal considerations. On 20 January 1976 Eisenmann's nephew, a Panamanian businessman, was arrested in Panama and exiled for antigovernment activities. Later, Eisenmann himself became an outspoken critic of ratification and eventually testified against the treaties before the Senate Foreign Relations Committee.[53] Leading members of the McGee committee therefore concluded (apparently with the concurrence of the State Department) that different auspices should be found for organized business support, and the committee was abandoned. As a result, this most visible and often-noted symbol of corporate political persuasion never even came into formal existence, much less into active service on behalf of the Carter administration.

The vehicle chosen to replace the McGee committee was the New York–based Council of the Americas. Founded in 1958, it was reorganized in the early 1960s by David Rockefeller to lend corporate support to the Alliance for Progress. By the mid-1970s the council had evolved into the principal umbrella organization linking the interests of two hundred Fortune 500–rank corporations, representing 95 percent of U.S. investment exposure in Latin America.

In the most general sense the council's main function has been to keep member companies apprised of economic and political developments that threaten to impinge on hemispheric trade and investment opportunities—in effect, to serve as an early warning system for the multinational corporate community. It has been guided in this task by some of the most influential business leaders in America: Rockefeller, George P. Shultz of Bechtel, Donald Kendall of Pepsi Co., Seymour Milstein of United Brands, Robert O. Anderson of Atlantic Richfield. The council's influence for the most part has been benign, smoothing rough spots in U.S.-Latin American relations and often acting as an advocate for Latin American interests on such issues as trade preferences and foreign aid. The council's role, in the words of Council president Henry Geyelin, has been to "anticipate areas of . . . confrontation between governments of the hemisphere and the private sector and to anticipate and develop a dialogue on them so that they do not become issues. . . . [We] look for a process which will lead to a convergence of understanding between the public and private sectors in the hemisphere."[54]

In the council, the Carter administration appeared to have its strongest and most natural constituency, an organization whose very raison d'être was to be on the lookout for the kind of trouble spots in hemispheric relations epitomized by the festering Canal dispute.[55] As for the treaties themselves, the "U.S. business community's involvement in this issue is inevitable," one council document suggested. "At stake is the investment climate in Panama ($1.8 billion in total U.S. investment in 1977) and Latin America, continued access to the Canal, and the avoidance of possible anti-U.S. violence. The business community is the most exposed element of the U.S. presence in Latin America, and would bear the brunt of any anti-U.S. reaction."[56] Well over a year before the start of Jimmy Carter's presidency, and two years prior to its formal endorsement of ratification, the council agreed to set up a special task force for the first time in its history, to support the renegotiation of the 1903 treaty.

Its first public statement on Panama was issued in October 1975, when the council endorsed the negotiations and the principle of new treaties with Panama. By early 1976 public opposition, stirred by the Reagan campaign and by moves in the House to block the ongoing treaty talks, prompted more decisive action. Early discussions indicated growing concern that no organization had stepped forward publicly to defend and rally support for the negotiations. In off-the-record conversations held in council chambers in November 1975 Geyelin complained that the "U.A.W., U.S. Chamber of Commerce, U.S. Council of Churches and many others have publicly come out for renegotiation but nobody is doing anything about it. We need to answer emotional rhetoric threatening to cut off negotiations."[57] Accordingly, Geyelin sent a general letter appealing for support to the "number one" list, that is, to the top executives in the member corporations. Following personal calls from Rockefeller, Gallagher, and Council chairman August Marusi of Borden Inc., the task force came into formal existence on 13 January 1976, "to carry out a public education program to stimulate a climate of public opinion in support of the negotiating process."[58]

Through the months leading to the September 1977 treaty signing the activity of the task force was intermittent. In July 1976 Geyelin sent a vigorous telegram to Capitol Hill urging defeat of the Snyder Amendment on the House floor. In the fall he led a delegation of council members to Panama for meetings with Torrijos and with American negotiator Ellsworth Bunker. In the spring of 1977 the task group prepared a scrupulously evenhanded brochure weighing the pros and cons of ratification, which was distributed to national organizations around the country.

By the beginning of 1978, as it became apparent that the council would have to bear by itself the principal burden of representing the business community, the tempo started to increase.[59] The day-to-day work of the task force focused primarily on keeping member companies informed on the political fortunes of the treaties. During this period council members regularly traded information on economic conditions in Latin America for up-to-date political intelligence on swing senators, information that was ostensibly to be used to direct the personal lobbying efforts of individual chairmen and CEOs. During much of the ratification period council staff occupied an office in the majority leader's suite, frequently sat in on Democratic Policy Committee staff meetings, and regularly kept in touch with the foreign-policy staffs of supportive senators. Moreover, council briefing papers were thoroughgoing defenses of the administration's position on the economic and military aspects of ratification. As one staff member summarized the council's work: "There is a great deal of misconception, even among the most knowledgeable staffers, about Panama and private enterprise, for example, or Panama and U.S. banks. The Work Group has found that its most valuable function has been to provide information to Senators, staffers and committees."[60]

In September the council's executive committee finally attended to the formality of soliciting approval for a public endorsement. Over 95 percent of the council's board of sixty-five trustees endorsed ratification, and in back-to-back events in mid-January the council officially went on record in favor of the administration's position. On 18 January nineteen trustees met with President Carter in the Cabinet Room at the White House for an announcement similar to that held for the citizens committee, brief and ceremonial but not without consequence to an administration in active search of allies. On 20 January Geyelin testified before the Senate Foreign Relations Committee, citing the council's concern for the "compelling need to modernize our relations with Panama."[61]

How significant was the council? To Senator Ernest Hollings of South Carolina, the council's endorsement was "proof positive that hard-headed businessmen who know the facts understand that these treaties are in the best interests of the United States."[62] To John Jackley, who worked on the staff of the Washington-based task group, its contribution was to "give the senators breathing room on the right, and therefore the flexibility to decide the issue on its merits."[63]

To Geyelin, the council was decisive in attracting and holding the support of key Republican swing votes in the Senate. "We were the only business organization that took a position and as such we acquired a degree of clout. We had a lot of credibility since we were, in effect, *the* spokesman for the business community. I think we had a terrific amount of impact, especially with some influential moderate Republicans who looked to the business community for its support on the issue."[64]

Given the potential that existed for corporate influence on the issue, the council's lobbying effort needs to be assessed in more prudent terms. The council had enormous resources at its disposal, and, as Geyelin notes, it was the only business organization that actually endorsed the new treaties. For the most part, however, it had much more to do with information than with direct lobbying. While the position it took may have helped legitimize the administration's case in the Senate, the political support for ratification that came through the council was only nominal. The council did almost no direct lobbying on the issue; the potential influence of the council's stable of two hundred chief executives thus went almost entirely untapped. Moreover, from among seventy-five of the largest corporations in America, which were members of the Panama task force, the council managed to raise a war chest of only $35,000. The average of $500 per multinational corporation provides a striking index of how little direct significance was attached to the passage of the treaties. Thus, like the McGee committee that preceded it, the council looked a considerably more formidable political force than it actually was. By the time the contest on the Canal treaties was over, this strong voice of corporate America had mustered only the merest whisper on behalf of ratification.

The experience at the council was not untypical. The Business Roundtable accorded the treaties an even lower priority. Had they been a matter of major concern, the roundtable's formidable political influence—*Business Week* described the organization in 1976 as the "most powerful voice of business in Washington"—would have been a major asset to the Carter administration.[65]

The roundtable was formed in 1972, a defensive response, much as the Liberty League had been half a century earlier, to the sudden end of a long period of general prosperity and to the erosion of public confidence in the leadership of corporate America. The assaults of environmentalists and public-interest groups, revelations of corporate complicity in Watergate and in the overthrow of Salvador Allende, the oil crisis, inflation, and recession, all combined to produce in the early 1970s what Leonard and Mark Silk describe as "an era of business defensiveness mixed with hostility." Out of it grew the roundtable and an aggressive new approach to corporate lobbying.[66]

Foreswearing party politics and grass roots organizing, the roundtable relied primarily on the direct lobbying efforts of the chief executive officers of its 158 influential corporate members representing big steel, big oil, the big three automakers, the principal multinational banks, and the giant retailers, including Sears and Montgomery Ward.

"The guts of the Roundtable," as Chairman Irving Shapiro of DuPont explained, "is the fact that the Chief Executive Officer is the man who participates."[67] Given limited capacities for such direct participation, the roundtable chose its issues carefully; conspicuously absent among them in 1977 and 1978 were the Panama Canal treaties. As Washington director John Post later said, summarizing the roundtable's view of the Canal issue: "Frankly, we just didn't sense any deep feeling on this one way or the other. . . . It could have been a serious problem diplomatically. That's the way [Irving] Shapiro viewed it. But there was no fear the world would be turned upside down if the thing didn't pass. When the White House came to us for an endorsement, we told them not to appeal to us on that basis."[68] At the roundtable the treaties thus failed to produce a ripple of interest, much less any organized effort to persuade individual senators to vote for ratification.

Further evidence of the absence of strong business support comes from the record of two other leading business associations, the Chamber of Commerce and the National Association of Manufacturers, on whose support the administration had placed high hopes. Neither, however, ended up taking an official position on ratification because of the strength of internal opposition to the treaties.

Writing of the failure of the chamber and the NAM to adopt positions on trade legislation in the 1950s and 1960s, Bauer, Pool, and Dexter note that the institutional obstacles to garnering organization-wide support on controversial issues in such "catchall, multipurpose organizations" are nearly insurmountable: "Since such organizations are supposed to represent a wide range of interests in a wide range of businesses, special efforts are taken to avoid generating any avoidable internal conflict. Cautious procedures are employed for reaching a policy position, and spokesmen are confined to stating that position without elaborating, for fear that even the most cautious elaboration may produce dissention."[69]

At the chamber there was initially a favorable response to the process, if not to the finished product, of the treaty negotiations. In November 1975 the chamber's International Relations Committee, noting that "the terms of the present treaty no longer reflect many changes that have occurred in Panama, the United States and the world," recommended that the chamber's board formally endorse the negotiations then being conducted by the Ford administration, consistent with the Kissinger-Tack principles enunciated in 1974. Without a new treaty, the committee noted, "the Panama Canal issue could become a serious problem in U.S.-Hemispheric relations."[70] Respond-

157

ing favorably to the committee's recommendation, the full chamber formally announced its support of the Ford administration's efforts to renegotiate, "reserving, however, final judgment until details of the renegotiated treaty are made public."[71]

At the Carter White House, in 1977, the action by the chamber two years earlier was taken as an auspicious sign. "The Chamber will support, as an organization, if our initiative is similar to the 8 principles set forth by Henry Kissinger in Panama in February, 1974," wrote one White House liaison with the business community. As a result, "major support from individual members, both CEO's of large international companies and national companies can be enlisted.... "[72] Chamber president Richard L. Lesher wrote to the White House underscoring the point: "I believe that if these principles are followed, ... our membership would vote to proceed toward a final new agreement and we would be able to do some legislative support work."[73]

Anticipating the potential for controversy, the chamber adopted its seldom-used procedure of polling individual members to obtain a reading on prevailing sentiments in time for the board's annual fall meeting in mid-November. A mail poll conducted in October asking the chamber's mostly small-town members whether they would "favor a modified treaty with safeguards" produced lopsided results—only 13 percent in favor and 83 percent opposed.[74] In the meantime the chamber's International Policy Committee convened to consider its own position. Dominated by such corporate giants as General Electric, Marine Midland, General Motors, Rockwell International, Owens-Illinois, and Pepsi Co., it had no difficulty reaching a consensus. By unanimous vote the committee recommended that the chamber formally endorse ratification on condition that the treaty be amended to include the twin rights of expeditious passage and intervention in case of emergency.

When the board met on 17 November, it was thus obliged to weigh conflicting chamber sentiments that reflected the split in the national polls between "mass" and "elite" opinion. In the end the board decided to postpone adoption of the International Committee recommendation until its next regularly scheduled meeting in February. One compelling consideration was the fact that even though the October poll was based on but a small fraction of responses, it revealed, as the national polls had done, a considerably higher degree of intensity among opponents. In an organization that places a high premium on avoiding controversy, the presence of even a small vocal minority is often sufficient to preclude the adoption of a public po-

sition. In any case, the prevalent assumption among treaty proponents at the chamber was that they had time on their side. Waiting
would give the administration three more months to carry its arguments to the public, and the Senate time to take action on desired
amendments. There was thus reason to hope that by February opposition within the chamber might be reduced to acceptable levels.
As one chamber staffer wrote: "In view of the membership response
to date, it is felt that the staff should continue to develop a more
comprehensive reading of membership views. This would take into
account the fact that the more people know about the treaties, the
more likely they are to favor ratification. Therefore, the more time
we can allow for preparation of a formal Chamber position, the greater
the chances are that the bulk of the membership would support the
Committee recommendation."

Once again, however, optimism was misplaced. Another poll was
taken in February 1978, and the results were as damaging as before.
While majority sentiment this time actually favored an amended treaty
(by a margin of 53 to 47 percent), the intensity factor, the gauge to
which board members were most sensitive, remained skewed in favor
of members opposed to ratification. Fully 55 percent of those against
indicated they felt strongly about their opposition; only 9 percent of
those who supported the treaties registered comparable intensity.[75]
One member of the International Policy Committee staff summarized
the challenges posed by such opposition:

> On issues like the Ex-Im [Export-Import] Bank and trade reform, the
> board will go with a position even though there are dissenting views—
> from members of the steel and textile industries, for example—but in
> this case there is an understanding that the chamber publicly represents
> a free-trade position. But Panama is different.... It's not one of the
> chamber's bread-and-butter issues. It affects people like a religious issue.
> We wouldn't pass judgement in the chamber on school prayer, and we
> were well advised not to pass judgment on the Panama treaties—not
> with such a vocal minority waiting in the wings.... We approached the
> issue and evaluated it, but in the end we had no way to go but to back
> away from it.[76]

Thus when the board met in February, it was agreed, for the last
time, that no action should be taken on the recommendation of the
International Committee to support ratification of the Panama Canal
treaties.

The problems of finding a consensus were if anything even more formidable at the National Association of Manufacturers, where the division of opinion on foreign-policy issues between large and small member firms has produced a perpetual identity crisis. As one NAM official mused on the organization's schizophrenic makeup, "we're like a frequency scan searching for our place on the spectrum."[77] Through much of its eighty-year history the NAM has been viewed as a principal spokesman for small and medium-size industrial firms.[78] The majority representation of such firms, passionately devoted to free enterprise and given to expressions of xenophobia in matters of foreign policy, has given the association a distinctly conservative outlook. Through the 1930s and during the postwar years the core business support for such ultrarightist movements as the Crusaders for Economic Liberalism, Sentinels of the Republic, and the John Birch Society has been culled from the ranks of the NAM's smaller and family-run companies. Among such firms the Carter administration's case for giving away the Panama Canal was hardly likely to attract heartfelt support.

By the mid-1970s the relative balance of power between the NAM's large and small members had attained an unusual state of equilibrium. Seventy percent of the NAM's members were smaller businesses, but representation on the association's Board of Directors was evenly split, and on the Executive Committee representatives of the larger multinationals held a slight edge. This division of influence is telling, for in the end the Panama issue proved too divisive and too tangential to the direct interests of too many companies to make possible a consensus in favor of ratification. Nevertheless, the issue did not pass without a fight.

Spearheading efforts to secure the NAM's endorsement of the treaties was Association president Heath R. Larry, a former vice-president of U.S. Steel. Larry had been an outspoken critic of the Carter administration on the bread-and-butter issues of common situs picketing and labor law reform, but he was an early administration supporter on the treaties and an articulate defender of ratification within corporate circles. As he explained his views to the president:

Much of the rest of the world must surely view our existing presence in Panama as virtually the last vestige of colonialism in the world. To me this is hardly the proper image for a country which normally prides itself upon the fact that it has never been an example of either colonialism or imperialism. ... I consider the treaty no evidence of our national weakness—on the contrary, I believe it represents a statement of strength—representing our willingness as a nation to voluntarily bring ourselves into harmony with contemporary mores.[79]

That such views were not representative of the association quickly became apparent. That the effort to win acceptance for ratification within the organization would entail sizable political risks, however, would not become apparent until later. One source familiar with the NAM later observed that Larry "stuck his neck out a mile [on the treaties] and probably abridged his tenure at the NAM in the process."

With the treaties signed on 7 September and an association board meeting scheduled to begin on 23 September, Larry banked his hopes for garnering formal support from the NAM on an effort to circumvent standard consensus-gathering procedures. Securing an informal indication of support from a steering group of the International Relations Committee[80] and from the Executive Committee, and arranging for Ellsworth Bunker to be on hand to argue the administration's case, he marshaled all the available cards for a decisive meeting of the full board scheduled for the evening of 24 September. On the evening of the 23d the plan began to unravel. Challenged in private by conservative board members led by brewer Joseph Coors and California drugstore magnate Justin Dart, Larry was forced to agree to the addition of a second speaker to represent the views of treaty opponents. On twenty-four hours' notice Coors and Dart made arrangements for retired admiral William Mott to be flown to the Virginia resort where the meeting was in progress, in time for a back-to-back appearance with Bunker. After the presentations were made, the floor was opened for discussion, and it immediately became apparent that there would be more than sufficient opposition to defeat any resolution of endorsement. Faced with an imminent setback and with the possibility that a protracted, divisive discussion might even produce a resolution *opposing* ratification, treaty supporters quickly moved to table the issue. As a result the effort to secure speedy approval of the treaties was aborted, and with it the only real chance of success.

After the meeting the Panama issue was sent back through regular channels. It did in fact go before the full International Relations Committee in December, where ratification was endorsed by a 42 to 2 majority, reflecting the disproportionate representation on the committee by major multinationals. But in the more representative Policy Committee of the board the issue was quickly quashed, and in neither of its scheduled December and February meetings did the committee resolution make it to the full board. The story at the NAM thus largely paralleled that at the Chamber of Commerce, and the association retained its official neutrality on the Canal treaties throughout the ratification debate in the Senate.

The only apparent exception to the political reticence of the business community was a brief lobbying effort undertaken during the early months of 1978. In the end it too would only serve to reconfirm the low priority attached to the issue. In response to appeals for business support made directly by the White House, some informal work on behalf of ratification was undertaken by a spin-off group of about fifty Washington corporate representatives affiliated with a loose, unincorporated information group called the Energy Users Forum. For seven weeks, beginning in February 1978, the group met weekly for breakfast on Thursday mornings in the Pershing Room of the Army-Navy Club in downtown Washington, and with seed money raised through the roundtable and the NAM its members did vote counts and pooled political information on swing senators. The effort was directed by a former executive of Owens-Illinois.

At first blush it appeared the stuff conspiracies are made of—representatives of powerful corporations, clandestine meetings, quiet pressure to get the Senate to save the corporations and banks from catastrophic economic losses. Closer examination confirms the thesis that Panama was of no more than peripheral concern. As one member of the ad hoc Panama group recalled:

> The president asked us to help, and even though there was no vested stake in doing it, there was no compelling reason not to. It came at a time when there was no pressing business. It was a chance to do a favor for the president on the cheap. That's how things work.
>
> I would not want you to think this was a big deal for us. Basically, it was a "throwaway." We'd talk to a senator and say, by the way, we think Panama's a good vote. If you need another arrow in your quiver you can say you were contacted by big business on the issue.[81]

The ad hoc group met through February and March, and while contacts were made on the Hill, they were all by the Washington representatives of the participating companies. The effort apparently generated no calls either from relevant chairmen or CEOs or from the formidable network of company representatives and plant managers in the states who are routinely mobilized on matters of greater consequence. "When we really want to win one, we pull out all the stops," continues the member of the Panama group:

On Labor Law Reform we had a committee of 600 representatives, a grass roots operation, an issue research team, a legislative lobby group, a public relations apparatus. We funded Panama from our hip pockets. On Labor Law Reform the corporations made it clear that money was no object—and when you deal with the Chamber, which has a $29 million dollar base, the NAM, which has an $11 million base, plus the A.P.I. [the American Petroleum Institute], autos, paper, chemicals—you're talking a lot of money.

Panama wasn't like this: we did no selective lobbying, we didn't use the plant managers, we didn't set up contact groups in the field or put out press releases or write op-ed pieces. We didn't do that on Panama. It was a minor effort for us; it was not a major effort. It was one we could handle with our left hand. It was a fire hydrant filling a drinking cup.

Despite abundant circumstantial evidence to the contrary—the sheer scope of corporate investment, the special privileges enjoyed in Panama by the U.S. banks, even the influence of the corporate-led Trilateral and Linowitz commissions in helping shape the Panama policy— the record of corporate involvement in the ratification process attests to nothing more than perfunctory support. The McGee committee foundered even before it began. The Council of the Americas harnessed but a fraction of the political energies that could have been mobilized in support of the new treaties. At the Chamber of Commerce and the National Association of Manufacturers internal divisions precluded even a public endorsement of ratification. The treaties came and went virtually unnoticed at the Business Roundtable. Nor is there evidence of free-lance corporate lobbying by individual CEOs, though the possibility cannot be entirely discounted. Thus, by the end, the record of corporate involvement was one of moral support matched by almost total political passivity.

[7]

The wide disparity between appearance and reality has two explanations. One might be found by searching for some other issue, more important to the business community, that support on the treaties might have jeopardized. In fact there was such an issue, in the pending fight over legislation on Labor Law Reform. In the months during and after Panama that issue catalyzed the full energies of companies operating principally through the chamber, the NAM, and the roundtable in a way the Panama treaties did not. A White House aide explained the implications:

> The NAM decided to end up like the U.S. Chamber and the Business Roundtable and take no position at all [on the treaties]. They indicated that one of the major reasons was the linkage between the Panama Canal and Labor Law reform. [A NAM spokesman] said that most of the Senators who are with the NAM on labor law reform are against the Panama canal treaties and the board felt that they could not afford to antagonize these Senators over the Canal when the bigger issue of Labor Law reform is on the horizon.[82]

As one NAM official put it more succinctly, the association exercised some caution in approaching the treaties to "avoid having to cash in chips with the hardliners on Panama who were our angels on Labor Law Reform."

But while conversations with corporate officials confirm that Labor Law Reform was a partial constraint on corporate support for ratification, they also indicate a second, more basic explanation: the corporations and banks simply perceived no need to make a fight over the treaties. For all the dire predictions regarding the economic consequences of rejection, the very companies whose interests were most directly on the line in the region almost wholly discounted such warnings. They saw no strong, self-interested motive for political action. The simple fact is that the treaties were *not* a matter of direct concern to the business community and therefore not the object of an all-hands lobbying effort.

"Acquiescence was a convenience for the companies," says one former State Department official active in the administration's ratification campaign. "Sure, the profit picture was dependent on healthy relations with Latin America. The companies were getting the message locally.... But there was no sense of putting a price tag on the issue."[83] The Council of the Americas' Geyelin concurs: "There was a legitimate distinction beteen personal and business reasons for supporting ratification.... The CEOs supported the treaties because they were concerned citizens, not because of investment opportunities. They knew it was good for U.S. relations to have the matter resolved. It was as simple as that."[84] A spokesman for United Brands cited the same motives:

> There were relatively few companies that had a key interest in the treaties. We were one. No company representative worked more on the issue than I did. The chairman [Seymour Milstein] and the president

[Max Fisher] spoke out on it; we plugged it in letters to the stockholders; Milstein testified; we supported the ads run by COACT [the citizens committee]; I even helped with the information gathering and vote counting. We worked for it, but it wasn't the highest priority issue. . . . Sure there was an element of self-interest. Naturally, if the treaties had lost, we wanted to be able to say to Panama, "we supported the administration." But no one really thought much or talked much about the possible adverse consequences except in the most general terms. We really thought the chances of terrorism were minimal.

"There's no doubt that rejection would have been fuel for the Communists," this United Brands spokesman continues. "Communists in the unions could have stirred up trouble. We might have felt it in strikes or wage demands. I'm sure we would have taken a verbal shellacking. But the fact is, no one can take our place. There's no question in my mind that even if the treaties had been rejected, U.S. business would be in operation in Latin America today at the same level."[85]

If the reality that "no one can take our place" was true of United Brands and other U.S. companies in Panama, it was even more applicable to the banks themselves, the rewards of whose presence made political reprisals in the wake of rejection all but unthinkable. By the time of the treaty debate the banks had generated close to 8,000 local jobs (as many as the Canal itself), trained a native cadre of professionals, and through a "multiplier-effect" created a boom in construction and tourism and a demand for locally supplied services.[86] Moreover, the presence of the banks has helped divert a disproportionate amount of commercial bank credit to Panama. And recognition of the benefits of American investments in Panama has not been confined to Panama's commercial and professional classes, for as the rush of foreign banks has triggered a construction boom in Panama City, even Panama's Marxist-influenced trade unions have succumbed to the logic—or at least to the benefits—of this capitalist-induced prosperity.[87]

"I think the Latin American nations would have sponsored condemnatory resolutions in the OAS" in the wake of rejection, an American banking official in Panama reflected on the probable consequences of rejection.

Mexico, Venezuela, and Brazil would have sponsored measures in the UN. . . . But no one would have done anything about it. Why kill the goose that lays the golden egg? There are 115 banks here, ten to fifteen thousand employees. The banks have so much money they lend freely to the government of Panama and that lowers Panama's debt capacity. The Guardia [the Panamanian National Guard] is going to protect the banks.

As for the corporations, they have their fortunes heavily implicated in the Free Zone. They just have small offices that can easily be moved. But here again, the National Guard isn't going to ruin a good thing. [The Zone] hasn't grown by 28 percent a year by having a hostile environment.[88]

"Treaty or no treaty, Torrijos or no Torrijos, the banks will stay," concludes an executive of a Boston-based bank with extensive commitments in Panama and Latin America. "It's a fact of life."[89]

To argue, then, as the *Nation*'s Lernoux and others have argued, that "the real question in the ongoing controversy over a new treaty is whether the Canal is worth the multinationals' Latin empire" is largely to miss the point.[90] In fact the empire was not at stake. Despite the changing economic environment, the American corporate and banking presence in Latin America was too beneficial to sacrifice to a fit of postrejection anger. This single fact divides the appearance from the reality of business support for the Panama treaties. The most to be said is that such support as the issue did command was given largely out of personal conviction rather than economic need, and only to the degree that it did not impinge on other, more important priorities.[91]

Would more active corporate lobbying have helped? "Yes, it would have made a great deal of difference," said one White House lobbyist later. "I don't think we would have gotten 80 votes out of a corporate lobby but the 68 we needed would have been considerably easier if we had had it."[92] A key Senate staffer agrees: "If [big business] had launched a major campaign, we wouldn't have had the fight on the Hill we did."[93] That the administration did have such a fight hints again at the hazards involved in trying to secure congressional support on a controversial issue in the absence of both public and interest-group support.

[8]

One of the ironies of the Panama debate is that it boiled down to a contest between two groups of Republicans or, as Penny Lernoux rightly suggests, between two groups of Republican imperialists.[94] One group consisted of "economic" imperialists, the corporate and banking executives who understood the need for such tactical changes as were symbolized by the new Panama policy to preserve the old regime of free trade and open markets in Latin America. The other group consisted of traditional "territorial" imperialists, whose view of the world was largely congruent with Theodore Roosevelt's and who formed the core of the political lobby dedicated to the preservation of U.S. rights in the Canal Zone, and thus to rejection of the new treaties. Their most prominent spokesman was Ronald Reagan.

As we have seen, the first group was part of a large coalition of interests that, while supporting ratification, were only marginally effective as administration allies. The second group, to whom we now turn, drew skillfully on popular opposition to the new treaties to form one of the most powerful political lobbies in recent history.

What stands out in reconsidering the treaty debate is the remarkable disparity between the limited number and narrow range of those groups that assumed leadership of the opposition movement and the enormous influence they had on the final outcome of the debate—if not actually winning then at least making victory prohibitively costly for the Carter administration. The opposition was managed by a handful of umbrella organizations on the Right, working in concert with several veterans' and patriotic groups. It never enjoyed unified conservative support; influential leaders and writers such as William F. Buckley and George F. Will eventually broke ranks and supported the Carter administration. Moreover, despite Senator Paul Laxalt's optimistic estimate that the treaties were the "best political issue that could be handed to a political party in recent history,"[95] opposition leaders never elicited more than perfunctory support from the national Republican party.

Such apparently long odds notwithstanding, leaders on the "New Right,"[96] as one later recounted, "picked up the flag and set out to do battle with the American establishment," and, in one of the most successful enterprises of its kind in American history, nearly succeeded in defeating the treaties.[97] By the time the debate was over, they had created a political counterforce, manifested in a tidal wave of angry mail to Capitol Hill, that came close to offsetting the combined weight of "the Carter Administration, the Democratic leadership in both Houses of Congress, both living ex-Presidents . . . Big Labor, Big Business, Big Media, the big international banks, and just about every liberal political and cultural star you could name."[98] In the process, they threw popular resistance to the new treaties into sharp relief and nearly deprived the administration of the coveted prize of ratification.

During the two decades before the 1977 treaties were initialed, a tenacious rearguard action aimed at preserving American sovereignty in the Zone was led by a small but determined gerontocracy. Its chief spokesmen included Daniel Flood, the flamboyant congressman from Pennsylvania whose outspoken opposition to treaty reform earned him the title "Public Enemy Number One"in Panama;[99] Harold Lord Varney, former editor of the *American Mercury* and director of the ultrarightist Committee on Pan American Policy; Spruille Braden, controversial former U.S. ambassador to Argentina and assistant secretary of state, who warned that changes in U.S. treaty policy would constitute an invitation to Soviet control of the hemisphere; and Philip Harman, a self-described "fanatic on anti-Communism"[100] whose Southern California-based Canal Zone Non-Profit Public Information Corporation was a prolific source of antitreaty literature, and who first interested candidate Ronald Reagan in the Canal issue in 1975. These men and others worked through various small committees and personal networks to fend off treaty reform.

But if efforts to preserve the 1903 treaty were kept alive by older men, it was a group of younger men just coming of political age in the mid-1970s who fell heir to the task of defeating the new 1977 treaties. They were for the most part the self-appointed heads of new lobbying and fund-raising organizations that were formed to reunite the scattered remnants of the political Right.

Among the leaders of this new generation of American conservatives was Paul Weyrich, former aide to Colorado senator Gordon Allott, who with funds provided by Colorado brewer Joseph Coors founded the Heritage Foundation and the Committee for the Survival of a Free Congress. Another was attorney John T. Dolan, a graduate from the ranks of the Young Americans for Freedom, who founded and led the largest political action committee on the Right. Another was Howard Phillips, former Nixon administration official charged with the task of dismantling the Office of Economic Opportunity, who founded the Conservative Caucus, the principal vehicle on the Right for mobilizing manpower at the local level for conservative causes. The central figure in the resurgent Right, however, was Richard A. Viguerie, former executive secretary of the Young Americans for Freedom, whose reticence about making personal requests for contributions led to his perfecting the technique of mail solicitations and, by the time of the ratification debate, to the creation of one of the country's largest direct-mail empires.

As Viguerie later described it, the watershed in the creation of the New Right was Gerald Ford's appointment of Nelson Rockefeller to be vice-president in 1974. "I could hardly have been more upset if Ford had selected Teddy Kennedy," he wrote.[101] The choice convinced Viguerie and other young conservatives that the Republican party could no longer be a fit repository for conservative loyalties, and it prompted first thoughts of creating an independent conservative movement that would steer a course "between the gray-flanneled sobriety of organizations like the American Conservative Union and the 'crazies' of the John Birch Society and the Liberty Lobby."[102] Using Viguerie's direct-mail skills, and the financial backing of Coors and other conservative benefactors, Viguerie, Weyrich, Phillips, and others made an aggressive bid to bring together anticommunists, free marketeers, right-to-work advocates, antitaxers, antiabortionists, antigun-control advocates, antifeminists, moral majoritarians—"the whole brawling host of ambitious anti-liberals"[103]—under one roof.

It was not to be a coalition forged around a bargaining table in a smoke-filled room; rather, it would be fashioned inside the Viguerie computers. It held the potential to realign American politics fundamentally. The one missing ingredient was an issue with sufficient overarching appeal to unite all the hitherto disparate factions of the Right while attracting new recruits into the conservative movement from the "silent majority" of discontented Americans. For these purposes the Panama Canal treaties were all but made-to-order.

As Viguerie noted, the Right had in the treaties a "no-loss" issue.[104] It offered almost unlimited possibilities to tap a highly nationalistic constituency with strong anticommunist predilections, which, motivated by various status anxieties, was almost certain to be receptive to charges that the new treaties were a "sellout" by Eastern capitalists more concerned with profits than with the national interest. Even hints of perfidy on the part of the administration and its business allies offered a rare opportunity to discredit moderate Republicans and liberal Democrats, doing to "those who surrendered the Canal," as columnist Patrick Buchanan suggested, "what Yalta did [to] the Democratic party."[105] In a more fundamental sense the Panama issue provided the kind of catalyst to conservative action that the civil rights movement and the Vietnam War had given to liberals in the 1960s, and thus the chance to expand the revenue and membership base of the Right. In short, as Viguerie noted, even if the treaty were ratified, "we will have had the issue for eight or nine months, we will have rallied many new people to our cause [and] we will have given our supporters an issue, a cause to work for."[106]

The speed with which leaders of the New Right were able to translate latent public opposition to the new treaties into effective political action suggests just how receptive conservatives were on the issue. Ironically, the strategy of opposition leaders was essentially the same as the administration's, although it was based on entirely different assumptions. At the White House the ratification effort was designed to buy time, to keep undecided senators from declaring against the treaties while a massive public relations offensive was mounted to help make eventual votes in favor of ratification as free of risk as possible. On the Right the strategy was to consume time, with an eye fixed on the 1978 midterm elections and with a sure instinct that the closer the treaty vote came to the elections the riskier a vote for ratification would become. As Viguerie put it: "The closer it gets to election day, talking to Ham Jordan and [JCS chairman] General [George] Brown isn't going to be that effective when the Senator has by that time accumulated 80,000 letters, 20,000 phone calls, 10,000 telegrams against the treaties, or when 80 percent of his home-state press is hollering at him."[107]

The strategy of delay was largely effected by what Viguerie termed the "inside"team,[108] a group of twenty-odd Senate conservatives led by Nevada's Paul Laxalt. They worked in close cooperation with the directorate of organizations operated out of the "firebase"[109] of the New Right, Viguerie's Falls Church, Virginia, headquarters. Their strategy involved, first, an attempt to amend the treaties to death by attaching conditions unacceptable to the Panamanians. Second, it included an effort to keep issues extraneous to the treaties before public attention, in particular, allegations of involvement by the Torrijos family in illicit drug trafficking. While no damaging amendments were ever added to the treaty, and while no permanent harm was inflicted by the drug allegations, the strategy helped delay the final votes long beyond the point where the momentum of the administration's ratification drive began to flag. By the time the two treaties were voted on, the resources of the administration were exhausted, the patience of the Senate was worn thin, and key fence-sitters like Dennis DeConcini were still left without sufficient political cover.

But if the strategy of delay on Capitol Hill was successful, the heart of the effort to defeat the treaties was in its local manifestations, for it was from the grass roots that the force against ratification drew its political power. Viguerie later described this "outreach" side of the antitreaty drive, probably without exaggeration, as "larger than anything that's ever been done before outside the major two parties."[110]

Much of the locally generated opposition was orchestrated by two crosscutting conservative coalitions (the "outside" team): the Emergency Coalition to Save the Panama Canal, founded in August 1977 by the American Conservative Union, and the Committee to Save the Panama Canal. Together they coordinated one of the most costly, massive lobbying campaigns in U.S. history, complete with speakers' bureaus, rallies, newspaper ads, phone banks, billboards, bumper stickers, and, most important, millions of direct-mail appeals that, "using words like bullets,"[111] warned against the dangers posed by the new treaties and urged opponents to contact senators, to write to local editors, and to encourage local organizations to pass antitreaty resolutions.

The American Conservative Union alone sponsored hundreds of radio and television spots and produced a film—*There Is No Panama Canal . . . There is an American Canal in Panama*—watched by an estimated ten million viewers. The National Conservative Political Action Committee dispatched half-a-million letters; the American Security Council, two million; the Council on Inter-American Security, two million. The most active group, the Conservative Caucus, sponsored "Keep Our Canal" days in 48 states and 53 statewide training conferences to organize antitreaty activity on the local level, in addition to sending its own two million letters. Under the auspices of the Committee to Save the Panama Canal a "Truth Squad" of twenty leading, mostly congressional, treaty critics was dispatched on a four-day, 6,000-mile media blitz to talk to local reporters and lead local antitreaty rallies in Miami, St. Louis, Denver, and Portland, and to divert attention from the administration's own "January offensive." It was, as Viguerie noted later, a "prime example of how conservatives were learning invaluable lessons in the political major leagues . . . lessons which we would put to good use later in 1978."[112]

When it was all over, the aggregate statistics told an impressive story. The campaign to defeat the treaties generated over $3 million, mostly in the form of small individual contributions, and between seven and nine million direct-mail appeals. The response was a barrage of letters that "fell like snowflakes in a thick storm" on Capitol Hill and—just as leaders on the Right had anticipated—created political pressures that administration lobbyists were largely helpless to resist.[113]

[9]

Spokesmen and propagandists on the New Right marshaled a wide range of arguments to rally opposition to the new treaties. At one level such arguments were tied to tangible interests, that is, to assessments of the continuing military and economic value of the Canal. The military argument found its most publicized expression in a letter to President Carter coauthored by four former chiefs of naval operations, Arleigh A. Burke, Robert B. Carney, Thomas Moorer, and George Anderson. The four navy chiefs underscored the continuing strategic importance of the Canal, noting that it enabled the United States, with a one-ocean navy, to patrol two oceans effectively, and they warned of the direct and indirect consequences of relinquishing control of the waterway. "Our experience," they wrote the president, "has been that as each crisis developed during our active service—World War II, Korea, Vietnam and the Cuban missile crisis—the value of the Canal was forcefully emphasized by emergency transits of our Naval units and massive logistical support for the Armed Forces. The Canal provided operational flexibility and rapid mobility. . . . [I]t offers inestimable strategic advantages to the United States, giving us maximum strength at minimum cost."[114]

This argument was elaborated in countless opposition speeches and mailings. It was a particular rallying point for such veterans' organizations as the American Legion and the Veterans of Foreign Wars. They stressed, as naval theorists had stressed seventy-five years earlier, that the "nation's security is inseparably linked to that of the Western Hemisphere"[115] and that the security of the Western Hemisphere was contingent on continued U.S. control of the waterway. In addition, critics emphasized the economic importance of the Canal, citing its significance as the hub of thirteen major trade routes crossing the Caribbean and as a key artery for the shipment of important strategic minerals, including, by 1977, oil from Alaska bound for the East Coast.[116] Opponents thus successfully pressed the point that there could be no substitute for the retention of U.S. control over the Canal. To give it up, Governor Reagan argued, "would make about as much sense as it would for the U.S.S.R. to invite the U.S. Sixth Fleet to roam at will around the Black Sea."[117]

But as frequently as economic and military considerations surfaced in the case against the treaties, it was not such cool academic arguments that generated the heated emotions prevalent on the Right but a deep, visceral response to something more basic to the politics of ratification, namely, the decline of American power. After Vietnam, after OPEC's oil shock, after the rise of Soviet military power, after unmistakable signs of what Patrick Buchanan called a "headlong retreat" around the globe, the decision to give up the Canal was certain to provoke a supercharged reaction.[118] In the debate that followed, arguments over geopolitics and toll rates were largely subordinated to popular frustrations over the "vanished mastery" of the United States.[119] As a result, the debate ended up having less to do with the terms of the treaties themselves than with the wisdom of making such an important, and untimely, strategic concession.

What mobilized the political energies of literally millions of Americans was thus a determination to reverse two decades of retreat and concession by saying "no" in the most unequivocal terms to Panama and to world opinion. As New Hampshire governor Meldrum Thompson observed, the alternatives were to "stand brave and firm for freedom in this real world of spreading Communism" or to "crawl into historical obscurity in the face of the hysterical howling of world opinion."[120]

Perceptions of "retreat" in Panama were heightened by the appearance that the United States had been "bluffed and bullied out of the Panama Canal by a Marxist thug" with a gift for mobilizing world opinion.[121] It was an impression that reinforced public doubts about the political will of the Carter administration to stand up to threats of terrorism and blackmail. As William F. Buckley noted, it may have generated more popular dissatisfaction with the treaties than the actual relinquishing of the Canal itself. Buckley writes of an informal poll taken among members of the Young Americans for Freedom, an organization militantly opposed to the new Canal pacts: "They were asked 'If the revised Treaty had resulted from an American initiative rather than from a Panamanian initiative, would you alter your position on it?' Most seemed to agree that they would. This is to say that other considerations were relatively insignificant by comparison: considerations arising out of the economic cost to us of the Canal, and the residual military situation. What matters most is the symbolic act: we are being pushed around."[122]

Thus to understand the strength of the appeal produced by treaty opponents on the Right, one need only calculate the context within which the ratification debate occurred—the twenty-year-long recession of American power and prestige—and the extent to which it produced the hard disposition not to give ground. "Since the Bay of Pigs the United States has been in retreat," one critic spoke for a legion of treaty opponents. "Somewhere the line must be drawn—thus far and no farther. Sometime the resolution and the will of the American people must be made manifest. Panama is the place and now is the time."[123]

Under the circumstances it is not surprising that the Panama issue was quickly translated into an issue of national honor and that public opinion provided a rich lode for the Right to mine. Throughout the ratification debate leaders of the organized opposition skillfully played on public apprehensions over the loss of American power and prestige. Advertisements addressed to "men and women who are determined to make America No. 1 again" warned that Americans were being "victimized by a propaganda barrage from Jimmy Carter" designed to convince the nation that "there will be violence if we do not seek to alleviate the Panamanian people's concerns."[124] Fundraising letters cautioned "each and every single freedom loving American" against the "campaign to hoodwink the American people" with a "treaty which literally promotes national disaster for America."[125] They urged Americans to resist demands by "liberal Democrats" to " 'write off' the Canal like we were forced to 'write off' Vietnam, Cambodia and Laos."[126]

In some quarters these intimations of disloyalty spilled over into hints or outright allegations of conspiracy that implicated the administration in a master plot managed by "a clique of eastern financiers" and "multinational corporate lobbyists."[127] Right-wing tracts alternatively explained Wall Street intrigue to subvert the U.S. position in Panama as the product of a political debt owed to Torrijos for privileges granted under the 1970 banking decree and as an effort to divert Canal revenues to Panama to ensure repayment of "bad" loans made to Panama. In either case, by the time of the ratification debate "the Big Boys [were] more concerned with getting their loans paid off and their investments returned than with the national security of the United States."[128]

Writers on the Right embellished the theory in different ways, though the common thread was the supposition of a "Grand Design on the part of the [David] Rockefeller–[Henry] Kissinger–CFR [Council on Foreign Relations] crowd"[129] to "stage, in effect, a secret coup" to gain control of U.S.–Panama policy."[130] Driven by the prospect of financial gain, the argument ran, this axis of Establishmentarians pursued a carefully orchestrated strategy begun in 1974 with the formation of the Commission on United States–Latin American relations, chaired by "none other than the shadowy Linowitz,"[131] to recommend the immediate end of the 1903 treaty. The strategy progressed with creation of the Business and Professional Committee for a New Panama Canal Treaty and later business efforts designed to "mobilize the power and prestige of the hidden backers of ratification;"[132] with the "subversive penetration of the White House"[133] by Establishment puppet and fellow Trilateralist Jimmy Carter; and by the appointment of key members of the axis, including Vance, Linowitz, and Brzezinski, to top policy-making positions in the new administration. The conspiracy climaxed when the same clique banded together under the direction of the Harriman citizens' committee to force the treaties through an unwilling Senate, "working closely with President Carter in an attempt to subvert the will of the majority of the American people by using their corporate power and prestige to obtain ratification."[134]

"Not since the 1945 Conference at Yalta and Potsdam have political leaders of the United States so brazenly betrayed this nation and its citizens," summarized one organ on the Right.[135] The reaction was typical, and it reveals a strain of paranoia on the far Right that places it in the tradition of elements in the anti-Masonic, Jacksonian, populist, and McCarthy movements.[136] At the simplest level it operated as a general suspicion, described by journalist Henry Fairlie, that "the 'international banks' and the 'Establishment' and even something as vague as 'big business' will do almost anything . . . to sustain their financial and trading interests."[137] More potently it evoked fears of a vast, subtle force, manipulated by a secretive elite, that threatened the very life and values of the nation.

Leaders of the New Right were not reluctant to exploit these fears in their effort to defeat the treaties. "We're going to ride this hard," declared Richard Viguerie. "It's a sexy issue. It's a populist issue. And here's a populist President who's going to bail out David Rockefeller."[138] Given the antielitist character of the New Right, the conspiracy motif had great appeal. By describing the treaties as a crucial battle between the common man and the Establishment for the control of foreign policy, and for the preservation of American values, the Right issued a potent call to arms that strained even further the already taut emotions of the Canal debate. One writer crystalized the mood prevalent among treaty opponents:

> The people have had their fill of the politics of concession, appeasement, and surrender which these "ruling circles" have been following since World War II—Yalta, and Potsdam, and the Berlin Wall . . . Korea, the Bay of Pigs, Vietnam, Cambodia . . . and the impending sellout of Free China. The people have had enough of betraying allies while fawning on enemies. Now when they are told that we must give away our great canal on the Isthmus of Panama to a pipsqueak Marxist bully, they have dug in their heals, and with a voice of thunder that is rattling the windows on Capitol Hill the people have said—no—never.[139]

It was a powerful appeal, and it produced the very kind of political excitement so conspicuously absent among supporters of the new treaties.

[10]

Measured by almost any standard, the opposition to the Panama treaties was a striking success. Ironically, the issue ultimately did for the New Right what State Department and White House officials hoped in vain the treaties would do for the Carter administration: provide a broad new constituency, weaken the political opposition, and lay the groundwork for future legislative and electoral contests. In particular, the treaty debate proved to be a magnet to unite conservative factions scattered in the aftermath of the Goldwater candidacy and the Watergate debacle of the 1960s and 1970s. "Before Panama," notes one key figure in the antitreaty effort,

> the Right was developing cadres at all levels, reaching out to blue-collar families, ethnics and the like. Now Panama came and this was the test to see if we could put into practice what we'd been learning. Panama identified hundreds of thousands of closet conservatives; the issue did for conservatives what Vietnam did for liberals—it helped to identify conservatives and build alliances. Our political strength was demonstrated by the strength and nature of our loss.[140]

By the time of the Senate treaty votes over 400,000 names had been added to the membership rolls of the various organizations active in the fight against the administration, and financial contributions were up sharply.[141]

The treaty issue also gave leaders on the Right the opportunity to identify friends and foes: votes on ratification were judged a critical litmus test of loyalty to conservative principles. The Canal treaties, observed Viguerie, were a "touchstone issue—one of those great questions that have a way of telling you who is, and who isn't, in harmony with the deepest sentiments of the American people."[142] For those moderate and liberal senators from both parties who failed the test, the Right proved a constituency with a long memory. "Conservatives have one weapon the White House doesn't have—the ability to *punish*," warned Viguerie during the ratification debate. "We're going to look *very* carefully at the votes when all this is over and do an *awful* lot of punishing next election."[143] In fact, in the elections of 1978 and 1980, 20 of the 68 senators who voted for ratification were defeated in bids for reelections, including such bêtes noires of the Right as liberal senators Frank Church (D.-Id.), John Culver (D.-Iowa), George McGovern (D.-S.D.), and Thomas McIntyre (D.-N.H.). By November 1980 the dream of realigning American politics, of setting a new national agenda, and even of taking control of the Republican party seemed within reach. Viguerie writes, on the contribution of the treaty fight to the resurrection of the Right, that it helped develop "a great deal of confidence in ourselves," and gave conservatives the chance to watch as "our opponents became weaker."[144] Ultimately, it helped set the stage for Ronald Reagan's election to the presidency in 1980.

With respect to the treaties themselves, the organized opposition to ratification was a signal success. One congressional staff member compared the volume of mail that inundated Capitol Hill to the surfeit of information Army intelligence was forced to sift through after the Japanese diplomatic code was broken in the months before Pearl Harbor. "There was such a flood of response on the treaties that it became all but impossible for the senators to sort it all out, to filter out the relevant signals, to figure out exactly what the public mood was. The mail had a significant obfuscating effect that made the senators cautious about making public commitments for the treaties. It was a major constraint on the Senate."[145] Senator Thomas McIntyre wrote later that "There's no doubt in my mind that the mail generated by the Panama Canal treaties had an effect. . . . If it did not sway many votes, it surely encouraged the prolongation of the debate and invited the near destruction of the treaty by reckless amendments."[146]

Still, there are indications that the antitreaty lobby, for all its success in harnessing the public mood, could have been more successful, perhaps even successful enough to defeat the treaties in the Senate. As we shall see in the next chapter, the New Right had a significant opportunity to exploit the weakest point in the administration's defense of ratification, the economic costs of the new treaties. The administration was vulnerable on the economic issue throughout the ratification debate. Its own estimates of the costs of implementing the treaties—the impact on U.S. shipping, on jobs and port revenues, and on the U.S. taxpayer—were largely unsubstantiated or were at odds with the estimates of outside experts. Through the long ratification period the Right was never able to capitalize on the economic issue, and in failing to do so it may have missed an important chance to gain ground with undecided senators. As one administration official noted with relief after the ratification debate: "I think right up to the end, we were all pretty surprised that the opposition never really grabbed a hold of the economic issue. . . . We all kept watching for the other shoe to fall. . . . Goldwater raised it effectively on the floor but no one really followed it up. I think it was the major tactical blunder of the opposition."[147]

In addition to that failure the New Right may have further compromised its chances of winning by failing to find common ground with the conservatives of the Old Right. The arguments the New Right invoked against ratification and the tone it brought to the debate may have precluded building the partisan consensus necessary to defeat the treaties in the Senate.

Consensus was, in particular, a casualty of differing perspectives on the motives behind treaty reform and on the consequences of rejecting the new treaties. The protreaty Right reflected the more traditional conservative respect for the evolutionary processes of history. Commentators such as William Buckley embraced the administration's argument that the pressure for treaty reform in Panama expressed the anticolonial impulse that was the dominant political emotion of the postwar era. As a result they urged a policy of accommodation as the only prudent course of action in Panama. They argued that whatever the United States may have contributed to Panamanian independence, whatever benefits the Canal may have brought to Panama, old debts were an inappropriate basis for future policy. "Even if our eternal sovereignty were written in gold," wrote James T. Burnham, "our initial entry into the Panama picture prompted by angelic motives, and our 75 years' rule a model of enlightened humanitarianism, this would not prove that our national security and interest would best be served by staying on. Times change, and nations that fail to adapt to changes go under."[148]

As Buckley elaborated, an effort to cling to old rights under new circumstances would be to ignore the lessons of the past and to doom U.S. policy to futility.

> We departed from the Philippines without duress in 1946 because we made a decision in our own time in 1936. Had we not made it we surely would have experienced spiraling duress after 1946 as the British, French and Dutch did elsewhere. This involves a kind of sensitivity to history. Nationalism is perhaps the strongest force abroad in the world today. As Americans we can sympathize with that.... Conservatives are realists and here is a test of realism.... Politics is as much an art of timing as of substance and strength. It has ebb and flow. There is a tide in the affairs of men, which, taken at the ebb—is damned foolishness. The point is that at this juncture we should husband the frayed political and spiritual resources of the nation, not subject them to unnecessary demands.[149]

On the New Right, however, the treaties evoked a more doctrinaire response. Its leaders were in particular reluctant to accept an argument based on Panamanian nationalism. Governed by a more static concept of history and by the precepts of Cold War ideology, leaders of the opposition interpreted the pressures for changes in the 1903 treaty as the product of outside—that is, Communist—influence. They described efforts to wrest the Canal from American control as part of a blueprint for Marxist subversion of the hemisphere, depicting concessions made in the 1977 treaties as the strategic and moral equivalent of concessions made at Munich in 1938. The substance of the opposition critique was thus an urgent plea to preserve the grant of sovereignty in the 1903 treaty as a means of shoring up U.S. rights in Panama, as a means of preserving the legitimacy of the U.S. presence in the Zone, and as the only viable means of preventing the domino effect in Latin America. "If Panama goes," warned Hanson Baldwin, a former journalist whose arguments were embraced by the Right, "all our positions in [the Caribbean] may eventually follow."[150]

The dominant motif on the New Right was thus the specter of appeasement, and the dominant rhetorical allusion was to the politics of Neville Chamberlain. Fears of betrayal were reinforced by apocalyptic estimates of the stakes in the ratification debate. Antitreaty spokesmen continually raised the possibility of "dismemberment of the United States" as the consequence of ratification, arguing that once the Canal was ceded, Mexico would be emboldened to demand the return of the Southwest, Russia the return of Alaska, and France the return of the Louisiana Territory. "Once Panama is gone," one critic sounded the alarm, "the Pandora's box would be opened for the loss of Puerto Rico and the Virgin Islands ... and by then the irreversible process would be so familiar and Americans so conditioned to the dismantlement of the country that they would hardly care what came next—Hawaii, Alaska, Florida...."[151] The angry, overwrought rhetoric evoked by such a prospect identified liberals and traditional conservatives alike as perpetrators of an act tinged with treason, and it produced what Howard Phillips described as a desire "to get revenge on the people who go against us." Such fears, not surprisingly, kept the New Right isolated, precluding any possibility of finding common ground among new and old conservatives. As the eight months of the debate repeatedly illustrated, one man's graceful accommodation to the inevitable was another's ignominious retreat, and between these alternative perspectives lay an almost unbridgeable gap.

The decision of the New Right to spearhead such forceful opposition undoubtedly entailed certain risks. Leaders of the organized opposition generally understood that if rejection were achieved, and if violence and closure of the Canal ensued, the administration would not have hesitated to use the Right as scapegoat. In the aftermath of violence in the Zone, one congressional staffer suggests, the Right would have been "eaten alive."[152] "If there *had* been riots in Panama, I'm sure the administration would have held us accountable," says a member of the Viguerie organization. "There was a sense of caution if we were to win; we knew we had to be prepared. We had lengthy discussions as to what might happen. In the end we just agreed that we would not let ourselves be branded as purveyors of violence."[153]

In retrospect, it seems highly unlikely that the New Right could have bought immunity from the almost certain consequences of rejection at the low cost of mere verbal disclaimers of responsibility. Thus the Right probably gained far more from losing than it ever could have gained from winning, as leaders of the opposition privately acknowledge.

Among all interest groups active in the ratification debate the Right had by far the most significant influence. Notwithstanding its narrow political base, it produced a show of opposition to the new pacts that brought the ratification contest to a near-standstill, illustrating the practical ramifications of Senate minority leader Howard Baker's observation that "those who are opposed to [the treaties] are really opposed to them, and those who are for them are just sort of."[154] As Viguerie wrote later, "The New Right fought Big Government, Big Business, Big Labor, and Big Media to a standstill for almost two years."[155] In the process it raised the ante so high that in order to win in the Senate the administration was obliged to forfeit the political capital necessary for later congressional initiatives. Thus while the administration finally won the battle, it was in a very real sense the Right that won the war. After Panama, after the administration's brief, unsuccessful experiment with a revisionist foreign policy, it was the Cold War traditionalists who once again assumed the prerogative of setting the terms of the national foreign-policy debate.

CHAPTER 6

Interest Groups, II:
The Economics of Ratification

By a remarkable accident of timing, the debate over ratification of the Panama Canal treaties began at the precise moment when, for the first time in its history, the Canal ceased to be a profitable enterprise. Its long-term economic significance to the national interest, if not to several important private interests, suddenly became an open question. As the Carter administration was generally quick to point out, the historic commercial importance of the Canal was diminishing fast by 1977 as a result of various circumstances, none of which was foreseen when the negotiations began in 1964, and all of which were culminating just as arrangements to transfer the waterway to Panama were nearing completion. The fact underscores a major irony of the ratification debate: just as political emotions on the Canal were turning up, the economic significance of the Canal was turning down. As *Business Week* wrote in 1976, "When [the Canal] was in its heyday nobody paid much attention. But now that people are fighting not to give it up, the thing isn't worth worrying about."[1]

There were, however, two broad groups of interests that continued to regard the Canal as something well worth worrying about. One was the coalition of organizations on the New Right whose interest was largely the product of a conservative, Cold War ideology. The other, to which we now turn, was a collection of commercial, mostly maritime, interests for whom the declining status of the Canal was a matter of tangible economic interest. Their concerns and their potential political implications constitute an important chapter in the story of ratification politics. They included, first, a group of American-flag shipowners primarily active in trade between the East and Gulf coasts and the Orient, and in what remained of the once-lucrative inter-coastal trade; second, a number of public port authorities scattered along the North Atlantic and Gulf coasts of the United States; and third, a variety of midwestern farm interests whose exports entered the world market through the Mississippi Valley river system and the Panama Canal.

These were the only parties directly affected by the outcome of the Senate debate. Prevalent among them was a growing sense of vulnerability to a pattern of declining traffic and rising tolls that was established in the early 1970s and which they feared the new Canal treaties would exacerbate. Throughout the ratification period they repeatedly sought assurances from the administration that the stepped-up annuities to Panama prescribed in the treaties would not translate into toll increases that would divert yet more traffic from the newly beleaguered Canal. Failing to secure more than pro forma responses, they became critics, if not always of ratification itself then at least of the failure of the administration to document its sanguine assessment of the long-term economic implications of ratification.

Their persistence in holding the administration to account on the economics of ratification raised questions that eventually challenged the faith of even strong supporters of the treaties in the Senate. That the administration chose, in effect, to ignore the line of inquiry pursued by the maritime interests (and that leaders of the New Right failed to utilize these same arguments to shore up their own attack on the administration's position) offers an instructive lesson in ratification politics. It is a story of risks thoughtlessly taken and of opportunities needlessly lost; of an administration maladroit in tending to the reasonable needs of important interest groups and of conservatives unable to distinguish reality from the mythology they helped to create. In the end a small group of congressional conservatives on the House Merchant Marine Committee *did* embrace the concerns of the maritime industry, and by using them to exact important concessions from the administration on legislation to implement the treaties, they clearly demonstrated the risks and the opportunities the situation held.

[1]

From its opening in 1914 the Canal was a consistently sound, self-sustaining business enterprise. The height of its prosperity was attained in the decades after World War II when, under the jurisdiction of the Panama Canal Company, transits and earnings reached record levels. By the early 1970s, for the first time in history and well into the period of the negotiations, the Canal was approaching its estimated total capacity of 26,000 vessels per year. Then, almost without warning, the company's fortunes took a sudden, dramatic downturn. Between 1973 and 1977 it suffered operating losses of over $60 million, while the number of transits dropped by nearly 25 percent. For the first time in the Canal's sixty-year history the company, required by law to remain self-sustaining, was forced to raise tolls in back-to-back increases in 1974 and 1976.

The downturn was partly the result of external influences, in particular the end of the Vietnam War, which dramatically reduced military transits; the reopening of the Suez Canal, which recaptured trade between Europe and the Near and Far East; and the recession of 1973–75, which caused a general slowdown in world trade.

But the downturn also had less transient, more threatening causes, especially inroads being made by various new time- and cost-competitive shipping alternatives. One was the new class of "supertankers," which were first used to accommodate the transport of Persian Gulf oil after the closure of the Suez Canal and which eventually proved adaptable to other "bulk" commodities. The supertankers threatened to capture large amounts of the trade in coal and grain that, together with petroleum products, constituted half the total tonnage which passed through the Canal each year.

As supertankers began to divert bulk commodities, the "minibridge" system was providing an attractive alternative for the transportation of high-volume, nonbulk goods ranging from electronic equipment to automobiles.[2] If the advantage of the supertankers was capacity, then the advantage of the minibridge system was speed, for containers of such nonbulk goods could be shipped across the United States by rail at up to a week's savings on trips, for example, between the Orient and cities on the East Coast. Such time saving made the new system, not even dreamed of a decade earlier, a virtual overnight success.

The rapid emergence of these alternatives to the Canal, together with the disruptions caused by international political and economic forces, suddenly placed the Canal in a financially precarious position. They clouded the company's long-term outlook even as negotiations to relinquish the waterway were winding to a conclusion. A reduction in traffic helped produce higher tolls, which in turn weakened the Canal's competitive position and threatened ultimately to reduce traffic even further. Worse, recent developments had exposed the fundamental structural deficiencies of an enterprise burdened by a fixed technology and high fixed costs. Thus by the eve of the ratification debate it was at least an open question whether the Canal would ever regain its former commercial prominence. One consultant to the Canal Company assessed the stakes: "The Canal is no longer the prize it once was."[3] *Forbes* magazine concurred in 1976 that "from a purely economic point of view . . . the Panama Canal is more symbol than substance."[4]

As a general measure of the Canal's declining value, *Forbes's* assessment was doubtless correct. Nevertheless, for the interests whose livelihoods were directly pegged to the prosperity of the Canal, the issue had far more than symbolic significance.

The minibridge system took its stiffest toll among the major port cities of the North Atlantic and Gulf coasts, whose direct seaborne links to the Orient were gradually being replaced by rail links to the Pacific Coast. Imports such as cars and appliances, which would once have traveled the Canal to Houston or New Orleans, were being unloaded with growing regularity in Oakland or Long Beach or Seattle and shipped east by rail to regional distribution centers. Such losses presaged a major shift in the balance of economic power to West Coast port authorities. Back East, the arithmetic of lost jobs and lost revenues made such older port cities as Boston, New York, Baltimore, and New Orleans ever more solicitous of the declining health of the Canal, which for so long had linked their fortunes to the Orient.[5]

These losses were shared by several American-flag cargo fleets, which also lost trade to the minibridge system. Further deterioration of the Canal's competitive position only raised the dark possibility of their being forced out of the East and Gulf coast–Orient trade altogether or into the overcrowded competition for trade between the West Coast and the Far East. For the liners, as well, the trend was westward. Between 1970 and 1977 Gulf and North Atlantic ports lost nearly 20 percent of their liner cargo, while Pacific Coast ports registered increases of better than 50 percent.[6] The shipping companies also had to add up the losses that resulted from the diversion of bulk commodities to the supertankers, virtually all of which were (and remain) under foreign registry.

As for midwestern farm interests, they shared a rising concern over the possible effect of recent and future Canal toll increases on the export crop, 20 percent of which—primarily wheat, soybeans, corn, and sorghum—passed down the Mississippi Valley and through the Canal en route to the Orient. Continental fears were expressed by the American Farm Bureau Federation and the National Grange that such increases could eliminate the small competitive advantage enjoyed over exports from such countries as Argentina and Canada.

The maritime interests, in particular, accurately perceived that they were casualties of new forces which were reshaping old patterns of commerce and that their fortunes were destined to grow worse in direct proportion to the deterioration of the competitive position of the Canal. When these interests looked to the future, they found themselves, by a remarkable accident of timing, face to face with a scheme to give away the Canal altogether, and under circumstances that, because the scheme would necessitate raising tolls to increase annuity payments to Panama, threatened to make an already bad situation worse. Having been the unwitting victims of a nascent transportation revolution, they discovered that they were about to become victims of an incipient revolution in American policy toward the Third World as well. And because they were vulnerable, they were openly critical and not at all reassured by constant administration references to the Canal as "economically obsolescent."

While these interests never coalesced into a strong political force, the arguments they raised about the possible impact of the treaties on the long-term prosperity of the Canal, and the spectre they conjured up of lost jobs and revenue, along with the inability of the administration to mount an effective response, endowed them with at least potential political significance. In the interplay between Congress and the executive branch these groups eventually proved important. By embracing their arguments, opponents of ratification on the House Merchant Marine Committee were able to wage a successful last-minute fight to amend legislation implementing the treaties following Senate ratification. If treaty opponents on the New Right who orchestrated the movement against ratification had also embraced these discontents, they might well have exposed the vulnerability of the Administration's defense and done irreparable harm to the administration's case in the Senate, where but one vote separated victory from defeat.

[2]

What concerned the maritime interests in particular were specific provisions of the new treaties bearing on the toll structure. The Panama Canal Treaty[7] provided for a complicated, four-part formula for payments to Panama until the year 2000. The formula consisted of

(a) a flat 30 cents for every ton of cargo transiting the Canal;
(b) an unconditional annuity of $10 million;
(c) an additional $10 million earmarked to pay for various maintenance services formerly provided by the Canal Zone government;
(d) a conditional annuity of up to $10 million to be paid out of operating profits when they existed at the end of any given year.

The total was an estimated $60 to $70 million, up sharply from the annuity of $2.5 million paid under the existing treaty since 1955.

For those interested parties with a wary eye on rising tolls even before the treaties, such a sudden, large increase in payments to Panama was a source of major concern. Toll increases occasioned by inflation were one thing; inflation, at least, affected all forms of transportation impartially. But possibly drastic increases brought about for noninflationary reasons, just as many commodities were beginning to exhibit sensitivity to toll rates, raised doubts about the treaties from the very outset. In particular, the inclusion in the toll base of up to $10 million annually in profits for Panama during the transition period threatened to alter the first principle by which the Canal had been run since its opening.[8]

Lobbyists for the shipping companies fired the first volley, warning of a "very detrimental, if not fatal, impact on the future of the Canal resulting from overburdened tolls."[9] "We are concerned," testified James J. Reynolds of the merchant shipping lobby, "that these Article XIII provisions may be overly ambitious politically and economically unsound. The Canal has never been operated as a profit-making enterprise and to transform it into one now could well be counterproductive. . . . If tolls are unreasonably increased, cargo will increasingly find its way across the continental United States by rail."[10] The president of one Gulf-based steamship company wrote that "Shippers simply cannot accept another increase in tolls. . . . The projection that another increase could be tolerated completely ignore[s] recent developments brought about by intermodalism and mini-land-bridge."[11]

A group of Gulf Port administrators wired the president that the "costs of payments to the government of the Republic of Panama, if met by increased Panama Canal tolls may well result in decreased use . . . as well as burdening specific American exports . . . to such an extent as to price them out of world competition."[12] "Loss of the use of the Canal or prohibitive toll increases have the potential . . . to dislocate 22,500 jobs in Virginia," warned the commissioners of the state's Port Authority."[13] "Untold thousands of Texas jobs will be in jeopardy and the economic losses to the State could run into the billions if the U.S. Senate chooses to sign over the Panama Canal as is now contemplated," echoed the Texas state legislature: "If you . . . consider the entire labor force in any one of the cities of Waco, Abilene, Odessa or Tyler, you are speaking of approximately 50,000 jobs—and that's how many jobs could be impacted in major economic sectors of the Texas economy by the Canal changeover."[14]

From the farm states, the attorney general of Iowa cautioned that "the toll increase is going to have a tremendous effect on us. It's going to price some farmers out of the market."[15]

One port director summarized the underlying fear: "If forces other than cost factors are allowed to dominate the toll-setting decisions, tolls could reach a point where they seriously discourage the flow of traffic. For many commodities the Canal could quickly become just as dead as if it had been closed by an act of war."[16] A government consultant concurred in this bleak, worst-case scenario: "In the long term an imprudent toll increase could sour traffic growth and set in motion irreversible decisions. Loss of traffic coupled with growth of costs will result in higher unit costs and the need for further toll increases, providing a vicious cycle that would result in eventual financial collapse."[17]

Under growing pressure the administration was finally obliged to address the economic effects of ratification.

[3]

Responding to the warnings of the maritime industry, the administration gathered evidence to demonstrate that the estimated 30 percent increase in tolls required under the treaty would neither jeopardize the viability of the Canal nor disrupt existing traffic patterns.[18] The administration's case was drawn principally from the results of back-to-back studies conducted by two consultants long familiar with the operations of the Canal and the Canal Company. The first, Leonard Kujawa of Arthur Andersen and Company, was the leading expert on the operations of the Panama Canal Company and the author of more than fifteen reports written for the Canal Company over a period of nearly twenty years. The second was Ely M. Brandes of International Research Associates of Palo Alto. Brandes's expertise was in the area of traffic projections and commodity sensitivity, and he figured in the unfolding story of the new treaties at several key points.

By the account of Robert Crittenden, military assistant to the assistant secretary of the army during the Carter administration, it was

Brandes who was responsible in 1977 for convincing Panama's minister of planning, Nicholas Barletta, that unreasonable demands for annuity payments from the United States during the life of the Panama Canal Treaty would have an adverse and possibly crippling effect on traffic flows through the Canal. "After that," Crittenden recounts, "Barletta seemed to have a completely different view of what he could get from the U.S. out of the revenues of the Canal, and that seemed to be . . . a turn-around point in my opinion because he had another meeting with Ambassadors Linowitz and Bunker right after that in which he seemed to be asking much less."[19] During the ratification debates Brandes, like Kujawa, was to be hastily commissioned by the State Department, after years of service on retainer to the Canal Company, to comment on the financial viability of the new regime prescribed in the Panama Canal Treaty. During the debate in the House of Representatives on legislation to implement the new treaties, the same Brandes, this time retained by a coalition of Gulf and East coast port authorities, would be instrumental in forcing key concessions from the administration on matters relating to the composition of the new Panama Canal Commission and to various procedural aspects of the toll-setting process.

In the fall of 1977, however, both Brandes and Kujawa were in the service of the administration. Their conclusions appeared at face value to stamp the imprimatur of long years of expertise on the administration's estimate of the financial impact of ratification.

Kujawa's report, issued in January 1978, provided an estimate of the increased costs to be imposed on the new Panama Canal Commission under the terms of the new treaties. Kujawa concluded that even though the treaties would require a sharply stepped-up schedule of payments to Panama, the increases would be offset substantially by the divestiture of various services provided by the Canal Zone government under the 1903 treaty. By the terms of the proposed treaties the Canal Zone would cease to exist, and the functions provided under its auspices, ranging from schools and hospitals for Zonians to various commercial maritime services for transiting ships, were to be absorbed either by the government of Panama or the U.S. Department of Defense. Accordingly, Kujawa estimated that the cash requirements of the Canal to the five-year horizon of his study would be increased by only 20 percent, and that such an increase could be met by a one-time toll increase of 19 to 27 percent. The projection was comfortably within the range of the administration's own estimate of 30 percent.

The task of demonstrating that a 27 percent increase would not drive traffic away fell to Brandes. His estimates addressed increases ranging from a sensitivity threshold of 15 percent to a point of diminishing returns at 50 percent. Between 15 and 50 percent probable traffic losses would be more than offset by gains in revenue. Against Brandes's estimates, Kujawa's projected increases were easily accommodated. "Our own conclusion," Brandes testified, "is that for the next five to ten years a future Panama Canal Commission should have sufficient revenue resources available—actual or potential—to meet its costs. This means, in effect, that during that period the income required should either be available from toll revenues at current rates; or if necessary, those rates could safely be raised to obtain the additional amounts likely to be needed."[20]

The best news for the administration was modest but optimistic forecasts for increased traffic through the waterway during the life of the treaty. The projections were based on a partial resumption of historic growth patterns, but also on the new movement of Alaska North Slope oil bound for Gulf and East coast refineries, which was likely to be dependent on the Canal for the foreseeable future. Based on the influx of Alaskan oil, Brandes projected a growth rate in traffic for the balance of the century at "slightly more than 2 percent per year," while the Maritime Administration projected growth at a somewhat higher 3 percent per annum.[21]

Taken together, the Kujawa and Brandes reports provided solid support for the administration's argument that the treaties would not compromise the financial integrity of the Canal. As Kujawa concluded,

The financial viability of the Commission can be demonstrated for the period of 1979 through 1983 by combining the results of the two studies. Our estimates of the pretoll net cash requirements and the traffic and tolls revenue deficiency in the range of $182.5 million to $265.5 million will be incurred during the five-year study period. A one-time toll rate increase of 19% to 27% would be required for the period effective on or about the date the treaty enters force in order to offset this deficit. This level of tolls increase is evaluated in the IRA [International Research Associates] study as having only a nominal impact on the level of Panama Canal traffic.[22]

The Brandes and Kujawa reports were released in January 1978. The administration held out high hopes that presentations made thereafter to Congress would lay to rest the exaggerated fears of disruption and economic losses voiced by treaty opponents. If transit costs were to increase as a result of ratification, then at least their impact was now demonstrably small. Moreover, recourse was always available to the more fundamental argument that the alternative to ratification was the near-certain prospect of closure by terrorism—or by the threat of terrorism, which would just as quickly invoke the exclusionary clauses of most maritime insurance policies. As the Council of the Americas, a leading business association, pointed out, any juxtaposition of the cost of toll increases and the cost of closure was sure to lend compelling weight to the administration's argument. The only alternative to ratification, suggested the council, was the "certainty of uncertainty."[23]

[4]

In February the administration's chief treaty lobbyists expressed renewed confidence that the potential for damage to the administration's case had been contained. The Kujawa report, they wrote to the president, "should lay to rest virtually all the questions concerning traffic projections and toll increases."[24] In fact, as events were soon to demonstrate, the Brandes and Kujawa reports exacerbated the administration's difficulties by exposing the limits of its economic intelligence and the rather large measure of wishful thinking that entered into its long-term assessments of ratification.

The major problem with both reports was that they addressed only the short term. Both gave the Canal a clean bill of health through 1983, but they could give no real assurance with respect to the years 1983–2000 and beyond. The administration itself was silent on this point save for vague assurances dispatched to Capitol Hill in February over the signatures of Secretaries Vance and Brown and Secretary of the Army Clifford Alexander: "While the range of uncertainty increases for the later years of the Treaty period, we believe it is reasonable to expect that the Canal enterprise can meet all its operating costs, including payments to Panama required by the Treaty."[25]

Just *why* it was reasonable, no one could exactly say. The estimate represented a leap of faith even the State Department's own consultants were reluctant to accept. A "significant conclusion of our study," Ely Brandes reported, "is that beyond the next 5 to 10 years, we can give no assurance about the ability of the Canal to maintain itself on a financially supporting basis. Beyond ten years, the uncertainties simply become too numerous to permit a worthwhile forecast."[26] Added Kujawa: "The combination of increased payments to Panama, the divestiture of various profit making operations, inflation, the threat of mini-bridge and supertanker competition and diminishing growth rates ... give little basis for optimism regarding the financial viability of the Panama Canal Commission.... There is as much doubt as there can be assurance that the Panama Canal Commission will be financially viable."[27]

These doubts were just as evident among other witnesses representing the government. "The period 1979 through 1984 will not be a major problem," testified Governor Harold R. Parfitt of the Canal Zone, "in that adequate tolls revenue can be generated to recover all costs of operation." Nevertheless, he told a startled Senate Armed Services Committee, "I believe you should be alerted to the possibility that the Canal operation may not be self-financing in the out years."[28] Comptroller General Elmer Staats offered a similar conclusion: "IRA's results suggest that it would be very easy to cover costs in the short run by raising tolls; the real test is whether those costs can continue to be covered in the long run as shippers have time to respond."[29]

What complicated the administration's case further was the problem that made long-term projections impossible to begin with, namely, the absence of a draft of the legislation that would implement the treaties once ratified—legislation the comptroller general described as "the key determinant of the financial viability of the proposed Canal Commission."[30] At issue was a list of the specific operational and treaty-related costs that the commission would be legally bound to recover through tolls. It was one thing to hypothesize what revenue the new Panama Canal Commission could *earn*, critics charged, but that information was meaningless unless there was also some indication of what the commission would have to *spend*. In hearings before the Senate Foreign Relations Committee a shipping industry representative successfully pressed the point with Paul Sarbanes of Maryland, cofloor leader on the Panama treaties:

Melvin Shore: None of these studies, Senator, is on the point.... He [Ely Brandes] was never asked, if I heard him correctly, to comment on the costs of the Canal. ... He was commenting only on its ability to earn revenue. This is only half the question.

Sarbanes: You can take those figures and then draw your conclusions on the basis of the burden that is involved. But the refined raw material that is necessary, it seems to me is available.

Shore: But Senator, I submit that this is still only half of the equation. The other half is the demand upon the toll structure, how much it must raise. That is not available, as far as I know. Dr. Brandes has indicated in this morning's testimony that he was not asked to comment on that.

Sarbanes: . . . I understand the point and I think it is an important one.[31]

In fact neither Brandes nor Kujawa, nor anyone else, could comment on "the other half," that is, on the demand side of the toll structure, until the administration made up its mind about whether, for example, the commission would be required to carry over a $20 million annual interest payment to the U.S. Treasury for the government's net unrecovered investments in the Canal; or whether the 30-cent-per-ton payment to Panama was to be pegged to the U.S. Wholesale Price Index; or whether money should be provided by the commission to induce employees eligible for early retirement to stay on into the transition period. To be sure, these were enormously complex accounting questions, and it is not surprising that they escaped general public notice in the ratification debate. To the ports and shipping companies, however, they were fraught with significance because, depending on what set of recommendations the administration chose to make to the Congress on these matters, the toll base could be increased by as much as $50 million, with possible resulting toll increases of 5 or 10 percent. The equation between costs of the commission and toll levels, on one hand, and between tolls and traffic, on the other, was always foremost in the minds of port and shipping company officials. Given the new and growing toll sensitivity of many commodities, 5 to 10 percent could debatably be the difference between profit and loss—precisely the point that caused such concern among the affected maritime interests. As Brandes warned, once the initial planned increases were implemented, the "margin of relatively safe toll increases will have disappeared. Thereafter, even small toll increases may precipitate large traffic losses."[32]

With tolerances so fine the administration's unwillingness to clarify the subject quickly attracted growing controversy. One writer described the administration's attitude toward the economics of ratification as "cursory."[33] An official of the Port of Baltimore called it "nonchalant."[34] The merchant shippers testified that they were

most disappointed that the Administration is still not able or willing to unveil its detailed legislative proposals for implementing the operational provisions of the proposed treaty. It is still somewhat puzzling that the executive branch seems to have a large number of experts who apparently have the time and inclination to travel the width and breadth of the Nation extolling the merits of the treaty, and yet they have been unable to assemble a comparable group to review the toll structure to consider all of the economic aspects involved, and to put a package together in time to meet this subcommittee's well advertised hearing schedule.[35]

The International Longshoremen's Association complained that it was

> dismayed, to say the least, by the State Department's procedure in only *now* having a study completed to determine the feasibility of the financial commitments expected by the U.S. contained in the Treaty's text with regard to future toll increases and toll-setting policies. ... It is inconceivable to the ILA that such decisive factors as levels of future toll rates and overall toll-setting policies—matters of paramount importance to the American maritime industry in general and the longshore industry in particular—are left unresolved and unanswered.[36]

"We can only conclude," wrote a port official, "that the State Department has negotiated a Treaty without proper consideration of the effects upon the ports of the United States."[37]

As the ratification debate progressed in the Senate, there was clear and growing evidence among the various economically affected sectors of what the *Journal of Commerce* described as "massive resistance to passing the costs of diplomacy to canal users."[38] Trade associations and lobbying groups pressed their concerns in resolutions and dispatches to Capitol Hill urging that the treaties not be ratified "until the effects of commitments made for diplomatic purposes upon the toll levels can be shown to be non-detrimental or else ... removed from the toll base."[39] Legislatures in at least five states passed strongly worded resolutions demanding the same guarantees. In the Midwest four farm-state attorneys general joined leading conservatives as co-plaintiffs in a suit filed against the administration in federal court to block ratification, citing as injury trade losses that would result from tolls inflated by the costs of diplomacy.[40] The American Farm Bureau Federation urged the Congress "not to appropriate funds to implement the provisions of the Panama Canal Treaties."[41] On the eve of the Senate's final vote on the second treaty seven Gulf port authorities complained in space purchased in the *Washington Post* of "dramatic losses" that would result from the necessity "to pay the costs of international diplomacy."[42]

In spite of these widely shared doubts the maritime groups never became the juggernaut of an organized antiratification movement, and for reasons that suggest the reverse of the paradox which characterized the corporate response to ratification. As described in chapter 5, the multinational banks and corporations appeared to have a major stake in *supporting* ratification but in the end remained politically passive. The maritime groups had a major stake in *opposing* ratification (or at least in modifying the economic provisions of the treaties), but for entirely different reasons they also remained politically passive, at least through the ratification period. As a result formidable political power that could have been brought to bear on the outcome of the Senate debate either for or against ratification was never utilized. Through the long contest over the treaties the power of private economic interests lay essentially dormant. For the corporations there was a consensus for ratification but no strong incentive to act; for the maritime interests there was an incentive to act, but because of circumstances that conspired against political solidarity, there was no workable consensus to make effective political action possible.

One major handicap to solidarity was the absence of political support from the key shippers, whose stake in the outcome of the ratification debate was reduced by the economics of supertankers and the growing overland capacity of the railroads. As long as cost-competitive alternatives to the Canal existed for the shipment of bulk commodities, toll sensitivity was destined to be of little more than academic interest to such giant international merchants of farm commodities as Cargill or Continental Grain, or to the large oil companies that owned most of the coal exported from Hampton Roads to Japanese steelmakers.

For most of the oil companies there was a reverse logic at work. By the time of the ratification debate the "majors," like Sohio and Gulf, did find themselves heavily dependent on the Canal for the transport of Alaskan oil to Gulf states and Caribbean refineries. But because oil displayed no great toll sensitivity and because the absence of foreseeable alternatives made the Canal indispensable, the companies were highly receptive to warnings from the administration that failure to ratify could lead to closure by terrorism.[43] Thus the oil companies and the maritime groups were approaching the question from opposite frames of reference. As one port official noted, "for the oil companies tolls were not a factor; fear *was* a factor."[44]

But there were other, more basic forces working against unified opposition to ratification. Among the ports, for example, the western port authorities stood to profit no matter how the treaty issue was finally resolved.[45] Moreover, the public-sector status of all the port authorities limited the possibilities for political action. As an official of the Port of New Orleans put it: "We had a concern and we did our best to express it. But we are a public agency; we were not trying to get into politics."[46] For the East Coast ports the constraints were even greater. A Baltimore port spokesman explains that "As public institutions, we found it impolitic to oppose ratification in the face of the near unanimity in support which prevailed among the senators from the states we represent. We were on record that the treaties be fair with respect to procedures for setting tolls but that was as far as we felt we should go as public agencies who were charged with increasing and protecting port commerce—giving advice and consent to treaties."[47]

Meanwhile, the views of the oil companies were sufficient to ruin the potential for solidarity among the shipping companies, since nearly half of the lobby representing the owners of liners and cargo ships (the American Institute of Merchant Shipping) involved the "captive" fleets of such major oil companies as Shell, Amoco, Mobil, Gulf, and Exxon. As one industry official explained, "the oil companies have their own interests, which do not reflect the concerns of U.S. flagship operators."[48]

Moreover, virtually all the shipping companies in question were federally subsidized. As one AIMS official commented, it "would have ill become [the steamship companies] to oppose a venture supported by three presidents."[49] Admitted another, more directly, "a subsidized industry like we are doesn't want the White House on its back."[50]

For the shipping companies there was, finally, a strong individual mitigating factor in the person of James J. Reynolds, the president of AIMS and former assistant and deputy secretary of labor under Presidents Kennedy and Johnson. As there was deference within the industry to AIMS on the treaty issue, so there was deference within AIMS to Reynolds. "We went on faith thanks to one person—James Reynolds," said AIMS's legislative director. "He kept the industry from opposing all by himself."[51] As Reynolds explains:

> I had a much broader vision of the importance of the issue than any single constituent company. Having been in government, I understood why these treaties needed to be ratified. My effort was to convince AIMS . . . Our mission was not to object to ratification. That wasn't our purpose. I had some responsibility to avoid precipitous increases in tolls. I visited [Ellsworth] Bunker during the negotiation. I told him, "We're supporting you; you'll have no problems with us so long as tolls are not a revenue machine for Panama." I eventually met with [Sol] Linowitz informally. I think he understood our concern.[52]

Another AIMS official, Albert May, hinted at a stronger threat. "We made it known to State that there had to be some controls on tolls and that if State ignored this we would join the opposition. With some assurances we would not object to ratification."[53] Such undocumented assurances as the maritime industry were able to get were sufficient to convince Reynolds, who in January 1978 confessed to the Senate Foreign Relations Committee his view that "to reject this treaty would be a devastatingly improper thing to do."[54] Concluded May: "As long as the United States kept control of the Canal until the end of the century, and as long as the toll base was not loaded, we could live with it."[55]

Thus, for a variety of political, institutional, and personal reasons, the interest groups that had the only direct stake in the outcome of the ratification debate were neither able nor disposed to spearhead a drive to kill the treaties in the Senate. The anomaly that characterized their position was dissatisfaction (ranging toward bitterness in some quarters) over the unwillingness of the administration to lend a sympathetic ear to their concerns, mixed with an acceptance—often a grudging acceptance—of the ultimate logic of ratification.[56] In the last analysis, however, they were never destined to be spoilers. This much is clear. What is also clear is that the arguments they marshaled against the administration on the economic consequences of ratification had the potential to be powerful weapons in the hands of treaty opponents.

The administration had begun with an estimate by the American negotiating team that the costs of the treaties, including the new annuities to Panama, would require an increase in tolls of no more than 30 percent. At nearly every point its case was challenged. When the source of the estimate was questioned, the administration revealed that it was based on a three-year-old Brandes report that, like its revised 1968 version, made projections without factoring in any new demands on the toll structure, including the new annuities.

When the validity of the 30 percent estimate was challenged after the beginning of the ratification debate, the State Department hastily commissioned the reports by Brandes and Kujawa, which were completed only weeks before the first Senate vote. They evoked expressions of disbelief (Senator Claiborne Pell: "Would it not be more intelligent to do the study *before* we conclude the treaty?")[57] and cynicism (a port authority spokesman: "The fact that the study was commissioned by the State Department . . . leads me to wonder what would happen if its conclusions were extremely negative").[58]

When the results were presented to Congress, they were challenged as largely irrelevant to the real question of the long-term consequences of ratification, and they offered virtually no documentation to justify the administration's optimistic assumptions about tolls and traffic.

When the State Department gave assurances that it would not let tolls reach the point of diminishing returns, its own star witness, Ely

Brandes, testified that that point was nearly at hand. "There is danger," he warned. "We're not very far from the point when we will get declining returns."[59] "It is right on the ragged edge," concurred Governor Parfitt.[60]

When Agriculture Secretary Bob Bergland reassured farmers that tolls would only have to be raised 25 percent to meet treaty costs, the attorneys general from four farm states, exaggerating their own case, replied that payments to Panama would require toll increases of between 200 and 300 percent.[61]

When Ambassadors Linowitz and Bunker argued that "the Canal enterprise should be capable of generating revenues to meet these payments to Panama under the treaty,"[62] another key government witness, Governor Parfitt, before the Senate Armed Services Committee, publicly "doubted Canal tolls could be raised enough to pay Panama all the money provided under the treaties."[63] Said one Senate aide of the governor's testimony, "Parfitt has stuck a knife into the State Department's back."[64]

When requests were made for implementing legislation that would help clarify the long-term picture, they were repeatedly postponed by the administration. As one shipping industry representative said, summarizing the prevailing dissatisfaction with the administration's performance, "We were deeply concerned about the absence of implementing legislation. But we were more concerned about the lack of specifics and the unaccountable unwillingness of the administration to face the issue."[65]

In failing to address such concerns the administration took a potentially high risk. It exposed a vulnerable position that, if exploited, could have called into question its larger defense of ratification and increased the pressure on wavering swing votes in the Senate. Without hard data to lend credibility to long-term predictions in the way the Brandes and Kujawa studies had done for the short term, there was no effective way to respond to often wildly exaggerated claims, such as those of 200 percent toll hikes made by the farm state attorneys general. With only a little ingenuity, enterprising opponents on the New Right might have raised the frightening specter—based on figures farm and maritime groups were freely making in their own worst-case estimates—of serious damage to national trade and payments balances because of competitive burdens placed on agricultural exports, for example, or the more than 110,000 jobs and nearly $5 billion in revenue implicated in port operations in the politically important Gulf and East coast states.[66]

If Governor Parfitt's cautious revision of the administration's estimates was "a knife in the back of the State Department," a less restrained, more politically motivated assault on the administration's exposed flank might have produced irreparable harm. "I think the vulnerability was there," reflected Parfitt later.[67] If the Right had seized the economic issues (which were real) and relinquished its embrace of Theodore Roosevelt and notions of the Canal's mythical link to lost greatness, it could have dealt the government's effort a serious, perhaps fatal, blow. When the ratification debate was over, at least one White House staffer breathed a sigh of relief: "The numbers we presented in those hearings—the first Senate Foreign Relations Committee—were different than the numbers we put on briefing papers we sent to the Hill. At different times we said different things. If they had really been smart and put all that together they really could have hurt us. Instead, they focused on the military arguments—and they couldn't break the JCS."[68]

Senator Frank Church, one of the leading supporters of the administration, concurred in assessing the risks: "When the Senate Armed Services Committee got into the numbers, the treaty was imperiled. That's one reason why when I was chairman of the Senate Foreign Relations Committee during SALT we were determined not to get caught short. The confusion on the numbers was hurtful. It created the feeling that costs were being hidden. . . ."[69]

Just why the administration gave such an opening to the opposition remains unclear, though there is a scattering of clues. For one thing, at least some of the information necessary for long-term cost estimates was simply not available. For example, the United States agreed to pay as part of the total annuity up to $10 million from operating profits in any given year; but six months into the ratification debate there was still no agreement as to whether any unpaid balances from this conditional annuity were to accrue from year to year and to be paid off in the year 2000. If such were required, then up to $10 million extra would have to be figured into the toll base each year. As we have seen, this was one of the most controversial provisions of the treaties, and it was not finally resolved until *after* the treaties had been ratified. As late as February 1978 the president's congressional lobbyists were still trying to pin down the issue: "We have determined that Panama does not expect the second $10 million, if unpaid in those years when insufficient surpluses exist, to accrue to the end of the treaty period and be paid to Panama in a lump sum at that time. We are exploring means of getting written proof of that from Panama."[70]

In addition, administration lobbyists had been careful to buy at least minimal protection on the economic issues by agreeing to co-operate with Senator Russell Long of Louisiana, a chief spokesman for the Gulf Coast maritime interests, on an understanding designed to insulate the toll structure from extraneous costs.[71]

Finally, the decision to withhold implementing legislation until after the Senate debate on ratification reflected the administration's considered judgment that to anger a small group of vested interests would risk less in the way of political fallout than to raise the entire set of economic issues before the full Senate. As one State Department official put it: "It came down to the question, are you more vulnerable with or without it? Do you lose more one way or the other? I think we felt we were better off waiting until after the Senate debate."[72] As long as there was no evidence of a serious threat from the Right on the economic issue,[73] and as long as there were indications that the maritime industry, despite reservations, would not oppose the treaties outright, there was probably little to lose by such a course. On the other hand, to have laid out the draft legislation in the Senate and House before the ratification vote would only have complicated matters by drawing attention to the weakest link in the administration's defense of ratification. As one Senate staff aide suggested, "If the implementing legislation had been unveiled, it would have unleashed two hundred more questions."[74]

Thus the administration's efforts at damage control were successful, and the worst potential for serious problems went unrealized. The State Department was therefore afforded the luxury of playing the issue as loosely as possible, by telling the Senate, in effect, what it wanted to hear. As one Defense Department official later complained, "our inclination was to do as accurate a job as we could of identifying the costs associated with implementing the treaty. The State Department's point of view was to come up with the lowest number you possibly can and make it even a lower number than you think is right in order to have the lower number and therefore presumably engender less Congressional opposition."[75] Still, the administration gained little in aggravating the situation, as it did by treating the affected parties with such an indelicate hand. One port official complained, "They tried to steamroller us. They were always very nice to us but there was never any sense or spirit of compromise. They didn't have their case worked out. They didn't have their policies worked out. They just did what they wanted."[76] As the Port of Baltimore's director of tariffs and national port affairs, Richard A. Lidinsky, Jr., later recalled, the manner of dealing with the House of Representatives after the treaties were ratified was no different. "There was a lot of arrog-

ance. They never said, 'What are your views on it; let's work together.'
And once they got past the Senate they were impossible to live with.
I think they seriously misjudged the animosity in the House."[77]

In the end such misjudgments helped foster a successful defensive
alliance against the administration. Once the House had a legislative
role to play (after the treaties were ratified by the Senate), and once
the East Coast ports were freed from the political constraints imposed
by the protreaty views of their own senators, an effective political
force began to develop, a force that ultimately prevailed against the
administration in the long struggle in 1979 over legislation to implement the treaties.

In the spring of 1978 a coalition of ports led by Boston, New York,
Philadelphia, Baltimore, and New Orleans was formed to exact in the
implementing legislation concessions they were unable to obtain in
the treaties. Representing fifty-one ports in nineteen states, the coalition acquired the political muscle commensurate with the "great
impact" the ports had on the economies of their respective states,
protesting they could "not rely on mere promises that rates will remain stable for the next twenty-one years."[78] The ports hired a Washington representative, contacted none other than Ely Brandes to make
their case to the Congress, and successfully marshaled their forces to
secure three key concessions from the administration: representation
for the ports, shipowners, and maritime labor on the new Panama
Canal Commission; an elaboration of the procedural safeguards specified in the understanding to the treaty sponsored by Russell Long
of Louisiana; and a definitive guarantee that the contingent $10 million
would not be included in the toll base.[79] Lidinsky, one of the leading
members in the coalition, explains:

> The issue of tolls was the battle cry, but there were other issues like
> representation on the commission which were the immediate object of
> our interest. One major fear was that with the Panamanians running
> the Canal and having favorable representation on the commission we
> could face a runaway toll situation. Many people in the ports community
> were fearful the Panamanians couldn't run [the Canal] well; they were
> afraid the Americans would just take their pensions and run. There was
> obvious distrust of both the Panamanians and the administration on the
> part of the ports.
>
> We met months before the implementing legislation to map strategy.
> We knew this was our last chance. We knew we had to protect ourselves.
> State wanted its own types on the commission—total federal repre-
> sentation—and the Senate version reflected this. In the House version,
> working with [Representatives] Donally [D.-Mass.], Bauman [R.-Md.],

Murphy [D.-N.Y.], Mikulski [D.-Md.], and others, we were able to get representation from port authorities, steamship companies and labor. That was significant. We all had different interests; they all had to be represented.

Through our own presentations we were also able to get the [Merchant Marine] Committee to report out with our recommendations for procedural protections and we got the built-in annual payoff—the extra $10 million—out of the toll base. We retained [Ely] Brandes. He reworked the figures he did for State and made some projections and testified. He made an effective case for us.

The administration was in the middle. It told Panama one thing and the Hill another. But we stuck to it; we worked with the committee, and eventually the administration had to concede.[80]

By its unwillingness to provide some reassurance and to seek some reasonable accommodation, the administration eventually paid a much higher price than it needed to. The ports and the House Merchant Marine Committee would not separately have had the leverage they enjoyed together. As it was, the administration's actions inadvertently produced an ad hoc but powerful alliance, which was able to wrest from the administration what it could have conceded gracefully and perhaps on better terms all along. A pattern was thus set, one that was to be duplicated time and again on other Carter initiatives. Having made up its mind that the treaties were morally right, the administration in effect threw compromise to the winds. In the process it helped produce a political counterforce that compelled the relinquishment of positions already won, and at the cost of a lingering legacy of bitterness. "It didn't have to be this much of a problem for the administration," said Lidinsky. "If the House Committee hadn't taken the issue up we would have had much less influence. As it was, the committee kept coming back to us. They wanted more and more. . . . The point of the struggle over the implementing legislation was the power of solidarity and what it might have accomplished during the Senate debate. If the ports had opposed the treaty as well, it might have lost."[81] Whether this assessment is correct or not, it is clear that the administration bought more trouble than it ever needed to. By ignoring the concerns of the maritime groups, the administration laid the groundwork for collaboration. It is easy to see what might have happened during the Senate debate had leaders of the New Right been as alive to the possibilities as a group of congressmen on the House Merchant Marine Committee proved to be.

In retrospect it seems clear that the administration's otherwise skillful ratification performance was marred by only two major tactical misjudgments. The first was the decision to negotiate directly with Dennis DeConcini over the Arizona senator's condition to expand U.S. defense rights in Panama after the year 2000. The second was the failure to anticipate the risks involved in the economic provisions of the treaties. In the first instance the administration was saved by the Senate leadership and key Panamanian officials who negotiated the compromise wording that defused a serious last-minute crisis. In the latter instance the treaties were retrieved from the brink of disaster by the failure of opponents inside and outside Congress to do during the ratification debate what the maritime interests could not do for themselves, by capitalizing on the Administration's vulnerability. In neglecting to probe the weakest part of the administration's defense, the Right may have forfeited one of the best available opportunities to inflict serious, perhaps fatal, damage on the treaties.

The reasons for the Right's neglect are not altogether clear, even in retrospect. They may have had to do in part with the ideological nature of the opposition to ratification. Leaders of the Right may have missed an important opportunity, the State Department's Richard Wyrough reflected later, "because of the nature of their arguments—sovereignty and nationalism," which diverted them from giving "serious attention to whatever vulnerability the treaty package might have had in the economic area."[82] Concurred a congressional staffer, "They were captives of their own rhetoric."[83] A spokesman for the Right attributes the failure to other causes. "We *did* attempt to identify for each of the cities we visited how much shipping was implicated and what it would mean in terms of economic impact. The problem was that we couldn't find the data. If there was any one shortcoming in our operation, it was our research capabilities."[84]

Whatever the reason, the administration was fortunate that the price it finally had to pay was exacted during the implementation and not the ratification phase of the treaty debate. As it was, the best to be said of the administration's performance in handling the objections raised by the maritime interests is that it was, in Lidinsky's words, "a fly ball, bobbled but caught."[85] That the administration escaped essentially unharmed may finally be due to the fact, as White House lobbyist Beckel concludes, that "we were blessed by luck, luck, luck."[86] Without it, the treaties may not have survived.

Conclusion

Given the nearly unanimous international support that existed for the Panama Canal treaties, it is not surprising that news of ratification produced an outpouring of positive reaction around the world. In Latin America, especially, the new treaties were celebrated as a watershed in hemispheric affairs. According to Venezuela's president, Carlos Andrés Pérez, the Carter administration's commitment to ratification was an "act of heroism." "Carter is a 'god' in Latin America," wrote Brazil's *Folha de São Paulo*, his successful efforts "the proudest moment in this century for the United States." "This act of justice," editorialized the conservative *El Siglo* of Bogotá, "is a personal victory for President Carter who, in a hard fight with Congress, initiated a new era in international affairs."[1]

Among treaty supporters back home, the reaction to the belated Senate victory was no more restrained. "Senate ratification of the Panama Canal treaties is a pivotal moment in the history of the hemisphere," wrote the *Baltimore Sun*, echoing overseas estimates of the diplomatic ramifications of the Senate victory: "It signals a readiness by the United States to face up to the realities of the post-colonial world, a world in which the collective voice of small countries cannot be denied by even the most powerful of nations. President Carter can take justified pride in coming to grips with this imperative. The *New York Times* concurred: "Mr. Carter is right to hope for a new era of broadly shared American purposes in our approach to the world. . . . The Panama experience keeps that hope alive."[2]

Inside the administration, and among key allies in the Senate, ratification was greeted with particular enthusiasm. Not only was success judged the harbinger of a new era in hemispheric relations, but it was also expected to usher in a more productive era in relations with the Congress as well. In the "ebullient postmortems"[3] that followed the March and April 1978 votes, treaty supporters expressed confidence that the work of ratification had produced a solid base of congressional and public support for future foreign-policy initiatives and weakened, perhaps permanently, the forces of opposition on the Right. "This is a turning point for the Administration," Senate majority whip Alan Cranston (D.-Calif.) proclaimed, voicing the hopeful sentiments that prevailed among jubilant administration officials.[4]

The president himself concluded that the political momentum produced by ratification could be harnessed to ensure legislative success on other initiatives. As Godfrey Sperling, Jr., of the *Christian Science Monitor* wrote, success "colored his political judgment": "after achieving victory on the Panama Canal treaties, he became convinced that if he worked hard enough and felt the cause was right, he could win on anything—no matter how much opposition in Congress or elsewhere."[5] For the president's national security advisor, Zbigniew Brzezinski, success in the face of long odds produced a surge of confidence about the future: "We started with eight percent public support on this issue and only 25 senators. It shows [Carter] takes on the hard issues, sticks to it, and prevails. We'll do that on other foreign policy issues. Others should take note—we're going to deal with other issues the same way."[6]

As Sperling concludes, however, such optimism was "not grounded in political realities." After Panama, he notes, neither the president nor any other high administration official was quite prepared for the "hard sledding ahead" or for "Congress's growing animosity to [Carter] on whatever he initiated."[7] Instead, the most significant aspect of the Panama story is that despite the administration's successful ratification performance, the effect of victory was not to aid but to hinder the plans and high hopes of the administration. Despite universal international acclaim for the new treaties, the principal domestic legacy of eight months of intensive effort was a widespread misunderstanding of the purposes of the Carter foreign policy and pervasive doubts about the adequacy of the president as custodian of the nation's security interests.

As these pages have shown, two circumstances combined to rob the administration of the fruits of victory. One was the political consequence of the American public's historic attachment to the Canal and its pride in the enormous technical and humanitarian achievement represented by its construction. From 1959, when President Dwight Eisenhower made the first concession to Panamanian sovereignty in the form of the "two-flags" policy, until the eve of the

Carter presidency public opinion and policy within the executive branch had diverged on the question of transferring jurisdiction of the Canal to Panama. By 1975 and 1976 soundings of public opinion were registering huge majorities opposed to any plan to bring about such a transfer. In Congress feelings were so strong that three presidents—Nixon, Ford, and Carter—were placed on notice by the Thurmond Resolutions that a new treaty would face stiff opposition in the Senate, much as Woodrow Wilson had been put on notice in the form of the famous "Round Robin" sixty years earlier. It was thus inevitable that the political cost of finally bringing the treaties to a vote in the Senate would be abnormally high for Jimmy Carter.

The other circumstance that compromised the administration's Panama victory was timing. The ratification debate occurred at the very moment popular frustrations over America's declining role in the world were reaching a climax. Polling data compiled in the mid-1970s revealed that just as Jimmy Carter was preparing to implement the Trilateralist foreign-policy agenda, a rare (and for the Carter administration, untimely) tidal shift in public attitudes on foreign policy was just beginning to take shape in response to events that were undermining the prevalent assumption of American global dominance.

The notion of such dominance was nurtured in the unique period of American political, economic, and military hegemony in the years after World War II. So long as America's position in the postwar world remained ascendant, the belief in global dominance, infused with the historic conviction of American mission and moral leadership, became an inevitable part of the American outlook. But by the late 1960s and early 1970s new realities began to crowd out the old myths. As Thomas Hughes suggests, one result was a "counterrevolution of descending expectations."[8] Another was the political troubles of the Carter administration, epitomized by the Panama debate. By the time Jimmy Carter became president, his idealism, his altruistic view of foreign policy, and his deemphasis of security issues in favor of issues of morality and human rights were fundamentally at odds with the American mood. Writes Hughes:

> The most open and optimistic of Americans, Jimmy Carter came to office at a time when the United States was having its first deep experience of historical self-doubt. The decade of disillusionment from 1965–1975 has, in fact, left us with our first national sense of tragedy. In psychological terms, we have begun to experience the Europeanization of America—a permeating sense of limits, constraints, in some quarters even fatalism, hitherto un-American themes except, ironically, in the American South.[9]

Though perhaps not the first instance of "historical self-doubt" or "national tragedy," the Panama treaties did present a case of classic, though unavoidable, bad timing for Carter. For just as the administration sought to "give the Canal away," the issue became a vehicle on which the public projected its pervasive fears about America's declining role in the post-Vietnam world; just as the president sought to end the last vestige of American imperialism, Americans sought to hold onto the Canal as a means of controlling threatening centrifugal forces; just as the Carter administration sought to win public acceptance for the new Canal policy on the grounds that the Canal was ill-gotten, Americans, smarting from a perceived loss of moral leadership in the aftermath of Vietnam, were unwilling to bear the guilt implied in the administration's criticism of the original 1903 treaty. As one White House official summarized the inescapable problem for the administration, the Canal issue was "so symbolically important. It represented everything people were frustrated about."[10] In the "psychological confusion" that followed the Vietnam War, conceded another treaty supporter, Senator John Culver of Iowa, the treaties "could hardly be viewed in other terms than as a humiliation."[11]

For Jimmy Carter the essential problem was thus one of timing, for the very international circumstances that made the new treaties a necessity made popular disfavor a certainty. As a result, nothing worked right in the effort to sell the treaties: the administration's arguments fell flat; interest groups were unable to generate a ground swell of favorable opinion; the administration could not insulate supportive senators from hostile public opinion. Moreover, as chapter 4 has shown, it became impossible to fashion a public consensus behind ratification. As one spokesman for the New Right summarized the president's problem, in the end there were limits to what the president could do:

A wave can't crash on the beach until the elements converge: the moon, the tides, the seasons. No one, including the president, can control all the elements. The president can make a small wave. He can command the attention of the media and make a small wave. But the timing of the Carter agreement came during an intellectual malaise, during a period when the public had a growing uneasiness with Carter and his ability to handle events. The administration thought it could orchestrate a quick, swift victory, but under the circumstances that was all but impossible. It thought it had the capacity to make a wave, but it learned it couldn't.[12]

Like Woodrow Wilson sixty years earlier, Jimmy Carter was largely the victim of a shifting mood. For Wilson the reservoir of idealism that was the legacy of two decades of American progressivism and of the high-minded crusade to make the world safe for democracy gave way in the immediate aftermath of World War I to a mood of disillusionment and isolationism, in which Wilson's calls for a new crusade to save the peace found a diminishing public response. For Carter, as we have seen, the public mood was shifting just as the policy of accommodation was unveiled, if not to a new isolationism then at least to a new, less generous kind of unilateralism that was its rough moral equivalent and that complicated the task of nourishing popular support for Carter's idealistic foreign policies. Consequently, appeals to "what's expected of a great, generous nation," as one administration official put it, were largely irrelevant.[13] For most Americans the gains of the Panama policy were simply too intangible, the risks too apparent, and the assault on cherished beliefs too painful.

In the process of trying to win public approval for the treaties and for a new post-Vietnam consensus, the administration unwittingly contributed to a growing polarization between those who defined international relations in the old, familiar terms of containment and those who, like the president and his "Trilateralist" advisers, subordinated East-West confrontations to new economic and moral issues. The polarization was exacerbated by political misjudgments on issues including the Korean troop withdrawal, and later by the SALT ratification debate, the Soviet invasion of Afghanistan and the Iranian hostage crisis. But it was the effort to ratify the Panama treaties that triggered the fundamental foreign-policy debate that, as Michael Mandelbaum wrote, "crystallized differing visions of the international role of the world's most powerful country—divisions which will dominate U.S. politics through the end of the century."[14] Those divisions, it may be argued, are as consequential as that which separated isolationists and internationalists during the 1930s.

In the end, of course, the administration did win in the Senate. Still, what the administration gained was in nearly every respect a Pyrrhic victory. In exhausting its political capital, it was forced to relinquish its leverage on other issues. In its inability to convince Congress and the public of the rationale for the new treaties, it failed to lay the foundation for other foreign-policy successes. In failing to address growing public concerns over the loss of American global dominance, it helped convey a sense, unfairly perhaps, that the administration lacked the resolve to shape events to American purposes. Carter's "brief, fragile experiment in revisionism,"[15] as *Washington Post* columnist William Grieder described it, was thus compromised from the beginning. Its foundations were washed away in the flood of criticism unleashed by the very issue the administration hoped would provide it with longevity.

Public Opinion Polls:
Panama Canal Treaties

The following is a comprehensive list of opinion questions on the Panama Canal treaties asked by the major national polling organizations. The questions are categorized according to the informational content of their wording (see pp. 123-24). They appear here with the permission of the organizations concerned.

Category I: Questions referring to ownership and control

Do you favor the U.S continuing its ownership and control of the Panama Canal or do you favor turning ownership and control of the Panama Canal to the Republic of Panama? (Opinion Research Corporation)

	June 1975	Apr. 1976	May 1977	Feb. 1978
Turn	12	12	8	19
Keep	66	75	78	72
Und	22	13	14	9

Category II: Reference to transfer with qualifications

1. May 1976 (ORC) 29 App
   48 Dis
   23 Und

As you may know, when a treaty is negotiated with a foreign country the treaty has to be voted on by the U.S. Senate. If a treaty is negotiated turning over ownership and control to the Republic of Panama, do you think the U.S. Senate should approve or disapprove?

2. June 1976 (Roper)	26	Mod	Do you think the time has come for the U.S. to modify our 1903 Panama Canal treaty, or that we should insist on keeping the treaty as originally signed?
	46	Keep	
	28	Und	
3. June 1976 (CBS)	24	Agg	Do you agree or disagree with the statement that our government should eventually return control of the Panama Canal to the Government of Panama?
	52	Dis	
	24	Und	
4. Jan. 1977 (Roper)	24	Mod	Same Roper question as in June 1976.
	53	Keep	
	23	Und	
5. Mar. 1977 (Yankelovich)	29	Fav	Do you favor or oppose giving the Panama Canal back to the Panamanians even if we maintain our rights to defend it?
	53	Opp	
	18	Und	
6. May 1977 (Caddell)	27	Yes	Do you think the U.S. should negotiate a treaty with Panama whereby over a period of time Panama will eventually own and run the Canal?
	51	No	
	22	Und	
7. Aug. 1977 (Roper)	28	Mod	Same Roper question as in June 1976.
	44	Keep	
	28	Und	
8. Aug. 1977 (NBC)	27	Shd	Do you think the U.S. should sign a treaty which would eventually return control of the Panama Canal Zone to the government of Panama, or don't you think so?
	55	Not	
	18	Und	
9. Sept. 1977 (Roper)	27	Mod	Same Roper question as in June 1976.
	53	Keep	
	20	Und	
10. Sept. 1977 (Associated Press)	29	Yes	Last week, President Carter signed a treaty that means the U.S. would relinquish control of the Panama Canal by the year 2000. Now the Senate must decide whether or not to ratify the treaty. Do you think the Senate should approve the treaty concerning the Panama Canal?
	50	No	
	21	Und	
11. Sept. 1977 (Caddell)	26	Fav	The Government last week announced that we have concluded a treaty with Panama to return some parts of the Canal, the Canal Zone, and operating revenues of the Canal to Panama. From what you have heard, do you favor or oppose the treaty?
	49	Opp	
	25	Und	

12. Oct. 1977 (CBS)	29	App	The Senate now has to debate the
	49	Dis	treaties that President Carter signed
	22	Und	granting control of the Panama Canal

The Senate now has to debate the treaties that President Carter signed granting control of the Panama Canal to the Republic of Panama in the year 2000. Do you approve or disapprove of those treaties?

13. Oct. 1977 (Harris)	26	Fav	
	51	Opp	
	23	Und	

As you know, President Carter asked the U.S Senate to vote approval of a new treaty between the U.S. and Panama that will hand control of the Panama Canal back to Panama by the year 2000. Would you favor or oppose the U.S. Senate approving this treaty with Panama?

14. Oct. 1977 (NBC)	30	Fav	
	61	Opp	
	9	Und	

The new treaty between the U.S. and Panama calls for the U.S. to turn over ownership of the Canal to Panama at the end of the century. However, this treaty still has to be approved by the Senate. Do you favor or oppose approval of this treaty by the Senate? [This poll shows marginally higher percentages of both support and opposition than other polls in Category II because the question was asked only of those previously indicating "awareness" of the issue.]

15. Nov. 1977 (Roger Seasonwein Assoc.)	28	Fav	
	59	Opp	
	13	Und	

The Senate is now considering a new Panama Canal Treaty that President Carter has submitted to it. The treaty calls for Panama to become owner of the Canal in the year 2000. Are you inclined to favor or oppose this treaty?

16. Dec. 1977 (Caddell)	26	Fav	
	53	Opp	
	21	Und	

As you may know, the U.S. Senate is currently considering whether to approve or disapprove of the Panama Canal treaty, whereby the U.S. would turn over the Panama Canal to the government of Panama by the year 2000. From what you know right now, would you favor or oppose passage of that treaty?

17. Jan. 1978 (NBC)	28	Fav	
	62	Opp	
	10	Und	

Same NBC question as in October 1977.

18. Jan. 1978 (CBS)	29	App	
	51	Dis	
	20	Und	

Same CBS question as in October 1977.

19. Apr. 1978 (CBS)

30 App
53 Dis
17 Und

As you know, the Senate is considering the two treaties granting control of the Panama Canal to the Republic of Panama in the year 2000. It has already approved the first treaty and is preparing to vote on the second treaty. Do you approve or disapprove of those treaties?

20. Apr. 1978 (Harris)

29 Fav
60 Opp
11 Und

The second treaty provides for the United States giving control of the Panama Canal to Panama after the year 2000. Do you favor or oppose the U.S. Senate approving this second treaty with Panama on the Panama Canal?

21. June 1978 (Roper)

30 Shd
52 Not
17 Und

Do you think the Senate *should* have approved the Panama Canal treaties, or should *not* have approved them?

Category III: Reference to residual defense, territorial, or operational rights

1. Sept. 1977 (Gallup)

39 App
46 Dis
15 Und

The proposed new treaty between the U.S. and Panama calls for the U.S. to turn over ownership of the Canal to Panama at the end of the century. However, the U.S. will retain control over the land and installations necessary to operate and defend the Canal. Do you approve or disapprove?

2. Oct. 1977 (Gallup)

40 Fav
48 Opp
12 Und

The treaties would give Panama full control over the Panama Canal and the Canal Zone by the year 2000, but the U.S. would retain rights to defend the Canal against a third nation. Do you favor or oppose these treaties between the U.S. and Panama?

3. Nov. 1977 (Roper)

33 For
47 Agn
21 Und

In September, the Presidents of the U.S. and Panama signed two treaties which would gradually turn the Panama Canal over the the Panamanians, but would provide for the continued use and defense of the Canal by the U.S. Before these treaties can take effect, the U.S. Senate must act on them. Do you think the Senate should vote *for* the new treaties or *against* them?

4. Jan. 1978 (Gallup)	45 Fav 42 Opp 13 Und	Same Gallup question as in October 1977.
5. Mar. 1978 (NBC)	35 Fav 55 Opp 10 Und	The Senate has approved one of the Panama Canal treaties guaranteeing the right of the U.S. to intervene to defend the Canal. The second treaty, which spells out how control of the Canal will gradually be turned over to Panama by the end of the century has not been ratified. Do you favor or oppose approval of this treaty of the U.S. Senate?
6. Apr. 1978 (Harris)	49 App 41 Dis 10 Und	As you know, the U.S. Senate approved one of the two treaties with Panama on the Panama Canal by 68-32, one more than was needed. The first treaty made certain that after the year 2000, the Canal would be neutral in allowing ships from all countries, including the U.S., to go through the Canal. All in all, do you approve or disapprove of the U.S. Senate ratifying this treaty?

Category IV: Reference to rights guaranteed in the "leadership amendments"

1. Oct. 1977 (CBS)	63 App 24 Dis 13 Und	Suppose you felt the treaties provided that the U.S. could always send in troops to keep the Canal open to ships of all nations. Would you then approve of the treaties?
2. Dec. 1977 (Caddell)	49 Fav 30 Opp 21 Und	Let's say the Panama Canal treaty contained a clause which allowed the U.S. to defend the Canal forever. Would you then favor or oppose ratification?
3. Jan. 1978 (NBC)	65 Fav 25 Opp 10 Und	Would you favor or oppose approval of the Panama Canal Treaty if an amendment were added specifically giving the U.S. the right to intervene if the Canal is threatened by attack?
4. Feb. 1978 (NBC)	54 Fav 40 Opp 6 Und	Would you favor or oppose approval of the Panama Canal Treaty if an amendment were added specifically giving the U.S. the right to intervene if the Canal is threatened by attack and the right to send our warships to the head of the line in case of emergency?

5. Feb. 1978 (Harris)	56	App	The original treaties have been
	20	Dis	changed to allow the use of U.S. mili-
	24	Und	tary force to defend the Canal in an
			emergency and to allow U.S. warships
			priority in going through the Canal in
			an emergency. Do you approve or dis-
			approve with these changes in the
			Panama Canal Treaty?
6. Feb. 1978 (Caddell)	47	Fav	Same Caddell question as in December
	37	Opp	1977.
	16	Und	
7. Apr. 1978 (Harris)	44	Fav	The second treaty has been changed to
	39	Opp	allow the use of U.S. military force to
	17	Und	defend the Panama Canal in an emer-
			gency and to allow U.S. warships
			priority in going through the Canal in
			an emergency. With these new
			changes do you favor or oppose the
			proposed second treaty with Panama
			on the Panama Canal?
8. Apr. 1978 (CBS)	51	App	Two amendments have been added to
	35	Dis	the treaties. One allows the United
	14	Und	States to defend the Canal beyond the
			year 2000. The other amendment per-
			mits U.S. ships to go through the
			Canal first during a national emer-
			gency. With these amendments, do
			you approve or disapprove of the
			treaties?

Senate Votes on the Two Resolutions of Ratification

The U.S. Senate voted in favor of the Neutrality Treaty on 16 March 1978 and the Panama Canal Treaty on 18 April 1978. Both resolutions were passed by the same margin and with the same supporters and opponents.

YEAS (68): 52 Democrats; 16 Republicans*

Abourezk, S.D.	Gravel, Alaska	Metzenbaum, Ohio
Anderson, Minn.	Hart, Colo.	Morgan, N.C.
Baker, Tenn.	Haskell, Colo.	Moynihan, N.Y.
Bayh, Ind.	**Hatfield, Mark O., Ore.**	Muskie, Maine
Bellman, Okla.	Hatfield, Paul G., Mont.	Nelson, Wis.
Bentsen, Texas	Hathaway, Maine	Nunn, Ga.
Biden, Del.	**Hayakawa, Calif.**	**Packwood, Ore.**
Brooke, Mass.	**Heinz, Pa.**	**Pearson, Kan.**
Bumpers, Ark.	Hodges, Ark.	Pell, R.I.
Byrd, Robert C., W. Va.	Hollings, S.C.	**Percy, Ill.**
Cannon, Nev.	Huddleston, Ky.	Proxmire, Wis.
Case, N.J.	Humphrey, Minn.	Ribicoff, Conn.
Chafee, R.I.	Inouye, Hawaii	Riegle, Mich.
Chiles, Fla.	Jackson, Wash.	Sarbanes, Md.
Church, Idaho	**Javits, N.Y.**	Sasser, Tenn.
Clark, Iowa	Kennedy, Mass.	Sparkman, Ala.
Cranston, Calif.	Leahy, Vt.	**Stafford, Vt.**
Culver, Iowa	Long, La.	Stevenson, Ill.
Danforth, Mo.	Magnuson, Wash.	Stone, Fla.
DeConcini, Ariz.	**Mathias, Md.**	Talmadge, Ga.
Durkin, N.H.	Matsunaga, Hawaii	**Weicker, Conn.**
Eagleton, Mo.	McGovern, S.D.	Willliams, N.J.
Glenn, Ohio	McIntyre, N.H.	

*The names of Republicans are set in boldfaced type.

NAYS (32): 10 Democrats; 22 Republicans

Allen, Ala.	**Griffin, Mich.**	**Schmitt, N.M.**
Bartlett, Okla.	**Hansen, Wyo.**	**Schweiker, Pa.**
Burdick, N.D.	**Hatch, Utah**	**Scott, Va.**
Byrd, Harry F. Jr., Va.	**Helms, N.C.**	Stennis, Miss.
Curtis, Neb.	Johnston, La.	**Stevens, Alaska**
Dole, Kan.	**Laxalt, Nev.**	**Thurmond, S.C.**
Domenici, N.M.	**Lugar, Ind.**	**Tower, Texas**
Eastland, Miss.	**McClure, Idaho**	**Wallop, Wyo.**
Ford, Ky.	Melcher, Mont.	**Young, N.D.**
Garn, Utah	Randolph, W. Va.	Zorinsky, Neb.
Goldwater, Ariz.	**Roth, Del.**	

*The names of Republicans are set in boldfaced type.
Source: "Senate Backs Turning over Canal to Panama," *Congressional Quarterly Weekly Report*, 22 April 1978, p. 951.

C

Primary Sources

Interviews

Interviews Conducted by the Author

The persons listed here were interviewed on the understanding that their comments were for attribution. I specify in each case the date of the interview and the place where the interview was conducted.

Aldrich, Frank. First National Bank of Boston. Boston, Mass. 18 November 1981.

Barletta, Nicholas. Minister of Finance and Planning, Government of Panama. Washington, D. C., 16 December 1981.

Bauman, Rep. Robert. U. S. House of Representatives. Telephone Interview, 13 July 1982.

Beckel, Robert. Carter White House. Washington, D. C., 23 June 1981.

Bennet, Jr., Douglas J. U. S. Department of State. Washington, D. C., 18 May 1982.

Boggs, Michael. American Federation of Labor–Congress of Industrial Organizations. Telephone Interview, 7 October 1982.

Brandes, Ely. International Research Associates. Telephone Interview, 13 July 1982.

Bunker, Amb. Ellsworth. U. S. Department of State. Washington, D. C., 21 May 1982.

Burke, Barbara. American Institute of Merchant Shipping. Washington, D. C., 16 December 1981.

Butler, Landon. Carter White House. Washington, D. C., 22 October 1981.

Caplan, Joanna. U. S. Department of State. Washington, D. C., 2 April 1982.

Christopher, Warren. U. S. Department of State. Telephone Interviews, 3 August 1983 and 26 September 1983.

Church, Senator Frank. U. S. Senate. Washington, D. C., 20 May 1982.

Constant, Thomas. Panama Canal Company. Washington, D. C., 22 December 1981.

Culver, Senator John. U. S. Senate. Washington, D. C., 20 May 1982.

DeBuck, Dean. U. S. Department of State. Washington, D. C., 2 April 1982.

DeConcini, Senator Dennis. U. S. Senate. Washington, D.C., 28 September 1983.

Dockery, Robert. U. S. Senate Democratic Policy Committee. Washington, D. C., 25 May 1982.

Eisenmann, Richard. Business and Professional Committee for a New Panama Canal Treaty. Telephone Interview, 10 December 1982.

Eldridge, Joseph. Washington Office on Latin America. Washington, D. C., 23 October 1981.

Evans, Ernest. Senate Armed Services Committee. Washington, D. C., 20 August 1981.

Geyelin, Henry. Council of the Americas, Inc., New York, N.Y. 20 October 1981.

Graves, Edwin. Office of Senator Walter D. Huddleston. Washington, D. C., 1 August 1983.

Haar, Herbert. Port of New Orleans. Telephone Interview, 22 January 1982.

Hatfield, Senator Paul. U. S. Senate. Telephone Interview, 20 December 1983.

Hehir, Father Bryan. U. S. Catholic Conference. Washington, D. C., 9 November 1981.

Hodges, Senator Kaneaster. U. S. Senate. Telephone Interview, 11 January 1984.

Jackley, John. Council of the Americas, Inc.. Washington, D. C., 1 April 1981.

Johnson, Peter. U. S. Department of State. Washington, D. C., 2 December 1981.

Jordan, Hamilton. Carter White House. Washington, D. C., 21 July 1983.

Lewis, Gabriel. Panamanian Ambassador to the United States. Telephone Interview, 22 February 1983.

Lidinsky, Richard. Maryland Port Administration. Baltimore, Md., 23 November 1981.

Lieper, Jane. National Council of Churches. Washington, D. C., 19 October 1981.

Linowitz, Amb. Sol M. U. S. Department of State. Washington, D. C., 21 May 1982.

Lissy, David. United Brands Inc. New York, N Y., 20 October 1981.

Lucey, Laurie. Carter White House. Washington, D. C., 18 March 1981.

McCall, Richard. Office of Senator Hubert H. Humphrey. Washington, D. C., 17 May 1982.

McGee, Amb. Gale. U. S. Department of State. Washington, D. C., 1 December 1981.

May, Albert. American Institute of Merchant Shipping. Telephone Interview, 16 December 1981.

Mitler, Milton. Committee of Americans for the Canal Treaties, Inc. Washington, D. C., 1 December 1981.

Moore, Frank. Carter White House. Telephone Interviews, 3 October 1983 and 12 January 1984.

Morgan, Eduardo Ferrar. Embassy of Panama. Washington, D. C., 3 May 1978.

Moyer, Benton. First National Bank of Boston. Telephone Interview, 24 November 1981.

O'Neill, Harry. Opinion Research Corporation. Telephone Interview, 24 November 1981.

Parfitt, Governor Harold R. Panama Canal Company. Telephone Interview , 22 January 1982.

Pastor, Robert. National Security Council. Washington, D. C., 18 May 1982.

Post, John. Business Roundtable. Telephone Interview, 6 February 1982.

Purvis, Hoyt. Office of Senator Robert C. Byrd. Telephone Interview, 21 September 1983.

Reich, Otto. Council of the Americas, Inc. Telephone Interview, 23 September 1983.

Reiman, Richard. Carter White House. Washington, D. C., 23 October 1981.

Reynolds, James. American Institute of Merchant Shipping. Washington, D. C., 19 December 1981.

Rhatican, William. Richard A. Viguerie Co. Falls Church, 24 May 1983.

Rogers, William D. Arnold and Porter. Washington, D. C., 26 June 1983 and 4 October 1983.

Romani, Romano. Office of Senator Dennis DeConcini. Washington, D. C., 28 September 1983.

Roshco, Bernard. U. S. Department of State. Washington, D. C., 18 February 1981 and 15 December 1981.

Sarbanes, Senator Paul. U. S. Senate. Telephone Interview, 7 December 1983.

Schlosberg, William. Committee of Americans for the Canal Treaties, Inc. Washington, D. C., 19 October 1981.

Stokeld, Frederick, U. S. Chamber of Commerce. Washington, D. C., 22 December 1981.

Tate, Dan C. Carter White House. Washington, D. C., 20 May 1982.

Thompson, Robert. Carter White House. Telephone Interview, 3 October 1983.

Wyrough, Richard. U. S. Department of State. Washington, D. C., 14 May 1983.

Interviews Conducted by Jeffrey D. Neuchterlein

Commissioned by the Office of Congressional Liaison at the White House, Jeffrey D. Neuchterlein taped interviews during the summer of 1978 with the following participants in the ratification of the Panama Canal treaties. The tapes, and a paper based on them, were submitted to the Carter White House early in the following year. These materials now form part of the holdings of the Carter Presidential Library, Atlanta, Ga.

Beckel, Robert. Carter White House. Washington, D. C., 13 July, 20 July, and 10 August 1978.

Biloncik, Ricardo. Embassy of Panama. Washington, D. C., 1 August 1978.

Blumenfeld, Michael, and William Crittendon. U. S. Department of Defense. Washington, D. C., 12 July 1978.

Bunker, Amb. Ellsworth. U. S. Department of State. Washington, D. C., 24 June and 25 June 1978.

Camaur, Richard. U. S. Department of State. Washington, D. C., 29 June 1978.

Cutter, Curt. U. S. Department of Defense. Washington, D. C., 28 June 1978.

Dockery, Robert. U. S. Senate Democratic Policy Committee. Washington, D. C., 18 July 1978.

Kozak, Michael. U. S. Department of State. Washington, D. C., 26 July 1978.

Linowitz, Amb. Sol M. U. S. Department of State. Washington, D. C., 3 August 1978.

McCall, Richard. Office of Senator Hubert H. Humphrey. Washington, D. C., 17 July 1978.

Moss, Ambler. U. S. Department of State. Washington, D. C., 29 June 1978.

Pastor, Robert. National Security Council. Washington, D. C., 25 June 1978.

Pezzullo, Lawrence. U. S. Department of State. Washington, D. C., 11 July 1978.

Rainwater, Elizabeth. Carter White House. Washington, D. C., 13 July 1978.

Thibodeau, Catherine, and Amb. David Popper. U. S. Department of State. Washington, D. C., 10 July 1978.

Wyrough, Richard. U. S. Department of State. Washington, D. C., 25 June 1978.

Manuscript Collections

American Legion, Washington, D. C.

Carter White House. Seen in Washington, D. C., and subsequently transferred to the Jimmy Carter Presidential Library, Atlanta, Ga.

Committee of Americans for the Canal Treaties, Inc., Washington, D. C.

Council of the Americas, Inc., New York, N. Y.

U. S. Chamber of Commerce, Washington, D. C.

U. S. Department of State, Bureau of Public Affairs, Washington, D. C.

Notes

All quotations from White House documents and from the interviews that Jeffrey D. Neuchterlein conducted for the White House in 1978 are from notes made by the author while working for the Carter White House and in his possession. All original documents are now deposited in the Jimmy Carter Presidential Library, Atlanta, Ga. Polling data are cited with the generous permission of the following organizations: ABC News/*Washington Post* (New York, N.Y.), Cambridge Survey Research (Washington, D.C.), CBS/*New York Times* (New York, N.Y.), The Field Institute (San Francisco, Calif.), The Gallup Organization (Princeton, N.J.), Louis Harris Associates (New York, N.Y.), NBC News (New York, N.Y.), Opinion Research Corporation (Princeton, N.J.), Roger Seasonwein Associates (New Rochelle, N.Y.), The Roper Organization (New York, N.Y.), and Skelly, Yankelovich and White (New York, N.Y.). Permission has also been gratefully received to quote from documents in the files of the Council of the Americas, Inc. (New York, N.Y.), and the U.S. Chamber of Commerce (Washington, D.C.).

Preface

1. Thomas A. Bailey, *The Man in the Street: The Impact of Public Opinion on American Foreign Policy* (New York: Macmillan, 1948), p. 5.
2. There were two separate Panama pacts. One, the so-called Neutrality Treaty, voted on 16 March 1978, defined a regime of perpetual neutrality for the Canal and prescribed U.S. defense and transit rights after the year 2000. The Panama Canal Treaty,

Notes

voted 18 April 1978, defined transitional administrative arrangements until the year 2000, when the Canal will pass into Panamanian hands.

3. See Godfrey Sperling Jr., "Carter's View of a Good Start That Brought a Bitter End," *Christian Science Monitor*, 26 January 1981, p. 23.

4. Jimmy Carter, *Keeping Faith: Memoirs of a President* (New York: Bantam, 1982), p. 152.

5. Interview with Robert Beckel, Washington, D.C., 23 June 1981.

6. Quoted in Frank Friedel, *Franklin D. Roosevelt: The Apprenticeship* (Boston: Little, Brown, 1952), p. 139.

7. David McCullough, undated letter to President Jimmy Carter.

8. Interview with Senator Frank Church, Washington, D.C., 20 May 1982.

9. Harlan Cleveland, *The Third Try at World Order: U.S. Policy for an Interdependent World* (Aspen, Colo.: Aspen Institute, 1976), p. 2.

10. See, for example, William Watts and Lloyd A. Free, *State of the Nation, III* (Lexington, Mass.: D.C. Heath, 1978), pp. 3ff.; John E. Rielly, "The American Mood: A Foreign Policy of Self-Interest," *Foreign Policy* no. 32 (Spring 1979): 74ff.; and Eugene R. Wittkopf and Michael Maggiotto, "Elites and Masses: A Comparative Analysis of Attitudes toward America's Role in the World" (Paper prepared for the Annual Convention of the International Studies Association, Philadelphia, 18-21 March 1981).

11. Rielly, "The American Mood," p. 74.

12. Wiliam Watts and Lloyd A. Free, "Nationalism, Not Isolationism," *Foreign Policy* no. 23 (Autumn 1976): 4.

13. Kevin Phillips, *Post-Conservative America: People, Politics and Ideology in a Time of Crisis* (New York: Random, 1982), pp. 27-28.

14. See chap. 4.

15. Letter from Congressman George Hansen, undated, in Committee of Americans for the Canal Treaties, Inc., files, Washington, D.C.

16. Advertisement, "There Is No Panama Canal. . . ." *Mt. Pleasant (Texas) Daily Tribune*, August 1977, p. 11. Committee of Americans for the Canal Treaties, Inc., files.

Chapter 1. *Historical Background: The Divergence of Policy and Opinion*

1. Quoted in Newton S. Manross, "This Partition of the Waters Has Served Its End," *New Republic*, 24 September 1977, p. 7.

2. See especially Dwight Carroll Miner, *The Fight for the Panama Route: The Story of the Spooner Act and the Hay-Herran Treaty* (New York: Columbia University Press, 1940), p. 8.

3. Ibid.

4. Quoted in Henry F. Pringle, *Theodore Roosevelt: A Biography* (New York: Harcourt, Brace, 1956), p. 233.

5. The history of the 1903 treaty is recounted in rich detail in David McCullough, *The Path between the Seas: The Creation of the Panama Canal, 1870–1914* (New York: Simon & Schuster, 1977); Miles P. DuVal, Jr., *Cadiz to Cathay: The Story of the Long Struggle for a Waterway across the American Isthmus* (Stanford: Stanford University Press, 1940); Philippe Bunau-Varilla, *Panama: The Creation, Destruction, and Resurrection* (London: Constable, 1913); Pringle, *Theodore Roosevelt*; Walter LaFeber, *The Panama Canal: The Crisis in Historical Perspective* (New York: Oxford University Press, 1978); and Russell Warren

Howe and Sarah Hays Trott, *The Power Peddlers: How Lobbyists Mold America's Foreign Policy* (Garden City, N.Y.: Doubleday, 1977).

6. In 1901 President William McKinley appointed a group of engineers, designated the "Walker Commission," to conduct a feasibility study of possible canal sites. The commissioners preferred the Panama route, but because of the exorbitant price the French company was asking for its rights and assets, they eventually recommended that the canal be dug through Nicaragua. In 1902 legislation authorizing the Nicaraguan route (the Hepburn Bill) was approved by an overwhelming majority in the House. The skillful lobbying of Bunau-Varilla helped produce congressional support in 1903 for an amendment that reversed the intent of the Hepburn Bill (the so-called Spooner Amendment), which instructed the president to build through Panama pending a reduction in the French company's asking price and a satisfactory treaty arrangement with Colombia, of which Panama was then a province.

The lobbying duties were shared by William Nelson Cromwell, a Wall Street attorney who was also retained by the reconstituted French company. According to one undocumented version of the story, the company had been quietly taken over by 1903 by American interests representing the financial house of J. P. Morgan and Company, which had close ties both to Cromwell's New York law firm (Sullivan and Cromwell) and to the Roosevelt administration. See Murray N. Rothbard, "The Treaty That Wall Street Wrote," *Inquiry* 20 (5 December 1977): 9-14.

7. As Bunau-Varilla put it, "My desire was to put into [Secretary of State] Hay's hands a document which would allow him to say to his contradictors what they ought to hear without him having to take the responsibility for it." Bunau-Varilla, *Panama: The Creation*, p. 374. During the ratification debate of 1977–78 the precise definition of "sovereignty" was debated endlessly. The term is used here in its broadest sense, to describe the transfer of complete jurisdictional rights to the United States. By the terms of the 1903 treaty the United States obtained rights in the Canal Zone that it "would possess and exercise if it were the sovereign of the territory. ..." U.S., Department of State, *Construction of a Ship Canal to Connect the Waters of the Atlantic and Pacific Ocean*, Treaty Series 31 (Washington, D.C., 1938), p. 2.

8. Bunau-Varilla, *Panama: The Creation*, p. 378.

9. Ibid., p. 384.

10. McCullough, *Path between the Seas*, pp. 396-97.

11. Quoted in Duval, *Cadiz to Cathay*, p. 384.

12. Quoted in McCullough, *Path between the Seas*, p. 387.

13. Bunau-Varilla, *Panama: The Creation*, p. 381. By the terms of the so-called Hay-Herran Convention of January 1903 the United States was to obtain a renewable 99-year lease over a zone six miles wide at an annual rental of $250,000. See Miner, *Fight for the Panama Route*, Appendix C, p. 413.

14. Bunau-Varilla, *Panama: The Creation*, p. 381.

15. Quoted in "An Introduction to the Panama Canal Treaties," (Washington, D.C.: Committee of Americans for the Canal Treaties, Inc., 1977), p. 9.

16. William D. McCain, *The United States and the Republic of Panama* (Durham: Duke University Press, 1937), p. 225.

17. In the Hull-Alfaro Treaty of 1936, the first of two revisions of the 1903 agreement, the United States renounced rights granted in 1903 to expropriate additional Panamanian territory for Canal use, to intervene unilaterally to defend the Canal, and to guarantee Panamanian independence, thereby ending Panama's status as an American protectorate. The treaty also increased the annuity to Panama to $430,000. See Lester Langley, "Negotiating New Treaties with Panama," *Hispanic American Historical*

Review 48 (May 1968): 220-33. The 1903 treaty was revised a second time in 1955; see note 24 below.

18. Raul A. Arias, "Epilogue: Letter from Panama," *Saturday Review*, 24 July 1976, p. 14.

19. The phrase is from Paul Ryan, *The Panama Canal Controversy: U.S. Diplomacy and Defense Interest* (Stanford: Hoover Institution Press, 1977), p. 34.

20. LaFeber, *The Panama Canal*, p. 94.

21. As one American writer put it, "The obligarchy is deceitful; to the people of Panama it expresses Yankeephobia while simultaneously courting the favor of the United States." Sheldon B. Liss, *The Canal: Aspects of United States-Panamanian Relations* (Notre Dame: University of Notre Dame Press, 1967), p. 8.

22. LaFeber, *The Panama Canal*, p. 95.

23. Donald Dozer, *Are We Good Neighbors? Three Decades of Inter-American Relations, 1930–1960* (Gainsville: University of Florida Press, 1959), p. 270.

24. The "Treaty of Mutual Cooperation and Understanding" of 1955 increased the annuity to Panama from $430,000 to close to $2 million, provided greater access for Panamanian businesses to the Canal Zone, enabled the government of Panama for the first time to tax its own citizens working in the Zone, and ceded property owned outside the Zone worth $4 million. See Lester Langley, "U.S.–Panamanian Relations since 1941," *Journal of Latin American Studies and World Affairs* 12 (July 1970): 345.

25. John Major, "Wasting Asset: The U.S. Re-Assessment of the Panama Canal, 1945–1949," *Journal of Strategic Studies* 3 (September 1980): 142. Moreover, in Egypt's nationalization of the Suez Canal in 1956 the Panamanians doubtless saw what *Fortune* magazine described as some "fundamental analogies." As Lester Langley writes, "The abrupt Egyptian seizure of the Suez Canal prompted many Panamanians to believe that a similar struggle against 'colonialism' in the isthmus was unfolding and that under pressure the American government might release its firm grip on Canal supervision." See Langley, "U.S.–Panamanian Relations since 1941," p. 348, and "America's Troubled Canal," *Fortune,* February 1957, pp. 129ff.

26. Stephen S. Rosenfeld, "The Panama Canal: State-of-Mind Diplomacy," *Washington Post*, 3 December 1976, p. A29.

27. The most comprehensive treatment of the evolution of U.S. policy toward the Canal is to be found in Margaret E. Scranton, "Changing United States Foreign Policy: Negotiating New Panama Canal Treaties, 1958–1978" (Ph.D diss. University of Pittsburgh, 1980), on which I have drawn substantially for this chapter.

28. Stephen S. Rosenfeld, "The Panama Negotiations—A Close-Run Thing," *Foreign Affairs* 54 (October 1975): 2.

29. Scranton, "Changing United States Foreign Policy," p. 86.

30. Eisenhower writes this of his visit to Panama: "I left Panama with a feeling of impending disaster. ... I doubt that a treaty guarantee of rights in perpetuity can be sustained. What seemed felicitous to Panamanians in 1903 ... may be unacceptable to their great-grand children tomorrow. Our stubborn insistence upon the legality of the original guarantee might in itself be cause for revolt and bloodshed." Milton Eisenhower, *The Wine Is Bitter: The United States and Latin America* (Garden City, N.Y.: Doubleday, 1963), pp. 217, 226.

31. Quoted in LaFeber, *The Panama Canal*, p. 122.

32. Quoted in Special Analysis, Report no. 3, "The Panama Canal—Its Past and Future," 88th Cong., 2d sess. (Washington, D.C.: American Enterprise Institute, 24 April 1964), p. 36.

33. Lawrence O. Ealy, *Yanqui Politics and the Isthmian Canal* (University Park: Pennsylvania State University Press, 1971), p. 112.

34. Eisenhower, *The Wine Is Bitter*, p. 222.

35. *Congressional Quarterly Almanac* (Washington, D.C.: Congressional Quarterly Services, 1960), p. 219.

36. Editorial, "Surrender in Panama," *Chicago Tribune*, 28 June 1967, p. 12; the latter quotation is from Testimony of Daniel Flood, U.S., Congress, Senate, Committee on Foreign Relations, *Panama Canal Treaties*, Part 2, 95th Cong., 1st sess., 1977, p. 371.

37. Testimony of Daniel Flood in U.S., Congress, House, Committee on Foreign Relations, Subcommittee on Inter-American Affairs, *United States Relations with Panama*, 86th Cong., 2d sess., 1960, p. 8.

38. Testimony of Daniel Flood, *Panama Canal Treaties*, Part 2, p. 371.

39. Testimony of Daniel Flood, *United States Relations with Panama*, p. 4.

40. Quoted in Thomas J. McIntyre, *The Fear Brokers* (New York: Pilgrim, 1979), p. 309.

41. Quoted in Ealy, *Yanqui Politics*, p. 113.

42. Admiral James S. Russell, quoted in *United States Relations with Panama*, p. 107.

43. Quoted in Ibid., p. 43.

44. Samuel Flagg Bemis, "A Way to Stop the Reds in Latin America," *U.S. News and World Report*, 28 December 1959, reprinted in U.S. Congress, House, Committee on Foreign Affairs, Subcommittee on Inter-American Affairs, *The Communist Threat in Latin America*, 86th Cong., 2d sess., 1960, p. 45.

45. *El Dia*, 12 December 1959, quoted in *United States Relations with Panama*, p. 39.

46. Testimony of Daniel Flood, *United States Relations with Panama*, p. 11.

47. Quoted in LaFeber, *The Panama Canal*, p. 128.

48. Ealy, *Yanqui Politics*, p. 112.

49. See, for example, Gordon Connell-Smith, *The United States and Latin America: An Historical Analysis of Inter-American Relations* (London: Heinemann, 1974), and Richard J. Walton, *The United States and Latin America* (New York: Seabury, 1972).

50. The School of the Americas was established in 1949 as a center for counterinsurgency training for Central and South American officers and enlisted men.

51. Members of the task force included Lincoln Gordon of Harvard, Robert Alexander of Rutgers, and historian Arthur Whitaker of Pennsylvania. The task force was chaired by New Dealer Adolf Berle. See Arthur M. Schlesinger, Jr., *A Thousand Days: John F. Kennedy in the White House* (Boston: Houghton Mifflin, 1965), p. 195.

52. See Scranton, "Changing United States Foreign Policy," pp. 136-76.

53. Eisenhower, *The Wine Is Bitter*, p. 215. Accounts of the 1964 riots are to be found in the president's own memoirs, Lyndon Baines Johnson, *The Vantage Point: Perspectives on the Presidency, 1963-1969* (New York: Holt, Rinehart & Winston, 1971); Philip Geyelin, *Lyndon B. Johnson and the World* (New York: Praeger, 1966); and Alfred Steinberg, *Sam Johnson's Boy: A Close-up of the President from Texas* (New York: Macmillan, 1968).

54. Scranton, "Changing United States Foreign Policy," p. 195.

55. Thomas M. Franck and Edward Weisband, "Panama Paralysis," *Foreign Policy* no. 21 (Winter 1975-76): 186.

56. Scranton, "Changing United States Foreign Policy," p. 247.

57. James J. Kilpatrick, "Latin America Today—High Stakes Poker?" (Philadelphia) *Evening Bulletin*, 4 October 1965, p. 21.

58. Quoted in *Congressional Quarterly Almanac* (1967), p. 1040. See also Benjamin Wells, "150 in House Oppose Three Panama Canal Treaties," *New York Times*, 9 August 1967, p. A16.

59. Rep. Walter S. Baring, cited in *Congressional Quarterly Almanac* (1967), p. 1040.

60. Quoted in Russell Freeburg, "Terms Found Shocking by GOP Leader," *Chicago Tribune*, 8 July 1967, p. 1.

61. Editorial, "Asking for It," *Chicago Tribune*, 8 July 1967, p. 10.

62. Quoted in ibid.

63. Quoted in Langley, "U.S.-Panamanian Relations since 1941," p. 363.

64. Congressman Daniel J. Flood, in 89th Cong., 1st sess. (24 September 1965), 118 *Congressional Record*: 25156.

65. James J. Reynolds, quoted in U.S., Congress, House, Committee on Merchant Marine and Fisheries, Subcommittee on the Panama Canal, *Panama Canal Treaty Negotiations*, 92d Cong., 2d sess. 1972, pp. 265-66.

66. Ibid., p. 266.

67. Jeffrey D. Neuchterlein interview with Sol Linowitz, Washington, D.C., 8 August 1978.

68. Quoted in *Panama Canal Treaty Negotiations*, p. 21.

69. Quoted in *Panama Canal Treaties*, Part 2, p. 375.

70. As the *New Republic*'s TRB [Richard Strout] wrote in 1975, "Omar Torrijos keeps volatile students in check but it is agreed that if he desired he could turn on violence like a faucet." TRB, "Letting Go," *New Republic*, 9 August 1975, p. 2.

71. Quoted in Scranton, "Changing United States Foreign Policy," p. 344.

72. Larry K. Storrs, "Panama Canal," *Congressional Research Service* Issue Brief no. IB74138 (11 March 1976), p. 13.

73. Carlos Andrés Pérez quoted in Paul B. Ryan, *The Panama Canal Controversy: U.S. Diplomacy and Defense Interests* (Stanford: Hoover Institution Press, 1977), p. 117.

74. Rosenfeld, "The Panama Negotiations," p. 4.

75. LaFeber, *The Panama Canal*, p. 184.

76. Rosenfeld, "The Panama Negotiations," p. 5.

77. Quoted in Scranton, "Changing United States Foreign Policy," p. 391. Neither volume of the Kissinger memoirs—*White House Years* and *Years of Upheaval* (Boston: Little, Brown, 1979, 1982)—treats the subject of the Canal negotiations.

78. Quoted in Richard Hudson, "Storm over the Canal," *New York Times Magazine*, 16 May 1976, p. 79.

79. Named after secretary Kissinger and Panamanian foreign minister Juan Tack.

80. Jeffrey D. Neuchterlein, "The 1978 Panama Canal Treaties: The Record of the Carter Administration" (Paper submitted to the White House, 4 April 1979), p. 5.

81. Denison Kitchel, *The Truth about the Panama Canal* (New Rochelle: Arlington House, 1978), p. 80.

82. "Just how broad the opposition was was a question we were asking ourselves at the time," commented Ellsworth Bunker on Ford administration efforts in 1975–76 to size up the political landscape. Interview with Ellsworth Bunker, Washington, D.C., 25 May 1982.

83. Interview with Robert Pastor, Washington, D.C., 19 May 1982.

84. Editorial, "Giving up the Canal to Save It," *Newsday*, 12 August 1977, p. 17.

85. Rosenfeld, "The Panama Negotiations," p. 8.

86. Quoted in Franck and Weisband, "Panama Paralysis," p. 168.

87. Strom Thurmond, "For Perpetual U.S. Control over the Panama Canal," *New York Times*, 7 May 1974, p. 45.

88. U.S., Congress, House, "Foreign Relations Authorization Act, Fiscal Year 1977," *House Miscellaneous Reports on Public Bills IX*, 94th Cong., 2d sess., 25 June 1976, p. 5.

89. Quoted in James P. Lucier, "Panama Question: An Alternative to U.S. De-featism," *National Review*, 12 September 1975, p. 989.

90. LaFeber, *The Panama Canal*, pp. 187-88.

91. Robert Pastor, "Coping with Congress's Foreign Policy," *Foreign Service Journal* 52 (1 December 1975): 15ff.

92. The reticence at State was in keeping with the department's traditional practice of consulting with the Senate only *after* treaties were formally submitted for ratification.

93. "Foreign Relations Authorization Act," *House Miscellaneous Reports IX*, p. 38.

94. Pastor, "Coping with Congress's Foreign Policy," pp. 17-18.

95. Quoted in Ryan, *Panama Canal Controversy*, p. 62.

96. Ibid., p. 56.

97. Cited in Bureau of Public Affairs (Department of State) memorandum, 12 August 1977, p. 2. From notes in the author's possession.

98. Ryan, *Panama Canal Controversy*, p. 56.

99. Quoted in McIntyre, *The Fear Brokers*, p. 120.

100. Quoted in Jules Witcover, *Marathon: The Pursuit of the Presidency, 1972-1976* (New York: Viking, 1977), p. 402.

101. Kitchel, *The Truth about the Panama Canal*, p. 27.

102. TRB, "Letting Go," p. 2.

Chapter 2. *The End of Containment: The Foreign Policy of Jimmy Carter*

1. Jimmy Carter, *Keeping Faith: Memoirs of a President* (New York: Bantam, 1982), p. 155.

2. *The Presidential Campaign 1976*, Vol. I, Part I (Washington, D.C., 1978), p. 82.

3. Jimmy Carter, statement before the Foreign Policy Association, New York, 23 June 1976, quoted in "Exerpts from Carter's Speech and His Replies," *New York Times*, 24 June 1976, p. A22.

4. Bernard Gwertzman, "Some Major Differences," *New York Times*, 8 October 1976, p. A19.

5. Marquis Childs, "Disquiet over Carter's Intentions," *Washington Post*, 16 November 1976, p. A15.

6. Ibid., p. 8.

7. *Weekly Compilation of Presidential Documents* 12 (11 October 1976): 1456, my emphases.

8. Carter, *Keeping Faith*, p. 155.

9. Presidential Review Memorandum NSC 1, 21 January 1977, p. 1.

10. Quoted in Don Oberdorfer, "U. S., Panama Will Seek Early Accord on Treaty," *Washington Post*, 1 February 1977, p. A4.

11. "OAS Speech," *Congressional Quarterly*, 23 April 1977, p. 761.

12. The president himself indicates that "he had long had a special interest in Latin America, even as governor" and that he was "familiar with the Linowitz Commission report," but that it was probably not until the 12 January meeting with congressional leaders "that I decided to move so aggressively." Jimmy Carter, letter to the author, 23 January 1984.

13. Jeffrey D. Neuchterlein interview with Sol M. Linowitz, Washington, D.C., 3 August 1978.

14. Richard Ullman, "Trilateralism: 'Partnership' for What?" *Foreign Affairs* 55 (October 1976): 4, 13.

15. John B. Oakes, "The Trilateral Way," *New York Times*, 10 April 1980, p. A27.

16. C. Fred Bergsten, quoted in Jeremiah Novak, "The Trilateral Connection," *Atlantic*, July 1977, p. 57.

17. Christopher Lydon, "Jimmy Carter Revealed: He's a Rockefeller Republican," *Atlantic*, July 1977, p. 57.

18. The term is used by Michael Mandelbaum and William Schneider in "The New Internationalism: Public Opinion and American Foreign Policy," in Kenneth A. Oye et al., eds., *Eagle Entangled: U.S. Foreign Policy in a Complex World* (New York: Longman, 1973), pp. 91–122.

19. D. C. Watt draws a useful distinction between the "east coast Anglo-Saxon Protestant bankers and lawyers" who comprised the old Establishment and the more expansive "community" of full-time "professors, congressional aides, Foundation and 'think-tank' experts" that has superceded the old Establishment and from which this younger generation of scholars was largely drawn. Watt, "A Return to Americanism? The Foreign Policy of President Carter," *Political Quarterly* 48 (October–December 1977): 431.

20. Zbigniew Brzezinski, quoted in Carl Gershman, "The Rise and Fall of the New Foreign Policy Establishment," *Commentary* 70 (July 1980): 14.

21. [George Kennan], "The Sources of Soviet Conduct," *Foreign Affairs* 25 (July 1947): 566–82.

22. Marshal Schulman, "What Does Security Mean Today?" *Foreign Affairs* 49 (July 1971): 607.

23. Warren Manshel, "Judas and the Scapegoat," *Foreign Policy* no. 19 (Summer 1975): 147.

24. Gershman, "The Rise and Fall," pp. 13–24.

25. Samuel P. Huntington and Warren Demian Manshel, "Why Foreign Policy?" *Foreign Policy* no. 1 (Winter 1970–71): 3.

26. Stanley Hoffmann, quoted in Gershman, "The Rise and Fall," p. 14.

27. A representative sample of the work produced by this group of writers includes Stanley Hoffmann, *Primacy or World Order? American Foreign Policy since the Cold War* (New York: McGraw-Hill, 1978); Richard Rosecrance, ed., *America as an Ordinary Country: U. S. Foreign Policy and the Future* (Ithaca: Cornell University Press, 1976); Robert Keohane and Joseph Nye, *Power and Interdependence* (Boston: Little, Brown, 1976); Seyom Brown, *New Forces in World Politics* (Washington, D. C.: Brookings, 1974); Alastair Buchan, *The End of the Postwar Era: A New Balance of World Power* (London: Weidenfeld & Nicholson, 1974); George Kennan, *The Cloud of Danger: Current Realities of American Foreign Policy* (Boston: Little, Brown, 1977); Zbigniew Brzezinski, *Between Two Ages: America's Role in the Techtronic Era* (New York: Viking, 1970).

28. Stanley Hoffmann, "The Uses of American Power," *Foreign Affairs* 56 (October 1977): 28.

29. Zbigniew Brzezinski, "U.S. Foreign Policy: The Search for Focus," *Foreign Affairs* 52 (July 1973): 721.

30. Stanley Hoffmann, "Choices," *Foreign Policy* no. 12 (Autumn 1973): 7.

31. William Bundy, "International Security Today," *Foreign Affairs* 53 (October 1974): 24. The consummate expression of such linkage comes from one latter-day practitioner of containment, Ronald Reagan: "Let's not delude ourselves. The Soviet Union underlies all the unrest that is going on. If they weren't engaged in this game of dominoes, there wouldn't be any hot spots in the world." Quoted in Karen Elliott House, "Re-

agan's World: Republican's Policies Stress Arms Buildup, a Firm Line to Soviet," *Wall Street Journal*, 3 June 1980, p. 1.

32. Richard J. Barnet, *Roots of War* (New York: Atheneum, 1972), p. 335.

33. Brown, *New Forces in World Politics*, p. 117.

34. Arnold Wolfers, *Discord and Collaboration: Essays on International Politics* (Baltimore: Johns Hopkins Press, 1962), p. 73.

35. Joseph Nye, "American Power and Foreign Policy," *New York Times*, 7 July 1976, p. A33.

36. Hoffmann, *Primacy or World Order*, p. 115.

37. President's Commission for a National Agenda for the Eighties, *The United States and the World Community in the Eighties*, Report of the Panel on the United States and the World Community (Washington, D. C., 1980), p. 5.

38. Gershman, "The Rise and Fall," p. 21.

39. Address by President Jimmy Carter at the University of Notre Dame, 22 May 1977, reprinted in *Weekly Compilation of Presidential Documents* 13 (30 May 1977): 773–79.

40. Richard J. Barnet, "Carter's Patchwork Doctrine," *Harper's*, August 1977, p. 27.

41. Ibid., p. 28.

42. Stanley Hoffmann, "A View from at Home: The Perils of Incoherence," *Foreign Affairs* 57 (America and the World, 1978):464–65.

43. Peter Jay, "Regionalism as Geopolitics," *Foreign Affairs* 58 (America and the World, 1979): 489.

44. President Carter, Notre Dame address, p. 775. As Brzezinski describes it, "a traditional international foreign policy based largely on maneuver among the more powerful nation-states, a policy devoid of moral concerns for the less fortunate majority that inhabits this globe, will simply not suffice for shaping the future." Zbigniew Brzezinski, "The Deceptive Structure of Peace." *Foreign Policy* no. 14 (Spring 1974): 55.

45. See, for example, President Carter, Notre Dame address, p. 775.

46. Ibid.

47. Thomas L. Hughes, "Carter and the Management of Contradiction," *Foreign Policy* no. 31 (Summer 1978): 37.

48. President Carter, Notre Dame address, p. 775.

49. Hughes, "Carter and the Management of Contradiction," p. 43.

50. Jay, "Regionalism as Geopolitics," p. 489.

51. Hedley Bull, "Kissinger: The Primacy of Geopolitics," *International Affairs* 56 (Summer 1980): 484.

52. Jay, "Regionalism as Geopolitics," p. 488.

53. Kissinger, quoted in Robert Sutherland Litwak, *Detente and the Nixon Doctrine: American Foreign Policy and the Pursuit of Stability, 1969–1976* (Cambridge: Cambridge University Press, 1984), p. 3.

54. Ibid.

55. Michael Howard, *War and the Liberal Conscience* (London: Temple Smith, 1978), p. 342.

56. Litwak, *Detente and the Nixon Doctrine*, p. 191.

57. Ibid.

58. Kenneth A. Oye, "The Domain of Choice: International Constraints and Carter Administration Foreign Policy," in Oye et al., eds., *Eagle Entangled*, p. 19.

59. Ibid.

60. Polling results reported by William Watts and Lloyd Free indicate that between 1974 and 1976—that is, on the eve of the Carter presidency—there was a discernible

increase in public anxiety about the country's role in the world, a heightened sense of nationalism, and an "enhanced desire for national security" reflected in "a sharply increased willingness to support defense and military expenditures." Watts and Free, *State of the Nation III* (Lexington, Mass.: D. C. Heath, 1978), p. 203. Attitude surveys commissioned by the Chicago Council on Foreign Relations in 1978 confirm the growing apprehension about Soviet power and concern over the "declining position of the United States as the preeminent global power." *American Public Opinion and U.S. Foreign Policy* (Chicago: Chicago Council on Foreign Relations, 197), p. 4; John E. Reilly, "The American Mood: A Foreign Policy of Self-Interest, "*Foreign Policy* no. 32 (Spring 1979): 74.

61. President Carter, Notre Dame address, p. 774.

62. Rosecrance, *America as an Ordinary Country*, p. 11.

63. Hughes, "Carter and the Management of Contradiction," p. 55.

64. TRB [Richard Strout], "A Man, a Plan, a Canal: Panama," *New Republic*, 3 September 1977, p. 38.

65. Alan Howard, "The Real Latin American Policy," *Nation*, 15 October 1977, p. 365.

66. Ibid.

67. *The Americas in a Changing World: A Report of the Commission on United States-Latin American Relations* (New York: Quadrangle, 1974), and *The United States and Latin America: Next Steps. A Second Report by the Commission on United States-Latin American Relations* (New York: Center for Inter-American Relations, 1976).

68. *The Americas in a Changing World*, p. 4.

69. Abraham F. Lowenthal, "The United States and Latin America: Ending the Hegemonic Presumption," *Foreign Affairs* 55 (October 1976): 206.

70. *The Americas in a Changing World*, p. 18.

71. Fred Bergsten, "U.S.-Latin American Relations to 1980: The International Framework and Some Possible New Approaches," in *The Americas in a Changing World*, p. 189.

72. *The Americas in a Changing World*, pp. 11–12.

73. Ibid., p. 23.

74. *The United States and Latin America: Next Steps*, p. 1.

75. Lowenthal, "The United States and Latin America," p. 210.

76. *The United States and Latin America: Next Steps*, p. 14.

77. *The Americas in a Changing World*, p. 43.

78. *The United States and Latin America: Next Steps*, p. 4, my emphases.

79. *The Americas in a Changing World*, p. 28.

80. *The United States and Latin America: Next Steps*, p. 5.

81. *The Americas in a Changing World*, p. 30.

82. *The United States and Latin America: Next Steps*, p. 5.

83. Ibid.

84. Linowitz, quoted in Jeffrey D. Neuchterlein, "The 1978 Panama Canal Treaties: The Record of the Carter Administration" (Paper submitted to the White House, 4 April 1979), pp. 10–11.

85. Philip Wheaton, "Trilateralism and the Caribbean: Tying up 'Loose Strings' in the Hemisphere," in Holly Sklar, ed., *Trilateralism: The Trilateral Commission and Elite Planning for World Management* (Boston: South End, 1980), p. 407.

86. *The Americas in a Changing World*, p. 13.

87. Abraham F. Lowenthal, "Jimmy Carter and Latin America: A New Era of Small Change," in Oye et al., *Eagle Entangled*, p. 291.

88. Ibid.
89. "OAS Speech," pp. 760–61.
90. Lowenthal, "The United States and Latin America," p. 210.
91. Joseph Kraft, "Righting Our Foreign Wrongs, and Beyond," *Washington Post*, 10 March 1977, p. A23.
92. Lowenthal, "Jimmy Carter and Latin America," p. 291.
93. Neuchterlein interview with Linowitz.
94. The Platt Amendment to the Cuban Constitution of 1902 gave the United States broadly defined rights to intervene in the domestic affairs of Cuba. Its revocation by Franklin D. Roosevelt in 1934 signaled a new era in U.S. relations with Latin America.
95. Walter LaFeber, *The Panama Canal: The Crisis in Historical Perspective* (New York: Oxford University Press, 1978), p. 194.
96. Interview with Robert Beckel, Washington, D.C., 23 June 1981.
97. Neuchterlein interview with Linowitz.
98. Carter, *Keeping Faith*, p. 180.
99. Interview with Beckel.

Chapter 3. *Organizing for Victory*

1. Neuchterlein interview with Sol M. Linowitz, Washington, D.C., 3 August 1978.
2. Margaret E. Scranton, "Changing U.S. Foreign Policy: Negotiating New Panama Canal Treaties, 1958–1978" (Ph.D. diss., University of Pittsburgh, 1980), p. 422.
3. Neuchterlein interview with Linowitz.
4. One exception, involving the handling of a last-minute reservation sponsored by Arizona senator Dennis DeConcini, is described later in this chapter. The second is discussed in chapter 6.
5. Hay, quoted in Nicholas Von Hoffman, "The Panama Gamble," *Washington Post*, 22 September 1977, p. A35.
6. See Carolyn Teague, "Ratification of the Panama Canal Agreements Toughest Fight since Versailles," *Congressional Quarterly*, 14 January 1978, p. 54.
7. For a detailed discussion of polling on Panama see chapter 4.
8. Institute for Conflict and Policy Studies, "Press Release," 2 August 1977, p. 2. According to the institute's report, "Nearly all insist on firm Treaty provisions to protect U.S. security and commercial interests during the life of a new treaty as a *sine qua non*. They favor Treaty clauses that clearly guarantee the U.S. right to defend the Canal and to insure unimpeded and nondiscriminant U.S. military and commercial access to the Canal during and beyond the Treaty's duration." As the treaty debate began, there was serious question whether the wording of the August draft would accommodate these concerns.
9. I. M. Destler, "Treaty Troubles: Versailles in Reverse," *Foreign Policy* no. 33 (Winter 1978–79): 523.
10. A discussion of the "radically redistributed . . . power of government" may be found in Thomas M. Franck and Edward Weisband, *Foreign Policy by Congress* (New York: Oxford University Press, 1979). The quotation is from p. 7. The authors suggest that the Vietnam War marked the beginning of the fourth period of congressional dominance in American politics. The first, a reaction to the consolidation of executive power under Andrew Jackson, lasted from the presidency of Martin Van Buren (1837) until the Civil War. The second began after the Civil War administration of Lincoln and Johnson and extended until the end of the century. The third began during the

last half of Woodrow Wilson's second term and lasted until the New Deal of Franklin D. Roosevelt in 1933. The fourth, like the two preceding, followed a major American war. The authors suggest that the institutional changes in the post-Vietnam period may make the resumption of congressional power a permanent fixture in American politics. See also Cecil V. Crabbe and Pat Holt, *Invitation to Struggle: Congress, the President and Foreign Policy* (Washington, D.C.: Congressional Quarterly Press, 1980); Lee H. Hamilton and Michael H. Van Deusen, "Making the Separation of Powers Work," *Foreign Affairs* 57 (Autumn 1978): 17-39; and Douglas J. Bennet, Jr., "Congress in Foreign Policy: Who Needs It?" ibid., pp. 40-50.

11. Terence Smith, "Carter Nears End of Long Drive for Canal Treaties," *New York Times*, 1 February 1978, p. A4.

12. David Broder, "Straight Shooting on the Canal Treaties," *Washington Post*, 5 February 1978, p. B7.

13. Michael Mandelbaum, "Big Ditch Debate," *New York Times Book Review*, 4 February 1978, p. 11.

14. Editorial, "Soft Selling the Treaties," *Atlantic*, December 1977, p. 16; "A Breakthrough with Panama?" *Washington Post*, 18 May 1977, p. A14.

15. Joseph Aragon, memorandum to Hamilton Jordon, 30 November 1977.

16. Neuchterlein interview with Lawrence Pezzullo, Washington, D.c., 11 July 1978.

17. Jimmy Carter, *Keeping Faith: Memoirs of a President* (New York: Bantam, 1982), p. 164.

18. Martha Shirk, "Hard Sell on Panama Treaty Begins," *St. Louis Post Dispatch*, 21 August 1977, reprinted in U.S. Department of State, *ARA News Roundup*, 26 August 1977, p. 41.

19. Ibid.

20. Murrey Marder, "White House Preparing for Battle over Treaty," *Los Angeles Times*, 11 August 1977, p. 1.

21. Jordan, quoted in James T. Wooten, "White House Lobbying to Change Opinions on Canal," *New York Times*, 13 October 1977, p. A67.

22. Interview with Dan C. Tate, Washington, D.C., 20 May 1982.

23. Denison Kitchel, *The Truth about the Panama Canal* (New Rochelle: Arlington House, 1978), p. 178.

24. "A Panama Production," *Newsweek*, 19 September 1977, p. 46.

25. "Now for the Hard Part," *Time*, 19 September 1977, p. 20.

26. "Excerpts from Statements by Carter and Torrijos," *New York Times*, 8 September 1977, p. A10.

27. *Weekly Compilation of Presidential Documents* (12 September 1977): 1297.

28. Baker, quoted in "Carter's High Risk Move," *U.S. News and World Report*, 12 September 1977, p. 18.

29. Philip Nicolaides, "The Selling of the Panama Canal Treaties," 9 December 1977.

30. Morrie Ryskind, "The Panama Canal Treaties and Shades of Munich," *Human Events*, 17 September 1977, p. 13.

31. Laurence W. Beilenson, "An Open Letter to Senator S. I. Hayakawa Re. the Panama Canal Treaties," *Battle Line*, October–November 1977, p. 13.

32. "Carter's High Risk Move," p. 18.

33. Neuchterlein interview with Curt Cutter, Washington, D.C., 28 June 1978.

34. Interview with William Rhatican, Washington, D.C., 24 May 1983.

35. The task force was staffed by representatives from the White House congressional liaison, political, and press offices and from the State and Defense departments.

36. Karen DeYoung, "State Dept. Is 'Selling' Canal Treaties," *Washington Post*, 26 February 1978, p. A1.

37. Cited in Bureau of Public Affairs (Department of State) memorandum, 26 September 1977. From notes in the author's possession.

38. The administration's priority list included the following states: Kentucky, Pennsylvania, Delaware, Florida, Indiana, Tennessee, New Hampshire, Oklahoma, Georgia, West Virginia, Montana, Vermont, and Arizona.

39. Interview with Dean DeBuck, Washington, D.C., 2 April 1982.

40. Bureau of Public Affairs memorandum, 26 September 1977.

41. As *Time* noted in January, "Suddenly everyone was headed somewhere to talk about the Panama Canal treaties." "Squaring off on the Canal" *Time*, 30 January 1978, p. 25.

42. Interview with Landon Butler, Washington, D.C., 22 October 1981.

43. Carter, *Keeping Faith*, p. 162. A typical delegation, from Minnesota, included the commander of the Minnesota Veterans of Foreign Wars, a cross section of leading clerics of all faiths, a mayor, the chairman of the Mayo Clinic, the chairman of the University of Minnesota's Board of Regents, three college presidents, the president of the National Farmers Union, executives of major corporations including Pillsbury and Control Data, and, for good measure, baseball player Rod Carew of the Minnesota Twins.

44. Pat Ordovensky, "White House Meeting Quells State Group's Panama Doubts," (Wilmington) *Morning News*, 29 September 1977.

45. "Southerners Are Briefed on Canal Treaties," *St. Petersburg Times*, 31 August 1977.

46. John Herbers, "Kentucky Is Focus of Key Battle over Canal Treaties," *New York Times*, 15 January 1978.

47. Don Campbell, "Carter Courts Opinion Shapers on Canal Treaties," *Nashville Banner*, 4 November 1977, p. 11. See also Jim Blair, "Meeting with President Changes Mind," *Kentucky Post*, 26 August 1977; Ed Ryan, "Canal Briefing 'Impressive' to Kentuckians," *Louisville Courrier-Journal*, 24 August 1977; and Charles Osolin, "Some Treaty Foes Change Position," *Atlanta Constitution*, 31 August 1977.

48. Another forerunner of the Panama committee was chaired by elder statesman Henry L. Stimson to help mobilize public and congressional support for the Marshall Plan during the Truman administration.

49. Hamilton Jordan, memorandum to President Jimmy Carter, 30 August 1977.

50. Richard Rovere, "Notes on the Establishment in America," in Rovere, *The American Establishment and Other Reports, Opinions and Speculations* (New York: Harcourt, Brace, 1962), p. 10.

51. Advertisements for the Committee of Americans for the Canal Treaties, Inc. (COACT), appeared in the *New York Times, Washington Post, Los Angeles Times*, and *Baltimore Sun* on 1 November 1977.

52. Landon Butler, quoted in "The Great Canal Debate," *Time*, 20 February 1978, p. 19.

53. Jeff Stein and Stu Cohen, "The Selling of the Canal Treaties," *Boston Phoenix*, 13 December 1977, p. 42.

54. A complete list of citizens' committee names maybe found in the committee's printed handbook, *COACT: The Bi-Partisan Citizens Committee of Americans for the Canal Treaties* (Washington, D.C.: 1977), p. vii.

55. By the end COACT did send several direct-mail appeals totaling over 300,000

pieces. By contrast, bulk mailings from the Right totaled an estimated 5 to 10 million letters.

56. See Walter S. Johnson, *The Battle against Isolation* (Chicago: University of Chicago Press, 1944); Wayne S. Cole, *America First: The Battle against Intervention, 1940–1941* (Madison: University of Wisconsin Press, 1953); and John E. Wiltz, *From Isolation to War 1931–1941* (New York: Crowell, 1968).

57. Mark Lincoln Chadwin, *The Warhawks: American Interventionists before Pearl Harbor* (New York: Norton, 1968), p. 2. Another ally in the fight for ratification was Panama's UN Mission in New York, which hired a New York public relations firm to produce and mail a package of treaty material to a targeted audience of politicians, journalists, academics, and businessmen. In addition the Panamanian Embassy in Washington joined the issue in a limited fashion, sponsoring dinners for Senate staff members and scheduling Panamanian finance minister Nicholas Barletta into prestigious forums across the country to counter right-wing allegations of Marxist influence in Panama. Ultimately, the capacity to help was limited, as one embassy official conceded: "We were very conscious of the fact that we could not try to sell the treaties ourselves. . . . We knew it was impossible for a Panamanian to sell the treaties to an American because the treaties were already perceived as something on which the Americans were already giving in without getting anything in return. We were always sure that we were right, that we had a just cause. But one American will buy this type of merchandise only from another American, not from a Panamanian." Interview with Eduardo Ferrer, Washington, D.C., 3 May 1978. See Don Oberdorfer, "Panama Plans Intensive Public Effort to Push New Treaty," *Washington Post*, 24 March 1977, p. A2.

58. I. M. Destler, "Learning from Panama: An Analysis of Executive-Congressional Relations," *Background Paper* no. 2 (Washington, D.C.: Carnegie Endowment for International Peace, 11 June 1978), p. 10.

59. Baker quoted in Jeffrey D. Neuchterlein, "The 1978 Panama Canal Treaties: The Record of the Carter Administration" (Paper submitted to the White House, 4 April 1979), p. 76.

60. Cited in Bureau of Public Affairs (Department of State) memorandum, 24 May 1978. From notes in the author's possession.

61. Carter, *Keeping Faith*, p. 164.

62. Karen DeYoung, "Baker Says Canal Pacts Could Pass," *Washington Post*, 8 November 1977, p. A1. See also Robert G. Kaiser, "42 Senators Join Panama Pilgrimage," *Washington Post*, 10 January 1978, p. A1.

63. Quoted in Stein and Cohen, "The Selling of the Canal Treaties," p. 42.

64. Neuchterlein interview with Robert Beckel, Washington, D.C., 20 July 1978.

65. Neuchterlein interview with Ambler Moss, Washington, D.C., 29 June 1978. After the treaties moved to the floor, the administration expanded the mechanism for building close working relationships on the Hill by establishing a command center in a Capitol office manned by four State and Defense Department officials (the so-called Gang of Four). As a source of substantive information on the treaties, it became an effective complement to the lobbying effort, which, by March, was being operated out of the vice-president's Capitol office. As "Gang" leader Ambler Moss described it, one of the major advantages of being able to work "side-by-side" with Senate staff was "our having great credibility with them . . . and . . . our greater ability to understand what senators needed in what form."

66. See Destler, "Learning from Panama," p. 2.

67. U.S., Department of State, Bureau of Public Affairs, Office of Media Services, "Treaty Concerning the Permanent Neutrality and Operation of the Panama Canal,"

in *Texts of Treaties Relating to the Panama Canal*, Selected Documents No. 6A (September 1977), p. 17.

68. U.S., Congress, House, Committee on Merchant Marine and Fisheries, *New Panama Canal Treaty*, 95th Cong., 1st sess., 1977, p. 53.

69. U.S., Congress, Senate, Committee on Foreign Relations, *Panama Canal Treaties, Part 1*, 95th Cong., 1st sess., 1977, p. 30.

70. Carlos López-Guevara, quoted in U.S. Department of State cable issued with "News from U.S. Senator Bob Dole" (press release), 4 October 1977.

71. Carlos López-Guevara, quoted in Scranton, "Changing United States Foreign Policy," pp. 505, 506.

72. Ibid., p. 503.

73. The visiting delegation included Senators Church, Goldwater, Baker, Byrd, Case, and Sparkman.

74. "News from U.S. Senator Bob Dole."

75. Neuchterlein interview with Michael Kozak, Washington, D.C., 26 July 1978.

76. Herbert Hansell, memorandum to Warren Christopher, U.S. Department of State, Washington, D.C., 5 October 1977, quoted in Neuchterlein, "The 1978 Panama Canal Treaties, pp. 94-95.

77. With respect to the rights of priority passage, the leaders agreed that warships and auxiliary vessels would be assured transit through the Canal "as quickly as possible, without any impediment, with expedited treatment, and in case of need or emergency, to go to the head of the line of vessels in order to transit the Canal rapidly." U.S., Congress, Senate, Committee on Foreign Relations, *Senate Debate on the Panama Canal Treaties: A Compendium of Major Statements, Documents, Record Votes and Relevant Events*, 96th Cong., 1st sess., 1979, pp. 7-8.

78. Byrd, quoted in Destler, "Learning from Panama," p. 5.

79. Ibid., p. 7.

80. Church, quoted in Neuchterlein, "The 1978 Panama Canal Treaties," p. 108.

81. Sparkman, quoted in ibid., p. 100. See also *Senate Debate on the Panama Canal Treaties*, pp. 9-10.

82. *Senate Debate on the Panama Canal Treaties*, pp. 9-10.

83. The index was significant but, as chapter 4 demonstrates, highly misleading.

84. Complete polling results are discussed in chapter 4.

85. The White House count on 30 November 1977 showed 45 senators solidly committed to ratification, with 10 others leaning in favor. Nine were undecided, while 35 were either opposed or leaning against. Figures from Neuchterlein, "The 1978 Panama Canal Treaties," p. 119.

86. By the end the administration was successful in gaining the support of 11 Southern and border-state senators, including Baker (R.-Tenn.), Bellmon (R.-Okla.), Bentsen (D.-Tx.), Bumpers (D.-Ark.), Byrd (D.-W. Va.), Hollings (D.-S.C.), Huddleston (D.-Ky.), Morgan (D.-N.C.), Nunn (D.-Ga.), Sasser (D.-Tenn.), and Talmadge (D.-Ga.).

87. In addition to the minority leader Republican senators Case (N.J.), Javits (N.Y.), Pearson (Kans.), and Percy (Ill.) voted in the majority. The lone dissenter was Republican Robert Griffin of Michigan.

88. Carter, *Keeping Faith*, pp. 168, 176.

89. Neuchterlein, "The 1978 Panama Canal Treaties," p. 128.

90. James Reston, "The Voting Trade-Offs," *New York Times*, 21 September 1977, p. A19. One senator described the process more bluntly to a senate staff aide following the favorable report of the Foreign Relations Committee: "It ain't this that's going to

get this treaty ratified. Jimmy Carter is going to get this treaty not because of arguments but because of the deals. Without them it can't be done." Interview with Robert Dockery, Washington, D. C., 25 May 1982. As Congressional chief Frank Moore noted later: "By the end they were coming in with lists of demands, four or five senators. We had to put an informal task force to work on it. It was mostly appointments, weather stations, small projects, loose ends mostly but it kept us busy. As soon as one list was done they'd come back with another. Once this kind of thing starts you can't stop it." Telephone interview with Frank Moore, 12 January 1984.

91. Crabbe and Holt, *Invitation to Struggle*, p. 82. See also Martin Tolchin, "White House Woos Holdouts on Canal with Offers of Help," *New York Times*, 14 March 1978, p. A1, and "Let's Make a Deal," *Wall Street Journal*, 16 March 1978, p. 20.

92. Quoted in John Dillin, "How Carter Woos Votes on Panama," *Christian Science Monitor*, 13 February 1978, p. 1.

93. Quoted in Tom Fiedler, "How Senator Stone Switched on Panama Canal Issue," *Miami Herald*, 7 February 1978; U. S. Department of State, *ARA News Roundup*, Supplement no. 11 (13 February 1978), p. 24.

94. Quoted in Fiedler, "How Senator Stone Switched on Panama Canal Issue."

95. John Goshko, "The Realpolitik of the Panama Canal Treaties," *Washington Post*, 2 February 1978, p. A16.

96. For texts see "Text of Senate Changes in Pact," *New York Times*, 17 March 1978, p. A12.

97. "Panama: A Big Win," *Newsweek*, 27 March 1978, p. 42. See also William J. Lanouette, "The Plight of the Uncommitted on the Panama Canal Treaties," *National Journal*, 11 March 1978, pp. 385–87.

98. Quoted in Donnie Radcliffe, "Panama Question Mark," *Washington Post*, 14 April 1978, p. B4.

99. Linda Charleton, "New Senator with Knack for Rocking a Boat," *New York Times*, 13 April 1978, p. A10.

100. In addition to Byrd attendees at the luncheons included Vice President Mondale, Warren Christopher, Senate majority whip Alan Cranston of California, and cofloor leader on the Panama treaties Frank Church of Idaho, plus undecided senators Deconcini, Wendell Ford of Kentucky, Russell Long of Louisiana, Sam Nunn of Georgia, and Herman Talmadge of Georgia.

101. Quoted in "Dennis the Menace?" *Newsweek*, 24 April 1978, p. 28.

102. *Senate Debate on the Panama Canal Treaties*, p. 404.

103. DeConcini's foreign-policy advisor, Romano Romani, observed later that Christopher's cautious approach with DeConcini reflected a lack of urgency within the administration: "I think State thought that as long as the amendment was reduced to a condition, it really wouldn't matter to the Panamanians anyway" (interview with Romano Romani, Washington, D.C., 28 September 1983). Administration officials protest that every effort was made to secure a concession on the offending language.

104. Jordan later commented, "Lewis was a gentle man. He showed an outrage I'd never seen in him before. He made it clear that he could not in good conscience recommend that Torrijos accept the treaty on this basis." Interview with Hamilton Jordan, Washington, D.C., 21 July 1983.

105. Omar Torrijos to Jimmy Carter, 15 March 1978.

106. On Wednesday the 15th the seriousness of the situation was again underscored when Lewis, OAS Secretary General Alejandro Orfilia, and Panama's ambassador to the United Nations met with the president and told him in person of the grave risks implied in the DeConcini measure.

107. Despite publicly announced intentions to vote against the treaties, Senator Jennings Randolph (D.-W. Va.) indicated privately to administration officials that if needed to ensure ratification he would vote in favor of the treaties. Interview with Moore.

108. Quoted in "Canal Showdown," *Newsweek,* 24 April 1978, p. 27. As Christopher elaborated later, DeConcini held all the cards: "We knew it would be much easier for DeConcini to vote against the treaties so we had no leverage. He had three votes, Hatfield, Hodges [D.-Ark.], and his own, and he was dug in. We couldn't do any more." Telephone interview with Warren Christopher, 30 September 1983. Most administration vote counts showed Senators Hatfield and Hodges tied to the DeConcini amendment. Senator Hatfield confirms (telephone interview with Senator Paul Hatfield, 20 December 1983) that view, while Senator Hodges indicates that he would have voted for ratification with or without the DeConcini amendment (telephone interview with Senator Kaneaster Hodges, 11 January 1984).

109. Carter, *Keeping Faith,* p. 170. After the meeting two final attempts were made to persuade DeConcini to abandon the controversial language. The first was made by the president himself, who, with a "new sense of urgency," called DeConcini to warn that without a compromise "we could have blood on our hands" (interview with Senator Dennis DeConcini, Washington, D.C., 28 September 1983). The second was made by Christopher, who urged for the third time on Wednesday evening the removal of the offending language. DeConcini agreed to consider the matter again overnight, but on Thursday morning he phoned to say he had decided to stick with the original wording (interview with Christopher; see also Destler, "Learning from Panama," p. 20, and Franck and Weisband, *Foreign Policy by Congress,* p. 280). As DeConcini commented later, "I realized the treaty might be in jeopardy. I took it seriously. We talked about it. I knew it might defeat the treaty. But we had already downgraded the amendment to a condition and we felt that was all we could do. . . . We felt we had to make explicit what was implicit in the treaties" (interview with DeConcini).

110. Senator DeConcini quoted in 95th Cong., 2d sess. (16 March 1978), 124 *Congressional Record:* S3817.

111. "DeConcini Amendment Dims Outlook for Approval of Second Panama Pact," *Wall Street Journal,* 14 April 1978, p. 4.

112. Quoted in "Changes Called an Insult," *New York Times,* 10 April 1978, p. D9.

113. Quoted in "Last Test of a Battered Treaty," *Time,* 24 April 1978, p. 22.

114. Quoted in "Panama Indicates Possible Challenge to Panama Canal Treaty," *Washington Post,* 7 April 1978, p. A14.

115. Quoted in David Maxfield, "Senate Backs Turning Over Canal to Panama," *Congressional Quarterly,* 22 April 1978, p. 952. Baker warned, nevertheless, that "I think our friends in Panama ought to know that just a twitch of an eyelid, just the slightest provocation or expression that these treaties, or this treaty in this form, is not acceptable to Panama, and the whole thing could go down the tube." Quoted in "A New Peril Confronts Canal Pacts," *Washington Post,* 8 April 1978, p. A99.

116. Both senators are quoted in Neuchterlein, "The 1978 Panama Canal Treaties," p. 155.

117. Editorial, "The Whims of Dennis DeConcini," *Washington Post,* 13 April 1978, p. A24.

118. Quoted in "Warning by Panama to Carter Reported," *New York Times,* 11 April 1978, p. A1.

119. As one White House lobbyist noted later, "We were more concerned with maintaining our margin and with keeping the second vote intact than with strength-

ening the wording to satisfy Torrijos. While the guys who voted in favor of the first would probably vote in favor of the second, there was tremendous pressure on them. We were afraid we might not retain that margin. Thus we were not really serious about efforts to change the DeConcini language" (interview with Tate).

120. Neuchterlein, "The 1978 Panama Canal Treaties," p. 157.

121. "Canal Showdown," p. 26. As Senator Byrd put it more discretely, the purpose was "to develop language that would not be directed at the DeConcini reservation but at the same time would enunciate non-intervention principles." Quoted in David Maxwell, "Senate Backs Turning over Canal to Panama," *Congressional Quarterly*, 22 April 1978, p. 952.

122. Senator Church, quoted in 95th Cong., 2d sess. (4 April 1984), 124 *Congressional Record*: S9428.

123. *Senate Debate on the Panama Canal Treaties*, p. 484.

124. Quoted in Franck and Weisband, *Foreign Policy by Congress*, p. 283.

125. Quoted in "How the Treaty Was Saved," *Time*, 1 May 1978, p. 13.

126. Neuchterlein interview with Linowitz.

127. Neuchterlein interview with Ellsworth Bunker, Washington, D.C., 25 June 1978.

128. Interview with Richard McCall, Washington, D.C., 17 May 1982.

129. Destler, "Learning from Panama," p. 27.

130. Franck and Weisband, *Foreign Policy by Congress*, pp. 279, 281. Destler suggests the possibility that three or four votes in reserve were known to the Senate leadership. If this were so, the risks of calling DeConcini's bluff may have been justified. The administration's vote counts showed no such margin for risk (Destler, "Learning from Panama," pp. 20–21). Indeed the risk assessment was such that prior to the first vote neither DeConcini nor the Senate leadership was told of Torrijos's threat to scuttle the treaties, fearing a possible backlash from charges of blackmail (telephone interviews with Frank Moore and Robert Thompson, 3 October 1983).

131. Interview with Robert Beckel, Washington, D.C., 23 June 1978.

132. Neuchterlein interview with Beckel.

133. Interview with Beckel.

134. Quoted in Franck and Weisband, *Foreign Policy by Congress*, p. 281.

135. Carter, *Keeping Faith*, p. 172.

136. Destler, "Treaty Troubles," p. 55.

137. Destler, "Learning from Panama," p. 2.

138. TRB [Richard Strout], "Two Thirds," *New Republic*, 10 September 1977, p. 2.

139. Alexander Hamilton, "The Federalist: No. 70," in Hamilton, James Madison, and John Jay, *The Federalist Papers* (New York: New American Library, 1961), p. 423.

140. Interview with Tate. One State Department official noted that "The President is spending over half his day, every day, on Panama now and seems more committed to them [the treaties] than to any other issue according to those closest to him." Robert Beckel, memorandum to Douglas J. Bennet, Jr., U. S. Department of State, 2 September 1977, quoted in Neuchterlein, "The 1978 Panama Canal Treaties," p. 80.

141. The term is used in Bernard C. Cohen, *The Political Process and Foreign Policy: The Making of the Japanese Peace Settlement* (Princeton: Princeton University Press, 1957), p. 29.

142. Interview with Jordan.

143. Interview with Ernest Evans, Washington, D.C., 20 August 1981.

144. Quoted in Richard Strout, "Carter under Pressure to Speak out on Panama," *Christian Science Monitor*, 17 October 1977, p. 3.

145. Hodding Carter III, memorandum to Hamilton Jordan, 19 September 1977; Jody Powell and Hamilton Jordan, memorandum to President Jimmy Carter, 3 October 1977.

146. The president may have spent more personal time on the treaties than on any other issue, but because so much of it was before small White House briefings and in closed sessions with legislators and government officials, there was a widespread misperception that Carter did not place a high priority on the issue.

147. Les Brown, "Timing of Carter's Speech on TV Questioned," *New York Times*, 2 February 1978, p. A24. The speech attracted 40 million viewers, 30 million fewer than the previous month's State of the Union address.

148. TRB, "Two Thirds."

149. Interview with Douglas J. Bennet, Jr., Washington, D.C., 18 May 1982.

150. Interview with Beckel.

151. Destler writes that "of the 68 Senators who backed Carter on Panama, only 12 Democrats and 5 Republicans were with him on the three other votes most important to his foreign policy—Middle East arms, Turkey and the natural gas portion of the energy package" ("Treaty Troubles," p. 63).

152. Interview with Tate.

153. Interview with Beckel.

154. James Reston, "Carter's Nightmares," *New York Times*, 21 April 1978, p. B–1.

Chapter 4. *Panama and Public Opinion*

1. Jeffrey D. Neuchterlein interview with Robert Pastor, Washington, D.C., 18 July 1978.

2. Quoted in Austin Scott, "Byrd: Panama Treaties Would Lose This Year," *Washington Post*, 25 September 1977, p. A7.

3. Hamilton Jordan, memorandum to President Jimmy Carter, 13 December 1978.

4. Cambridge Survey Research, "Panama Canal: Summary of Public Opinion" (undated), Committee of Americans for the Canal Treaties, Inc., files, Washington, D. C.

5. Quoted in James P. Gannon, "Heat on Key Senators over Treaties Is Becoming Intense," *Wall Street Journal*, 19 January 1978, p. 1.

6. Quoted in Jeffrey D. Neuchterlein, "The 1978 Panama Canal Treaties: The Record of the Carter Administration" (Paper submitted to the White House, 4 April 1979), p. 66.

7. Quoted in Hedrick Smith, "After Panama, More Battles," *New York Times*, 20 April 1978, p. A1.

8. Quoted in "Ford Discusses Shift on Panama Pacts, Predicts Approval," *Washington Post*, 19 December 1977, p. A17.

9. U. S., Congress, Senate, Committee on Foreign Relations, *Panama Canal Treaties*, Part 4, 95th Cong., 2d sess., 1978, p. 28.

10. Henry Fairlie, "Galluping toward Dead Center," *New Republic*, 8 April 1978, pp. 19–20.

11. Terence Smith, "Carter Nears End of Long Drive for Canal Treaties," *New York Times*, 1 February 1978, p. A4.

12. Daniel Yankelovich, "Farewell to 'President Knows Best,'" *Foreign Affairs* 56 (America and the World, 1978): 676.

13. David Broder, "Straight Shooting on the Canal Treaties," *Washington Post*, 5

February 1978, p. B7. The other thing the administration proved adept at, according to Broder, was the "negotiation of necessary compromises with the Congress."

14. Quoted in Jack Anderson, "Carter Cabinet Press," *Washington Post*, 16 March 1978, p. DC9.

15. Jimmy Carter, *Keeping Faith: Memoirs of a President* (New York: Bantam, 1982), p. 167.

16. As the State Department's polling analyst Bernard Roshco notes, "It was a seller's market for trends." See Roshco, "Searching for Opinion Trends in Foreign Policy" (Paper delivered at the 9th annual Attitude Research Conference, Market Research Division, American Marketing Association, Tarpon Springs, Fla. 29 March 1978), p. 3.

17. *Panama Canal Treaties*, Part 5, p. 28.

18. Opinion Research Corporation poll, October 1977.

19. Bernard Roshco, "The Polls: Polling on Panama—Si; Don't Know; Hell, No!" *Public Opinion Quarterly* 42 (Winter 1978): 555.

20. Paul Laxalt, "[Advertisement:] The Panama Canal: An American Triumph or an American Defeat?" *San Diego Union*, 21 October 1977, p. B9.

21. Quoted in "Senator Baker Walks on the Water," *Economist*, 14 January 1978, p. 25.

22. Byrd, quoted in Bureau of Public Affairs (Department of State) memorandum, 22 August 1977, p. 2. From notes in the author's possession.

23. Smith, "Carter Nears End of Long Drive for Canal Treaties," p. 4.

24. According to Roshco, "The Polls: Polling on Panama," p. 556.

25. The only exception was one of ORC's own polls, published in February 1978.

26. Richard Strout: "Can Carter Mold Public Opinion?" *Christian Science Monitor*, 2 February 1978, p. 5.

27. Daniel Yankelovich, "How Not to Read the Polls," *Time*, 28 April 1978, pp. 72–73.

28. After August the first sentence was dropped, reflecting the completion of the negotiations. Roper later asked other questions, which are cited below but not included here because of different wording. Roper polls: June 1976; January, August, September and November 1977. (Since percentages have been rounded off to the nearest whole number, marginals may not total exactly 100 percent.)

29. In June the question was worded: "Do you agree or disagree with the statement that our government should eventually return control of the Panama Canal to the government of Panama?" In April the question was changed to reflect Senate action on the first treaty: "As you know, the Senate is considering the two treaties granting control of the Panama Canal to the Republic of Panama in the year 2000. It has already approved the first treaty and is preparing to vote on the second treaty. Do you approve or disapprove of those treaties?" CBS polls; June 1976: October 1977; January, April, 1978.

30. "Support for Israel Declines, Poll Finds," *New York Times*, 14 April 1978, p. A1.

31. NBC News polls: August 1977, October 1977, and January 1978.

32. The Harris Survey: October 1977, April and June 1978. For the wording of the October and April Harris questions, see Appendix A, category II.

33. Interview with Bernard Roshco, Washington, D.C., 15 December 1981.

34. Roshco, "The Polls: Polling on Panama," p. 562. Further, though less reliable, evidence on the point is to be found in the results of several state-wide polls conducted during the ratification period. Most were fairly rudimentary straw votes, and in only one of which I am aware were questions repeated to ascertain trends. These polls

suggest that the lessons of the national polls were not aberrations. See, for example, "Panama Canal Treaty Opposed," *Reno, (Nev.) Evening Gazette,* 10 February 1978, p. 1. Nevadans were opposed to ratification by a margin of 90 percent. J. R. Bardsley, "Majority in State Opposed to Treaties," *Portland Oregonian,* 12 March 1978, p. 2. The *Oregonian* reported 62 percent opposed, 27 percent in favor. J. R. Bardsley, "Utahans Oppose Relinquishing Panama Canal," *Salt Lake City Tribune,* 26 February 1978, p. A1. In Utah the percentages were 72 percent opposed and 16 percent in favor. "Treaties with Guarantees Attract Support," *Omaha (Neb.) World Herald,* 12 March 1978, pp. 1– 2. The *World Herald* sampled opinion three times with the following results: August 1977—64 percent opposed, 22 percent in favor; December 1977—59 percent opposed, 23 percent in favor; March 1978—62 percent opposed, 19 percent in favor. In Texas ORC found opinion opposed 79 percent to 11 percent with the caveat noted later, footnote 49. (Opinion Research Corporation, "Statewide Survey in Texas on Attitudes toward the Panama Canal Treaty," Study no. 69121, February 1978, p. 61). In California the Field Institute produced more favorable results, reflecting, in part, the comparatively more sympathetic view toward ratification that prevailed in the three Pacific Coast states. The small upward trend recorded by Field has its explanation in a phenomenon described later. In November 1977 and January 1978 Field asked: "The treaties call for the gradual transfer of control over the Canal to the country of Panama by the year 2000, with the U. S. retaining military defense rights. From what you have seen and heard, do you personally *approve* or *disapprove* of the treaties?" In November the response was 35 percent approve, 49 percent disapprove, 16 percent undecided. In January the results were 41 percent approve, 46 percent disapprove, and 13 percent undecided. (Mervin D. Field, "Panama Canal Treaties Not Supported by California Public," *California Poll,* Release no. 950, 4 November 1977; Release no. 955, 24 January 1978.)

35. Walter Lippmann, *Public Opinion* (New York: Macmillan, 1922); and Lippmann, *The Phantom Public* (New York: Harcourt, Brace and World, 1925).

36. Lippmann, *Public Opinion,* pp. 3, 21, 29.

37. Lippmann, *Phantom Public,* p. 32; Leo Bogart, *Silent Politics: Polls and the Awareness of Public Opinion* (New York: Wiley Interscience, 1972), p. ix.

38. Bogart, *Silent Politics,* quoted in Roshco, "The Polls: Polling on Panama," pp. 551–52.

39. "The Polls: Polling on Panama," p. 552.

40. Throughout the actual ratification period "awareness" levels in most of the national polls ranged between 75 and 80 percent.

41. The Gallup Organization, "The Gallup Poll," *Press Releases,* 23 October 1977 and 2 February 1978.

42. *Gallup Opinion Index,* Report no. 149, December 1977.

43. Bogart, *Silent Politics,* p. 18. For more detailed analyses of the influence of question wording on polling responses see Herbert H. Hyman, *The Secondary Analysis of Sample Surveys: Principles, Procedures and Potentialities* (New York: Wiley, 1972); Howard Schuman and Stanley Presser, *Questions and Answers in Attitude Surveys* (New York: Academic, 1981); and John P. Robinson and Robert Meadow, *Polls Apart* (Cabin John, Md.: Seven Locks., 1982).

44. The leadership amendments, jointly sponsored by the Senate majority and minority leaders, provided for intervention and priority passage rights in case of emergency after the expiration of the Panama Canal Treaty in the year 2000.

45. Caddell's question read: "The United States government has recently concluded a treaty with the government of Panama to return the Panama Canal and the Canal

Zone to Panama over time finishing by the year 2000. The U.S. would retain rights to defend the Canal and Panama agrees to maintain its neutrality and keep it open. From what you know about the treaty, do you generally favor or oppose it?" The results are as follows:

	Aug. 1977	Oct. 1977	Dec. 1977	Feb. 1978
Approve	25	30	35	37
Disapprove	61	55	49	46
No opinion	14	15	16	17

46. With the partial exception of the NBC data cited on p. 119.

47. "Thus," notes Caddell, "the public moves from 2–to–1 against the treaties to better than 2–to–1 in favor." Cambridge Survey Research, "Summary of Public Opinion."

48. ORC's follow-up question asked: "If the proposed treaty were changed by the Senate to ensure that U. S. ships would have top priority for passage in times of emergency, and to ensure that the U. S. could protect the Canal to guarantee that it remains neutral, would you then support or oppose the treaty?" See Opinion Research Corporation, "Statewide Survey in Texas on Attitudes toward the Panama Canal Treaty," p. 8.

49. Cambridge Survey Research, "Summary of Public Opinion."

50. Gallup, "The Gallup Poll," 23 October 1977, p. 1.

51. Gallup found that among the small percentage that could answer the three "knowledge" questions quoted above, support for ratification was significantly higher. Responses were marginally higher in all polls among the 75 to 80 percent who, throughout the ratification period, were simply "aware" of the treaty issue. Among all respondents in Gallup's October poll opinion ran against ratification 46 to 36 percent; among the 74 percent aware, opposition diminished to 48 to 40 percent; among Gallup's 7 percent "better informed" opinion ran in favor of ratification 51 to 46 percent. See *Gallup Opinion Index*, Report no. 149.

52. Walter LaFeber, "Covering the Canal; or, How the Press Missed the Boat," *More*, June 1978, p. 27.

53. Cited in Bureau of Public Affairs (Department of State) memorandum, 30 June 1978. From notes in the author's possession.

54. Jude Wanniski, "Panama and Pax Americana," *Wall Street Journal*, 7 April 1978, p. 16.

55. Cf. William Schneider, "A Matter of Pride and Property: Debating the Treaty," *Washington Post*, 12 February 1978, p. C4.

56. Both CBS and Roper gauged intensity with comparable results. Concluded Roper, "most proponents of the new treaty do not feel very strongly about modifying the treaty, but most opponents of the new treaty feel 'very strongly' against any change." Roper Reports, "Early Selected Results: 77–9," 21 October 1977. CBS elaborated: "Twenty-nine percent of the entire population both had an opinion on the treaties *and* claimed that their opinions were strong enough to sway their votes the next time their Senators were up for reelection. Those individuals were . . . more likely to be found among opponents of the treaty. A full three-quarters of that intense group opposed the unclarified Panama Canal treaties, while only one-fourth supported the agreement." CBS/*New York Times* Poll, October 1977. See also Everett Ladd, "The Great Canal Debate," *Public Opinion*" March–April 1978): 33. CBS reported that among conservatives and those in lower education categories the tendency to hold political can-

didates accountable on a single issue was greater than among other demographic groups. This measure of intensity may not, therefore, be uniformly applicable. Many treaty supporters may well have expressed their intensity in other ways, invalidating comparisons reported above. Telephone interview with Kathleen Frankovic, New York, N. Y., 12 January 1981.

57. Thomas A. Bailey, *The Man in the Street: The Impact of American Public Opinion on Foreign Policy* (New York; Macmillan, 1948), p. 7.

58. The data are to be found in The Roper Organization, *Roper Reports*, vols. 76–5, 76–6, 76–7, 77–10, 78–3, and 78–4. (Since percentages have been rounded off to the nearest whole number, marginals may not total exactly 100 percent.) That the issue had but transient salience is suggested by the fact that a mere 4 percent of the respondents in a June 1976 Roper poll felt strongly enough about the Panama issue to influence a voting decision in the upcoming mid-term elections; within six months after ratification the issue had once again dropped to insignificance in issue rankings.

The measure of salience with respect to an issue of foreign policy needs, as always, to be put into perspective. While 45 percent of Americans followed the Panama treaties closely in March 1978, 68 percent followed the level of prices. While 43 percent followed closely in February, 84 percent followed "this winter's weather reports and forecasts." See The Roper Organization, *Roper Reports*, vols. 78–3 and 78–4. Still, as foreign policy issues go, 45 percent was respectable. At the same time Arab-Israeli relations attracted only 42 percent close attention; events in Rhodesia and South Africa, only 19 percent; and affairs in the Horn of Africa, but 9 percent.

59. The overall proportion of respondents having an opinion either pro or con increased from 73.5 percent to 81.2 percent. The complete Roper data are to be found in The Roper Organization, *Roper Reports*, vols. 76–6 and 77–10. The cross-tabulation (#05–RS–172) was run by the Roper Center, Office of Archival Development and User Services, Storrs, Conn., 21 December 1981.

60. Herbert H. Hyman and Paul B. Sheatsley, "Some Reasons Why Information Campaigns Fail," *Public Opinion Quarterly* 11 (1947): 417.

61. Quoted in ibid., p. 296.

62. *Gallup Opinion Index*, Report no. 150, January 1978.

63. Cambridge Survey Research, untitled, undated. From notes in the author's possession.

64. On differences in the behavior of "attentive" and "mass" publics see Gabriel Almond, *The American People and Foreign Policy* (New York: Praeger, 1960); James Rosenau, *Public Opinion and Foreign Policy* (New York: Random, 1961); Eugene R. Wittkopf and Michael Maggiotto, "Elites and Masses: A Comparative Analysis of Attitudes toward America's Role in the World" (Paper prepared for the Annual Convention of the International Studies Association, Philadelphia, 18–21 March 1981); and R. W. Oldendick and B. A. Bardes, "Mass and Elite Foreign Policy Opinion," *Public Opinion Quarterly* 46 (Autumn 1982): 368–82.

65. Raymond Bauer, Ithiel de Sola Pool, and L. A. Dexter, *American Business and Public Policy: The Politics of Foreign Trade* (New York: Atherton, 1963), p. 468. The administration's problem may have been exacerbated by the president's declining popularity, which dropped 26 points (from approval ratings of 66 percent to 40 percent) between mid-August, when the treaty was concluded, and April, when it was finally ratified. See The Gallup Organization, "Presidential Popularity: A 43 Year Review," *The Gallup Opinion Index* no. 182 (October–November 1980): 6, 14.

66. The term is Lloyd Free's and is discussed in Albert Cantril and Charles Roll, *Polls: Their Use and Misuse in American Politics* (New York: Basic, 1972), pp. 55–57.

67. The Harris Survey, "Public Opposes Canal Treaties," 20 October 1977, p. 2.

68. Ibid., p. 3.

69. Cambridge Survey Research, "An Analysis of Public Attitudes toward the Panama Canal Treaties," 8 October 1977, p. A4.

70. Mervin D. Field, "Panama Canal Treaties Not Supported by California Public," *California Poll* no. 950, 4 November 1977, p. 4.

71. Roger Seasonwein to Joseph Aragon, 22 November 1977.

72. Field, "Panama Canal Treaties Not Supported by California Public," p. 4.

73. Cambridge Survey Research, untitled, undated. Committee of Americans for the Canal Treaties, Inc., files, Washington, D.C.

74. Gallup Poll, 23 October 1977.

75. Harris, "Public Opposes Canal Treaty," p. 3.

76. Cambridge Survey Research, "Public Attitudes toward the Panama Canal Treaties."

77. Gallup Poll, 23 October 1977.

78. Field, "Panama Canal Treaties Not Supported by California Public," p. 4.

79. Caddell reported that 56 percent of all respondents to one poll cited the issue, expressed in one form or another, as the principal reason for opposition. Cambridge Survey Research, untitled, undated. Committee of Americans for the Canal Treaties, Inc., files. See also Harris, "Public Opposes Canal Treaties," p. 3; Field, "Panama Canal Treaties Not Supported by California Public," p. 4.

80. Cambridge Survey Research, untitled, undated. Committee of Americans for the Canal Treaties, Inc., files.

81. David McCullough to President Jimmy Carter, 21 October 1977.

82. As research reported by Paul Lazarsfeld and others has shown, prior exposure to a subject has an important effect in conditioning attitudes, even when, in controlled experiments, both those with and those without prior exposure are exposed to the same information. Writes Lazarsfeld: "We found in every case that the group who reported prior exposure to the information had a different attitudinal reaction from those without prior exposure. One could assume that this difference reflected the influence of the information on those previously exposed, except that . . . *both* groups, before being asked the attitude question, had been supplied with identical descriptions of the information in question." Lazarsfeld, quoted in Hyman and Sheatsley, "Some Reasons why Information Campaigns Fail," p. 296.

83. As Hyman and Sheatsley wrote in 1947, for example, the capacity to disseminate information outstrips the capacity to absorb it. "To assume a perfect correspondence between the nature and amount of material presented in an information campaign and its absorption by the public, is to take a naive view, for the very nature and degree of public exposure to the material is determined to a large extent by certain psychological characteristics of the people themselves." Hyman and Sheatsley, "Some Reasons Why Information Campaigns Fail," p. 291.

Chapter 5.   *Interest Groups, I: A Policy without a Constituency*

1. A fourth category of interest groups, comprised primarily of maritime interests, is discussed in chapter 6.

2. Interview with Robert Beckel, Washington, D.C., 23 June 1981.

3. Quoted in "Now for the Hard Part," *Time*, 19 September 1977, p. 21.

4. "The Panama Canal Treaties," *Crisis*, December 1977, p. 457.

5. George Meany, "The Canal—Facts, Not Emotions," *American Federationist*, November 1977, p. 2.

6. As noted in Marjorie Hunter, "White House is Lobbying Unusually Hard on Canal Pacts," *New York Times*, 1 September 1977, p. A2.

7. Telephone interview with Michael Boggs, Washington, D.C., 7 October 1982.

8. New Directions letter (undated), Committee of Americans for the Canal Treaties, Inc., files, Washington, D.C. Sponsors of the effort mounted by New Directions included the AFL-CIO; World Federalists; Americans for Democratic Action; Democratic National Committee; Center for Inter-American Relations; Washington Office on Latin America; United Methodist Church; Church of the Brethren; Coalition for a New Foreign and Military Policy; American Friends Service Committee; National Council of Churches; American Federation of Federal, State, County and Municipal Employees; International Union of Operating Engineers; United Auto Workers; Communications Workers of America; and the United Association of Plumbers and Pipefitters.

9. Interview with Joseph Eldridge, Washington, D.C., 19 October 1981.

10. "Resolution Adopted by the 1976 General Conference of the United Methodist Church [Washington, D. C.] in Portland, Oregon." Committee of Americans for the Canal Treaties, Inc., files.

11. Statement of the Executive Committee, Southern Baptist Convention, (Nashville, Tenn.), 1977.

12. National Council of Churches, (Washington, D.C.), Resolution of the Executive Committee, 9 September 1977, quoted in Testimony of William P. Thompson, U. S. Congress, Senate, Committee on Foreign Relations, *Panama Canal Treaties*, Part 3, 95th Cong., 1st sess., 1977, p. 352. See also National Council of Churches, "Resolution on Panamanian-U. S. Relations," 11 October 1975, and "Observations and Affirmations," National Council of Churches' Delegation to Panama, 3–7 April 1976, Committee of Americans for the Canal Treaties, Inc., files.

13. Quoted in testimony of Morris Levinson, *Panama Canal Treaties*, Part 3, p. 371.

14. See Adon Taft, "Churches Pressure Politicians," *Miami Herald*, 21 September 1975, p. 12A.

15. Alfred O. Hero, Jr., *American Religious Groups View Foreign Policy: Trends in Rank-and-File Opinion, 1937–1969* (Durham: Duke University Press, 1973).

16. See David Hollenbach, *Claims in Conflict Retrieving and Reviewing the Catholic Human Rights Tradition* (New York: Paulist, 1979); J. Lloyd Mecham, *Church and State in Latin America: A History of Politico–Ecclesiastical Relations* (Chapel Hill: University of North Carolina Press, 1966); Penny Lernoux, *Cry of the People* (Garden City, N.Y.: Doubleday, 1981); and Alan Riding, "The Sword and the Cross," *New York Review of Books*, 28 May 1981, pp. 3–6.

17. Brian H. Smith, S. J., "Religion and Social Change: Classical Theories of New Formulations in the Context of Recent Developments in Latin America," *Latin American Research Review*, Summer 1977, p. 8; see also Smith, "Churches and Human Rights in Latin America," *Journal of Inter-American Studies* 21 (February 1979): 89–127.

18. Renato Poblete, "From Medellín to Puebla," *Journal of Inter-American Studies* 21 (February 1979): 35.

19. Hero, *American Religious Groups View Foreign Policy*, p. 205.

20. Marcos G. McGrath, "Ariel or Caliban?" *Foreign Affairs* 52 (October 1973): 75–95.

21. Interview with J. Bryan Hehir, Washington, D.C., 9 November 1981.

22. Statement on U.S.-Panamanian Relations, U.S. Catholic Conference, 10 No-

vember 1976. Committee of Americans for the Canal Treaties, Inc., files. As Father Hehir, associate secretary of the Office of International Justice and Peace of the U. S. Catholic Conference, notes, "Once you get a local bishops' conference to come across on an issue like that, the other [in this case, the American] bishops take their responsibilities very seriously." Interview with Hehir.

23. McGrath, "Ariel or Caliban?" pp. 91–92.

24. Marcos G. McGrath, letter to the author, 12 July 1982.

25. Ibid.

26. As one index of such support, the roster of the Harriman citizens committee included a remarkable cross section of the most influential business leaders in the nation. See Table 2.

27. Council of the Americas, "Reasons for Supporting the Panama Canal Treaties," (undated), Council of the Americas, Inc., files, New York, N.Y.

28. Murray Rothbard, "The Treaty That Wall Street Wrote," *Inquiry*, 5 December 1977, reprinted in U.S. Congress, House, Committee on Ways and Means, Subcommittee on the Panama Canal, *Panama Canal Treaty Ramifications*, Part 2, 95th Cong., 1st sess., 1977, pp. 111–12.

29. While not up to its pre-World War II high, American private investment in the region was large ($22 billion in 1975) and growing (up 50 percent from 1970), and by the time of the ratification debate third only to Western Europe and Canada. See "U.S. Total Direct Foreign Investment and Rates of Return, 1970–1975," *Business International*, 14 January 1977, pp. 14–15. Figures for Europe in 1975 were $49.6 billion; for Canada, $31.1 billion. In Panama per se there was $1.825 billion in direct foreign U. S. investment, an increase of 45.9 percent since 1970 and the fourth highest in Latin America. U. S. investment was higher only in Brazil, Mexico, and Venezuela. As for trade, Panama absorbed over a third of its total imports from the United States ($307 million of $861 million in 1977). For all of Latin American U. S. exports totaled over $16.5 billion. See *Business Latin America*, 27 December 1978, p. 414.

30. As Assistant Secretary of State Terence Todman explained to one group of corporate chiefs: "It is private citizens in the business world who are often pioneers in . . . grasping the changing realities of the world in which we must deal." Todman, address to the Third Annual Central American Conference, Council of the Americas, 15–17 February 1978. Council of the Americas, Inc., files.

31. The phrase is from Isaiah Frank, "Big Business in the Third World: Gains on All Sides," *Christian Science Monitor*, 10 July 1981, p. 23. See also Frank, *Foreign Enterprise in Developing Countries* (Baltimore: Johns Hopkins University Press, 1980); Richard J. Barnet and Ronald E. Müller, *Global Reach: The Power of the Multinational Corporations* (New York: Simon & Schuster, 1974); Robert Gilpin, *U.S. Power and the Multinational Corporation: The Political Economy of Foreign Direct Investment* (New York: Basic, 1975).

32. See Raymond Vernon, "International Investment and International Trade in the Product Cycle," *Quarterly Journal of Economics* 80 (May 1966): 190–207; Barnet and Müller, *Global Reach*, pp. 129–33.

33. C. Fred Bergsten, Thomas Horst, and Theodore Moran, *American Multinationals and American Interests* (Washington, D. C.: Brookings, 1978), pp. 338–39. Writes Bergsten, Third World countries "no longer simply ask themselves whether they want foreign direct investment or not but pursue, instead, a two-track policy of first attracting investment (through the use of tax and other inducements, if necessary) and then harnessing it to assure that it will promote their national interests." Frank, *Foreign Enterprise in Developing Countries*, p. 146.

34. Todman, address to the Third Annual Central American Conference. One of

the most noteworthy statements of support for the treaties came from the holding company formed in 1969 around the United Fruit Company, whose activities for fifty years epitomized American commercial imperialism in the Western Hemisphere. In its manner of dealing with the politically neutered "banana republics" of Central America and with the occasional, invariably futile, outbreaks of political liberalism in the region, the company, described by Walter LaFeber as North America's "gift to radical Latin American nationalism," spawned a body of fact and legend that still underlies the appeal of militant anti-Americanism in the region. Against this background, the testimony of United Brands Chairman Seymour Milstein before the Senate Foreign Relations Committee is revealing. The treaties are a sign, Milstein testified, "that we have come to appreciate the need for cooperation and accommodation in dealing with our neighbors and that the day has passed when smaller, less developed countries will tolerate anything less than the controlling voice in their own destinies. We believe [ratification] is the right thing to do." *Panama Canal Treaties*, Part 4, p. 403.

35. Statement of Augustine R. Marusi, Council of the Americas, Inc., *1977 Annual Report*, pp. 4–5. Council of the Americas, Inc., files.

36. Within the Carter administration there was never any secret that new accommodationist policies in the Third World were designed to respond to economic as well as moral imperatives. As the *Washington Post Magazine* depicts the administration's most avid practitioner of accommodation Andrew Young: "when he arrived at the United Nations, the press was so busy chronicling his controversial misstatements that a story of astounding significance was virtually overlooked. For Chief Capitalist Andrew Young had converted the U. N. Mission into a virtual free market clearinghouse. Day in and day out, largely hidden from public view, he was joining the unlikeliest of couples—bloated American multinationals and struggling Third World governments— with all the wile and finesse of a Yiddish matchmaker.

"By the time he left office last fall, Andy Young had become the middleman for literally billions of dollars of trade commitments between U. S. corporations and Third World countries. He had developed more success than any single person in the government in breaking down trade barriers with developing nations." Andrew Alexander, "The Preacher," *Washington Post Magazine*, 27 July 1980, p. 11.

As Young himself explained the rationale for the policy: "I think that whenever we have the possibility of contributing toward development what we are doing, really, is creating stable conditions under which American goods and services will eventually be desired. My approach to Africa is in some ways like the Japanese approach to Asia, and my approach to foreign aid is not necessarily humanitarian. It is in the long-range interest of access to resources and the creation of markets for American goods and services." Quoted in Kai Bird, "Co-Opting the Third World Elites: Trilateralism and Saudi Arabia," in Holly Sklar, ed, *Trilateralism: The Trilateral Commission and Elite Planning for World Management* (Boston: South End, 1980), p. 340.

37. U.S., Congress, Senate, Committee on Foreign Relations, *International Debt, the Banks, and U. S. Foreign Policy*, 95th Cong., 1st sess., 1977, p. 1.

38. In nonoil-producing countries such deficits jumped from $9 billion in 1973 to $36.5 billion in 1975. Ibid.

39. *International Debt*, p. 1.

40. The business of recycling "petrodollars," that is, currency earned by the oil-producing nations, provided the banks with a major new source of profits. The twenty or so banks that dominated American foreign-branch activity were deriving higher and in some cases a majority of operating profits from foreign operations by the mid-1970s. Between 1970 and 1974 the international earnings of American banks rose at a com-

pound annual rate of 36 percent; the growth in international earnings accounted for fully 81 percent of total earnings increases. At Chase Manhattan such earnings as a percentage of total earnings during the same period rose from roughly 30 percent to 50 percent. Among leading growth sectors was Latin America. In Panama itself government indebtedness to American banks had by 1976 increased to $356 million. See Alan Howard, "The Real Latin American Policy," *Nation*, October 1977, p. 368; U. S. Department of State, "Fact Sheet, Revised," 24 March 1978, p. A2; Thomas Hanley "How Profitable Are U. S. Banks Overseas?" *Banker*, September 1975, pp. 1086, 1088; U. S., Congress, House, Committee on Banking, Currency, and Housing, *Financial Institutions and the Nation's Economy*, book 2, part 4, 94th Cong., 2nd sess., June 1976, p. 813.

41. As recently as the early 1960s most international banking in the United States was characterized by a few large banks managing foreign loans through correspondent banking networks or lending overseas from home offices with domestic funds. Because such lending had obvious negative balance-of-payments implications, the Federal Reserve restricted it. But in 1963 the Federal Reserve opened the doors for overseas branches to do foreign lending with foreign deposits, especially the sizable pool of Eurodollars that were increasingly making their way to Latin America. The Fed's revised ground rules began a surge in overseas banking activity by U. S. banks: in 1964 only eleven banks had overseas branches, with assets totaling $3.5 billion; by mid-1974, on the eve of the Senate's ratification debate, over 125 U. S. banks operated through foreign branches with assets totaling over $180 billion. G. J. Crough, *Transnational Banks and the International Economy* (Sydney: University of Sydney, 1977), pp. 13–14. In Latin America itself the number of U. S. branch banks, which grew only from 31 to 88 between 1918 and 1965, burgeoned in the seven years following to 227.

42. Sidney Wise, "Freedom Proves Lure to the Big Banks," *Times* (London), 25 April 1977, reprinted in *Panama Canal Treaty Ramifications*, Part 2, p. 14. See also Robin Pringle, "Service Centre for the Americas," *Banker*, October 1975, pp. 1203ff.; "Panama," *Banker*, May 1979, pp. 65–66; "Panama: The Mouse that Roared," *Euromoney*, September 1978, pp. 51–52; "Singapore of the West," *Euromoney*, June 1977, pp. 175ff.; Robin Pringle, "Banking in the Land of Balboa," *Banker*, October 1977, 1195–1201.

43. *Panama Canal Treaty Ramifications*, Part 2, pp. 285–301.

44. Between 1970 and 1975 the total number of foreign banks in Panama jumped from 21 to 75. Between 1967 and 1976 total assets rose 3,000 percent from $346 million to $10 billion. Howard M. Wachtel, *The New Gnomes: Multinational Banks in the Third World* (Washington, D. C.: Transnational Institute, 1977), p. 3.

45. In addition to privileges accorded foreign banks, foreign companies in Panama enjoyed the benefits of doing business in the second-largest free zone in the world, near the port city of Colón.

46. Rep. Gene Snyder (D.-Ky.), quoted in *Panama Canal Treaty Ramifications*, Part 2, p. 3. See also Philip Wheaton, "Trilateralism and the Caribbean: Tying Up 'Loose String' in the Western Hemisphere," in Sklar, *Trilateralism*, pp. 408–9.

47. Penny Lernoux, "U. S. Imperialists, Old and New," *Nation*, 3 April 1976, p. 392.

48. Ronald Steel, "Rough Passage," *New York Review of Books*, 23 March 1978, p. 14.

49. See Lernoux, "U. S. Imperialists, Old and New," p. 393.

50. Report of the Temporary Chairman, Business and Professional Committee for a New Panama Canal Treaty, undated, Council of the Americas, Inc., files. This discussion is based on interviews with Gale McGee (23 October 1981), Richard McCall (17

May 1982), and Richard Eisenmann (2 December 1982). See also Russell Warren Howe and Sarah Hays Trott, *The Power Peddlers: How Lobbyists Mold America's Foreign Policy* (Garden City: Doubleday, 1977), p. 123.

51. Richard Eisenmann, memorandum to Senator Gale McGee, 13 November 1975, Council of the Americas, Inc., files. Attendees included Upjohn Corporation, National Cash Register, Shell Oil Company, Gulf Oil Company, Rockwell International, Bank of America, Sears Roebuck, Firestone, Pan American World Airways, Bankers Trust, Pfizer, Caterpillar, Braniff Airlines, First Chicago Corporation, Chase Manhattan Bank, General Electric, the U. S. Chamber of Commerce, and Knight-Ridder Newspapers, Inc.

52. Business and Professional Committee for a New Panama Canal Treaty, "Proposal," undated. Council of the Americas, Inc., files.

53. Within months of his efforts "to divert ... congressional attempts to stop negotiations and to work in enlisting our multinational corporations to support treaty negotiation," Eisenmann confessed to a change of heart. Appearing before the Foreign Relations Committee in October 1977 Eisenmann explained how he, "as so many in the United States and even in Panama," had been "misled" in his early support for new negotiations. Disturbed by reports of human rights violations by the government of Omar Torrijos, he condemned the State Department for an "unbelievable lack of information or selective standards of ethics" in negotiating a treaty with "one of the most corrupt and arbitrary dictatorships in Latin America," and urged the Senate to reject the new treaties. See *Panama Canal Treaties*, Part 3, p. 281.

54. Testimony of Henry Geyelin, *Panama Canal Treaties*, Part 4, pp. 147–48.

55. Geyelin describes the connection between diplomacy and economics in these terms: "History has shown that unresolved political issues can generate a widespread xenophobia which not only disrupts U. S. diplomatic relations but creates an unfavorable trade and investment environment. ... A responsible new arrangement designed in conjunction with Panama will signify to the Latin American nations a new level of U. S. practical maturity and sincere intentions for cooperation with all nations." Geyelin, quoted in John M. Goshko, "Drawing Battle Lines on the Canal Issue, Multinational Firms May Back Ratification," *Washington Post*, 22 August 1977, p. A4.

56. "Why These New Panama Canal Treaties Support U. S. Interests," Talking Points, Meeting of the Executive Committee and Panama Canal Working Group, Council of the Americas, 28 September 1977. Council of the Americas, Inc., files.

57. Quoted in Council of the Americas, undated, untitled memorandum. Council of the Americas, Inc., files.

58. Otto Reich, memorandum to Washington Liaison Group, 19 Dember 1977. Council of the Americas, Inc., files. The task force was initially conceived as a vehicle for raising funds from individual member companies to support a public relations campaign. Eventually the Executive Committee took over full financial support of the task force as part of the council's general budget.

The chairman of the task force, John F. Gallagher, vice-president of international operations at Sears, Roebuck of Chicago, was a corporate executive well-schooled in the cost of anti-American politics in developing nations. For decades Sears was (and remains) one of the most visible manifestations of the American corporate presence in Latin America, and its operations have been regular targets of anti-American terrorist activity. In 1975 and 1976, on the very eve of the Panama debate, dozens of American businesses including numerous Sears retail outlets were damaged or destroyed by Puerto Rican nationalists threatening to "continue dealing bigger and bigger blows to the Yankee invader and his imperialist financial investment. ..." (Kenneth G. Slocum,

"Puerto Rican Arsonists Plague U.S. Concerns Operating on Island," *Wall Street Journal*, 11 September 1968, p. 17.) Violence in Puerto Rico and elsewhere had obvious, transferable lessons and did little to diminish corporate interest in assuaging the frustrated nationalism of Panamanian patriots intent on regaining the Canal.

59. As the council's Washington director, Otto Reich, wrote: "Despite the appearance of prominent businessmen on the Harriman Committee, business has not communicated this support directly to members of the Senate. The Council is in a prime position to focus their support where it will have the most impact. ... I think we should make a concerted effort to organize and identify the members of the business community who are willing to support the treaties, and secondly, we should direct this support toward the U.S. Senate." Otto J. Reich, memorandum to Henry R. Geyelin, 6 January 1978, Council of the Americas, Inc., files.

60. John Jackley, memorandum to Henry Geyelin and Otto Reich, undated, Council of the Americas, Inc., files.

61. Testimony of Henry Geyelin, *Panama Canal Treaties*, Part 4, p. 146.

62. Quoted in Council of the Americas, President's Letter, 22 February 1978, p. 3. Council of the Americas, Inc., files.

63. Interview with John Jackley, Washington, D.C., 1 April 1981.

64. Interview with Henry Geyelin, New York, N.Y., 20 November 1981.

65. "Business' Most Powerful Lobby in Washington," *Business Week*, 20 December 1976, p. 60.

66. Leonard Silk and Mark Silk, *The American Establishment* (New York: Basic, 1980), pp. 252–58.

67. Quoted in "Business' Most Powerful Lobby in Washington," p. 60. As *Business Week* suggests, the "Roundtable commands an access to politicians and the political process that eclipses the lobbying powers of such old time groups as the U.S. Chamber of Commerce and the National Association of Manufacturers."

68. Interview with John Post, Washington, D.C., 6 February 1982.

69. Raymond Bauer, Ithiel de Sola Pool, and L. A. Dexter, *American Business and Public Policy: The Politics of Foreign Trade* (New York: Atherton, 1963), p. 333.

70. Report of the International Relations Committee to the Board of Directors, U. S. Chamber of Commerce, "The Renegotiation of the Panama Canal Treaty," 20 October 1975, p. 1. U. S. Chamber of Commerce files, Washington, D. C.

71. U.S. Chamber of Commerce Press Release, 12 November 1975. "Chamber Backs Administration Efforts to Renegotiate Panama Canal Treaty," U.S. Chamber of Commerce files.

72. Richard Reiman, memorandum to Landon Butler, 27 June 1977.

73. Richard L. Lesher, letter to Richard Reiman, 28 June 1977.

74. Gordon Cloney, memorandum to Frederick Stokeld, 7 November 1977. U.S. Chamber of Commerce files.

75. U.S. Chamber of Commerce, "Summary of Responses to February, 1978, Membership Poll on Panama Canal Treaties," pp. 5, 8. U.S. Chamber of Commerce Files.

76. Interview with Frederick Stokeld, Washington, D.C., 18 December 1981.

77. This account is based on interviews with three individuals familiar with the NAM who have chosen to remain anonymous.

78. Philip H. Burch, Jr., "The NAM as an Interest Group," *Politics and Society* 4 (Autumn 1973): 97-130. As Bauer, Pool, and Dexter have demonstrated in their discussion of the more complex issue of trade, there were important divergences of views both between *types* of industries (chemicals and textiles, for example, were protectionist, while auto manufacturers were exponents of free trade) and even *within* industries.

With respect to Panama the division was more simply between large and small firms— or between managerial and family-run businesses. Though not without exception the larger, manager-run firms were more likely to be active in the international market and therefore more sensitive to the larger implications of an issue like Panama. There may have been sociological factors at work as well. "The larger the firm he represents," Bauer, Pool, and Dexter write, "the more must a man see things with what may be called 'the broad view,' . . . As we noted repeatedly in this study, the concern of the head of a big business is largely with the external environment, whereas that of the head of a small business is with internal management." Bauer, Pool, and Dexter, *American Business and Public Policy*, pp. x, 161-62.

79. Heath R. Larry, letter to President Jimmy Carter, 26 August 1977.

80. The full committee was not scheduled to meet until December.

81. Anonymous source.

82. Stephen Selig, memorandum to Hamilton Jordan, 21 February 1978.

83. Interview with Peter Johnson, Washington, D.C., 2 December 1981.

84. Interview with Geyelin.

85. Interview with David Lissy, Washington, D.C., 20 October 1981.

86. See Harry Johnson, "Panama as a Regional Financial Center: A Preliminary Analysis of Development Contribution," *Economic Development and Cultural Change* 24 (January 1976): 261-86.

87. Interview with Nicholas Barletta, Washington, D.C., 16 December 1981.

88. Telephone interview with Benton Moyer, 24 November 1981.

89. Interview with Frank Aldrich, Boston, Mass., 18 November 1981.

90. Lernoux,"U.S. Imperialists, Old and New," p. 392.

91. One Council of the Americas document corroborates the point: "The treaties are the main items of priority of the Carter Administration's foreign policy. If the corporations support it, they will have leverage with *other matters of more direct importance* such as Cuban claims, disclosure of investment information, taxation of foreign source income, etc." (My emphasis.) "Reasons for Supporting the Panama Canal Treaties," Council of the Americas information sheet, undated, Council of the Americas,Inc., files.

92. Interview with Dan C. Tate, Washington, D.C., 20 May 1982.

93. Interview with McCall.

94. Lernoux, "U.S. Imperialists, Old and New," p. 391.

95. Quoted in Robert Lindsey, "Reagan Backers Dominate California GOP Meeting," *New York Times*, 3 October 1977, p. 3.

96. The term "New Right" will be used here, as it is by Kevin Phillips, to distinguish "social-issue" conservatives from "business" conservatives on the "Old Right." See William J. Lanouette, "The New Right—'Revolutionaries' out after the 'Lunch-Pail' Vote," *National Journal*, 21 January 1978, p. 91.

97. Richard A. Viguerie, *The New Right—We're Ready to Lead* (Falls Church, Va.: Richard A. Viguerie Co., 1981), p. 65.

98. Ibid.

99. Walter LaFeber, *The Panama Canal: The Crisis in Historical Perspective* (New York: Oxford University Press, 1978), p. 128.

100. Ibid., p. 213.

101. Quoted in Godfrey Hodgson, "Anatomy of the Right," *New Republic*, 31 January 1981, p. 30.

102. Quoted in "Richard A. Viguerie—The Man in the Middle of the Right," *A*

Citizen's Guide to the Right Wing (Washington, D.C.: Americans for Democratic Action, n.d.), p. 22.

103. Hodgson, "Anatomy of the Right," p. 30.

104. Viguerie, *The New Right*, p. 65.

105. Quoted in ibid., p. 66.

106. Quoted in William J. Lanouette, "The Panama Canal Treaties—Playing in Peoria and in the Senate," *National Journal*, 8 October 1977, p. 1560.

107. Quoted in ibid.

108. Viguerie, *The New Right*, p. 66.

109. Mary McGrory, "Is Panama Treaty GOP Road to Power? *"Washington Star*, 27 September 1977, p. 5.

110. Quoted in "The New Right: Many Times More Effective Now," *Congressional Quarterly*, 24 December 1977, p. 2649.

111. Thomas J. McIntyre, *The Fear Brokers* (New York: Pilgrim, 1979), p. 43.

112. Viguerie, *The New Right*, p. 68.

113. Charles Evans Hughes, quoted in Bernard Cohen, *The Public's Impact on Foreign Policy* (Boston: Little, Brown, 1973), p. 143.

114. Arleigh A. Burke, Robert B. Carney, Thomas Moorer, and George Anderson, letter to President Jimmy Carter, 18 June 1977, reprinted in U.S. Congress, House, Committee on Merchant Marine and Fisheries, subcommittee on the Panama Canal, *U.S. Interest in Panama Canal*, 95th Cong., 1st sess., July 1977, pp. 126-27.

115. Paul B. Ryan, *The Panama Canal Controversy: U.S. Diplomacy and Defense Interests* (Stanford: Hoover Institution Press, 1977), p. 48. One of the most influential expressions of military opposition was a statement issued by 309 retired flag-rank officers on 18 October 1977 under the aegis of the Retired Officers Association. Claiming that they were not "muzzled" by political considerations like the Joint Chiefs, the signatories warned of the danger of entrusting the vitial asset of the Canal to Panamanian jurisdiction. Retired Officers Association News Release, 18 October 1977, Committee of Americans for the Canal Treaties, Inc., files.

116. Ryan, *Panama Canal Controversy*, p. 48.

117. Quoted in "Where Ford and Reagan Stand on the Issues—In Their Own Words," *U.S. News and World Report*, 1 March 1976, p. 17.

118. Patrick J. Buchanan, "International Shrinking Violet," *Human Events*, 27 August 1977, p. 655.

119. George Will, "A Vote for the Canal Treaties," *Newsweek*, 6 February 1978, p. 92.

120. Meldrum Thompson, "Keep Our Canal," *Members Report* (Conservative Caucus), September 1977, p. 2.

121. Patrick J. Buchanan, "Sold Down the Canal and Paying for the Privilege," *New York Daily News*, 16 August 1977, p. 18. As Buchanan explains, "Sixty years ago this country would have responded to threats of riots and sabotage not with negotiations. General Torrijos would have been fortunate to make it to the foothills of the jungle before his successor was sworn in—with a Marine holding the Bible."

122. William F. Buckley, Jr., "On the Right," *National Review*, 30 September 1977, p. 113.

123. Hanson Baldwin, "The Panama Canal: Sovereignty and Security," in *"A New Treaty for Panama?" AEI Defense Review* no. 4 (August 1977): 30.

124. Advertisement, "The Panama Canal," *San Diego Union*, 21 October 1977, p. B9.

125. Undated letter, Rep. George Hansen, American Legion files, Washington, D.C.

126. Letter by Ronald Reagan, 5 December 1977, Committee of Americans for the Canal Treaties, Inc., files.

127. George Nicholas, "Rocky's CIA Switched Signals on General Torrijos, "*Spotlight*, 3 October 1977, p. 14. The most elaborate descriptions of the Panama "conspiracy" emanated from the ultraRight, from publications such as the *Spotlight* and from spokesmen like New Hampshire governor Mendrum Thompson and the Conservative Caucus's Howard Phillips. Among the "mainstream" organizations on the New Right, hints of conspiracy were more often implicit than explicit.

128. Undated letter by Rep. Larry McDonald, Committee of Americans for the Canal Treaties, Inc., files.

129. Herman Dinsmore, "Plan to Give Away the Panama Canal—First Step to Dismemberment of U.S.," *National Educator*, August 1978, p. 1.

130. Nicholas, "Rocky's CIA," p. 14.

131. Ibid.

132. "Final Issues in the Panama Canal Giveaway," *Phyllis Schlafly Report* 2 (April 1978): 1.

133. Nicholas, "Rocky's CIA," p. 14.

134. Congressman George Hansen, in 95th Cong., 1st sess. (4 January 1978), 124 *Congressional Record*: E7545.

135. "The Selling of the American Canal Treaties," *Don Bell Reports*, 3 February 1978, p, 1.

136. See Richard Hofstadter, *The Paranoid Style in American Politics* (New York: Knopf, 1964), pp. 1-9. See also David Brion Davis, "Some Themes of Counter-Subversion: An Analysis of Anti-Masonic, Anti-Catholic, and Anti-Mormon Literature," *Mississippi Valley Historical Review* 47 (September 1960): 205-24.

137. Quoted in Alan Crawford, *Thunder on the Right: The 'New Right' and the Politics of Resentment* (New York: Pantheon, 1980), p. 89.

138. Quoted in Lanouette, "The Panama Canal Treaties," p. 1560.

139. Philip Nicolaides, "The Selling of the Panama Canal Treaties," *Register*, 9 December 1979, p. 3.

140. Interview with William Rhatican, Washington, D.C., 24 May 1983.

141. Viguerie, *The New Right*, p. 70.

142. Ibid., p. 15.

143. Quoted in Lanouette, "The New Right: 'Revolutionaries' out after the 'Lunch-Pail' Vote," p. 1560.

144. Viguerie, *The New Right*, p. 71.

145. Interview with Ernest Evans, Cambridge, Mass., 20 August 1981.

146. McIntyre, *The Fear Brokers*, p. 92.

147. Jeffrey D. Neuchterlein interview with Curt Cutter, Washington, D.C., 28 June 1978.

148. James T. Burnham, "Panama or Taiwan?" *National Review*, 16 September 1977, p. 1043.

149. William F. Buckley, Jr., "The Proposed Treaty: Preliminary Thoughts," *National Review*, 2 September 1977, p. 982.

150. Hanson Baldwin, "The Panama Canal," p. 15.

151. Dinsmore, "Plan to Give away the Panama Canal," p. 4.

152. Interview with Robert Dockery, Washington, D.C., 25 May 1982.

153. Interview with Rhatican.

154. Quoted in "Canal Passage Still Dubious," *New York Times*, 8 January 1978, p. D2.

155. Viguerie, *The New Right*, pp. 69-70.

Notes

Chapter 6. *Interest Groups, II: The Economics of Ratification*

1. "Is the Panama Canal Worth It?" *Business Week*, 6 December 1976, p. 84.

2. In the minibridge system containers were off-loaded on one coast and shipped to the other—or to intermediate, inland destinations—on railroad flatcars. The term "land-bridge" is used to designate such service between Europe and the Orient.

3. Quoted in "Is the Panama Canal Worth It?" *Business Week*, p. 84.

4. "The Canal without Rhetoric," *Forbes*, 15 November 1977, p. 93.

5. Between 1973 and 1977 the North Atlantic ports actually mounted a long, expensive, and ultimately fruitless legal battle against the minibridge at the Federal Maritime Commission (*Council of North Atlantic Shipping Associations v. U.S. American Mail Lines, Ltd.*, FMC 73-38 [1977]).

6. John R. Immer, "Liner Cargo Changing Patterns," *American Seaport*, December 1978, p. 11.

7. The Panama Canal Treaty, the first of the two treaties concluded in 1977, defined the transitional administrative arrangements for the Canal through the end of the century.

8. Under the 1903 treaty tolls were set by an arrangement, prescribed by Congress, that was cost- and not profit-based, with any excess after capital and operating expenses earmarked for the U.S. Treasury to amortize the existing debt on the Canal.

9. Testimony of James J. Reynolds, U.S., Congress, Senate, Committee on Foreign Relations, *Panama Canal Treaties*, Part 4, 95th Cong., 1st sess., 1977, p. 391.

10. Testimony of James J. Reynolds, U.S., Congress, House, Committee on Merchant Marine and Fisheries, Subcommittee on the Panama Canal, *Panama Canal Treaty Ramifications*, Part I, 95th Cong., 1st sess., 1977, pp. 209, 211.

11. W. T. Amoss, Jr., quoted in *American Legion Bulletin*, 26 September 1977, p. 7.

12. Anita Schrodt, "Gulf Port Officials Warn of Canal Pact Opposition," *Journal of Commerce*, 30 September 1977, reprinted in U.S. Department of State, *ARA News Roundup*, Supplement no. VI, 26 October 1977, p. 18.

13. State of Virginia, Board of Commissioners of the Virginia Port Authority, *Resolution 77-21*, 12 October 1977.

14. Statement by House Speaker Bill Clayton, Texas, House, *Economic Impacts of the Proposed Panama Canal Treaties on Texas*, 15 March 1978.

15. Quoted in Joseph S. Helewicz and James A. Rousmaniere, Jr., "The Panama Canal: Who'll Pay the Freight?" *Baltimore Sun*, 23 October 1977, p. K7.

16. Testimony of W. Donald Welch, executive director of the South Carolina State Ports Authority, U.S., Congress, House, Committee on Merchant Marine and Fisheries, Subcommittee on the Panama Canal, *Canal Operation under 1977 Treaty*, 96th Cong., 1st sess., p. 477.

17. Testimony of Leonard Kujawa, *U.S. Interest in Panama Canal*, p. 70.

18. The 30 percent figure was used by the State Department to estimate additional revenues needed to meet increased treaty- and nontreaty-related costs through the year 2000.

19. Jeffrey Neuchterlein interview with Robert Crittenden, Washington, D.C., 27 July 1978.

20. Testimony of Ely M. Brandes, *Panama Canal Treaties*, Part 4, p. 128.

21. The Brandes estimate is from ibid., p. 122; the Maritime Administration's estimate is from the testimony of Howard Casey in ibid., p. 121.

22. Leonard Kujawa, "Analysis of the Estimated Cash Requirements of the Panama Canal Commission, 1979–1983," Arthur Andersen and Company, January 1978, p. 6.

23. Council of the Americas, "Panama Canal Treaty Economic Issues Briefing Paper," mimeo. (New York, 1977). Council of the Americas, Inc. files, New York, N.Y.

24. Frank Moore, Robert Beckel, and Robert Thompson, memorandum to the president, 1 February 1978.

25. Cyrus Vance, Harold Brown, and Clifford L. Alexander, Jr., to U.S. Senate, 10 February 1978. Committee of Americans for the Canal Treaties, Inc. files, Washington, D.C.

26. Brandes, *Panama Canal Treaties*, Part 4, p. 125.

27. Testimony of Leonard Kujawa, *Panama Canal Treaty Ramifications*, Part I, pp. 135, 136.

28. Testimony of Harold R. Parfitt, U.S., Congress, Senate, Armed Services Committee, *Defense Maintenance and Operation of the Panama Canal Including Administration and Government of the Canal Zone*, 95th Cong., 2d sess., 1978, p. 313. The "out years" refers to the years after 1983.

29. Testimony of Elmer B. Staats, *Defense Maintenance and Operation of the Panama Canal*, p. 373.

30. Ibid., p. 369.

31. Testimony of Melvin Shore, *Panama Canal Treaties*, Part 4, pp. 170, 367.

32. Testimony of Ely M. Brandes, *Canal Operations under 1977 Treaty*, Part II, p. 1498.

33. William G. Hamlin, Jr., quoted in ibid., Part II, p. 1493.

34. Testimony of Richard A. Lidinsky, in ibid., Part II, p. 1493.

35. Reynolds, *Panama Canal Treaty Ramifications*, p. 212.

36. Written Statement, International Longshoremen's Association, *Panama Canal Treaties*, Part 4, p. 590.

37. Shore, ibid., Part 4, p. 163.

38. *Journal of Commerce*, 20 September 1977, quoted in the *American Legion National Security/Foreign Relations Bulletin*, 26 September 1977, p. 7.

39. Shore, *Panama Canal Treaties*, Part 4, p. 161.

40. Complaint at p. 10, *Helms et al. v. Vance*, 432 U.S. 907 (1977).

41. American Farm Bureau Federation, "Farm Bureau Policies," Washington, D.C., 1979, p. 35. Maryland Port Authority Files, Baltimore, Md.

42. Advertisement, "Not Even Bowie Kuhn Would Have Allowed This Trade," *Washington Post*, 15 April 1978, p. A17.

43. The companies explored a number of transcontinental pipeline alternatives but for various economic and environmental reasons none looked likely to materialize by the time of the ratification debate. The other alternative, the sale of Alaskan oil to Japan, was effectively prohibited by the Jones Act (the Merchant Marine Act) of 1920. Limiting oil exports to American bottoms and ships manned only by American crews made the importation of American oil not economically feasible for the Japanese.

44. Interview with Richard A. Lidinsky, Baltimore, 23 November 1981.

45. As the *Los Angeles Times* wrote: "If the U.S. approves the treaties relinquishing control of the Canal, tolls will be increased to such an extent that they will drive traffic away.... If the United States rejects the treaties political unrest could be stepped up in the Canal Zone and will have an equally deterimental effect on Canal trade.... Either way, the West Coast wins...." William G. Rempel, "More Shipping Seen for Southland Ports," *Los Angeles Times*, 8 February 1978, p. 31.

46. Telephone interview with Herbert R. Haar, Jr., 22 January 1982.

47. Interview with Lidinsky.

48. Telephone interview with Albert May, vice president of AIMS, 17 December 1981.

49. Interview with James J. Reynolds, Washington, D.C., 19 December 1981.

50. Interview with May.

51. Interview with Barbara Burke, Washington, D.C., 17 December 1981.

52. Interview with Reynolds.

53. Interview with May.

54. Reynolds, *Panama Canal Treaties*, Part 4, p. 396.

55. Interview with May.

56. According to Reynolds, the difference between public positions on treaty reform taken by AIMS in 1967 and 1977 was the growing realization within the executive committee that, whatever the deficiencies of the new treaties, they represented an idea whose time could be postponed only at serious risk of violence. Interview with Reynolds.

57. Senator Claiborne Pell, quoted in *Panama Canal Treaties*, Part 1, p. 298.

58. Shore, quoted in ibid., Part 4, p. 168.

59. Quoted in Helewicz and Rousmaniere, "The Panama Canal: Who'll Pay the Freight?" p. K7.

60. Testimony of Harold R. Parfitt, *Panama Canal Treaties*, Part 1, p. 298.

61. Helewicz and Rousmaniere, "The Panama Canal: Who'll Pay the Freight?" p. K7.

62. Testimony of Linowitz and Bunker, *Panama Canal Treaty Ramifications*, Part 1, p. 9.

63. Quoted in Adam Clymer, "Charge Canal Pacts Will Cost Taxpayers Millions," *New York Times*, 2 February 1978, p. A14.

64. Quoted in Jeremiah O'Leary and Walter Taylor, "Canal Treaty Costs: A New Row?" *Washington Star*, 5 February 1978, p. A12. As Governor Parfitt observed later: "Some of [the State Department's] numbers were done, very frankly, without close consultation with us. And it caused us some problems because there was always the pressure to come in line. But we didn't do it when we disagreed." Telephone interview with Governor Harold R. Parfitt, 22 January 1982.

65. Interview with Burke.

66. Atlantic-Gulf Ports Coalition memorandum to House/Senate Conference Committee members, undated, p. 1. Maryland Port Authority Files.

67. Interview with Parfitt.

68. Jeffrey D. Neuchterlein interview with Robert Beckel, 20 July 1978. The point was underscored by one key congressional staffer: "The numbers kept changing. We kept saying and thinking, 'For God's sake make this the last time. . . . ' The issue was just a matter of degree but with only one vote separating, degrees count." Interview with Robert Dockery, Washington, D.C., 19 May 1982.

69. Interview with Senator Frank Church, Washington, D.C., 20 May 1982.

70. Moore, Beckel, and Thompson memorandum to the president.

71. The Long Understanding mandated that tolls be adjusted according to "1) the costs of operating and maintaining the . . . Canal; 2) the competitive position of the use of the Canal in relation to other means of transportation; 3) the interests of both Parties in maintaining their domestic fleets; 4) the impact of such an adjustment on the various geographical areas of each of the two Parties; and 5) the interest of both Parties in maximizing their international commerce." U.S., Congress, Senate, Committee on Foreign Relations *Senate Debate on the Panama Canal Treaties: A Compendium of Major Statements, Documents, Record Votes and Relevant Events*, 96th Cong., 1st sess., 1979, pp. 401-2.

72. Interview with Richard Wyrough, Washington, D.C., 14 May 1982.

73. As Wyrough observed: "There were two occasions when we were concerned that the economic arguments might be used. Once was in the fall and once was between the two Senate votes in the spring.... We were obviously relieved that the threat didn't materialize either time." Ibid.

74. Interview with Dockery.

75. Neuchterlein interview with Michael Blumenfeld, Washington, D.C., 27 July 1978.

76. Interview with Haar.

77. Interview with Lidinsky.

78. Ibid.

79. Atlantic-Gulf Ports Coalition, Press Release, 15 February 1979, p. 2. Maryland Port Authority files.

80. Interview with Lidinsky.

81. Ibid.

82. Interview with Richard Wyrough, Washington, D.C., 25 June 1978.

83. Interview with Richard McCall, Washington, D.C., 17 May 1982.

84. Interview with Rhatican.

85. Interview with Lidinsky.

86. Interview with Robert Beckel, Washington, D.C., 23 June 1981.

[Conclusion]

1. All three quotations appear in "President Carter's Visit to Panama," U.S. International Communications Agency, *Foreign Media Reaction*, Current Issues, no. 9, 27 June 1978.

2. Editorial, "Ratification!" *Baltimore Sun*, 19 April 1978, reprinted in U.S. Department of State, *ARA News Roundup*, Final Supplement, Part II, 24 July 1978, p. 19, and editorial, "Navigating beyond the Canal," *New York Times*, 20 April 1978, p. 22.

3. Editorial, "Panama: Some Second Thoughts," *Washington Post*, 21 April 1978, p. A28.

4. Quoted in David M. Maxfield, "Senate Backs Canal Neutrality Treaty, 68-32," *Congressional Quarterly Weekly Report*, 18 March 1978, p. 675.

5. Godfrey Sperling, Jr., "Carter's View of a Good Start That Brought a Bitter End," *Christian Science Monitor*, 26 January 1981, p. 23.

6. Brzezinski quoted in Jeffrey D. Neuchterlein, "The 1978 Panama Canal Treaties: The Record of the Carter Administration" (Paper submitted to the White House, 4 April 1979), p. 166.

7. Sperling, "Carter's View of a Good Start That Brought a Bitter End."

8. Thomas L. Hughes, "Carter and the Management of Contradictions," *Foreign Policy* no. 31 (Summer 1978):39.

9. Ibid.

10. Interview with Robert Beckel, Washington, D.C., 23 June 1981.

11. Interview with Senator John Culver, Washington, D.C., 20 May 1982.

12. Interview with William Rhatican, Washington, D.C., 24 May 1983.

13. Joseph Aragon, quoted in Martha Shirk, "Hard Sell on Panama Treaties Begins," *St. Louis Post Dispatch*, 21 August 1977, reprinted in U.S. Department of State, *ARA News Roundup*, 26 August 1977, p. 41.

14. Michael Mandelbaum, "Big Ditch Debate," *New York Times Book Review*, 4 February 1978, p. 11.

15. William Grieder, "The Foreign Policy We Really Didn't Try," *Washington Post*, 16 November 1980, p. L1.

Index

Index

Library of Congress Cataloging in Publication Data

Moffett, George D., 1943-
    The limits of victory.

    "Written under the auspices of the Center for International Affairs, Harvard
University"—P.
    Bibliography: p.
    Includes index.
    1. Panama Canal Treaties, 1977. 2. Treaties—Ratification. I. Harvard Uni-
versity. Center for International Affairs. II. Title.
JX1398.73.M63   1985   341.44'6'02667307287   84-14920
ISBN 0-8014-1737-6 (alk. paper)